"Only If You Are
Really Interested"

"Only If You Are Really Interested"

Celebrity, Gender, Desire and the World of Morrissey

NICHOLAS P. GRECO

McFarland & Company, Inc., Publishers
Jefferson, North Carolina, and London

LIBRARY OF CONGRESS CATALOGUING-IN-PUBLICATION DATA

Greco, Nicholas P., 1973–
  "Only if you are really interested" : celebrity, gender, desire and the world of Morrissey / Nicholas P. Greco.
    p.   cm.
  Includes bibliographical references and index.

  ISBN 978-0-7864-6274-2
  softcover : 50# alkaline paper ∞

  1. Morrissey.   2. Singers — Great Britain — Biography.
  I. Title.
  ML420.M635G74   2011
  782.42166092 — dc22   [B]   2011017222

BRITISH LIBRARY CATALOGUING DATA ARE AVAILABLE

© 2011 Nicholas P. Greco. All rights reserved

No part of this book may be reproduced or transmitted in any form or by any means, electronic or mechanical, including photocopying or recording, or by any information storage and retrieval system, without permission in writing from the publisher.

On the cover: Morrissey (photograph by Jake Walters)

Manufactured in the United States of America

McFarland & Company, Inc., Publishers
  Box 611, Jefferson, North Carolina 28640
    www.mcfarlandpub.com

This book is dedicated to Antonella and Serafina ... well, the pleasure, the privilege is mine.

Table of Contents

Acknowledgments   ix
Preface   1
Introduction   3

1. "That's the Story of My Life": Morrissey's Career, Controversies and Comeback   17
2. "The Songs That Saved Your Life": Critical Reception of the Works of Morrissey   33
3. "Let Me Kiss You": Celebrity, Gender And Desire   77
4. "The Boy Racer": Morrissey's Changing Gender Identity in Music Video   109
5. "At Last I Am Born": Morrissey in Live Performance   130
6. "We'll Let You Know": Inactivity and the Musical World of Morrissey   142
7. "The Harsh Truth of the Camera Eye": Morrissey's Enigma Through Mediated Performance   160

Conclusion   180
Chapter Notes   193
Bibliography   205
Index   213

Acknowledgments

I would like to thank my colleague Dr. Will Straw, without whom this book would not have been possible. His support and advice in the development of this book have been invaluable. My thanks also go to my colleagues at Providence College, who constantly put up with me. I wish to especially thank Dr. Michael Gilmour for his valuable guidance in this project.

My utmost love goes to Antonella, my wife and best friend, without whose support I could not continue. Her sacrifices have allowed me to study, inquire, teach and carry on as I do. I must also acknowledge Serafina Persephone Greco, my daughter, who listened to Morrissey from her earliest moments of existence, I think. It is to Antonella and Serafina that this work is dedicated.

Finally, this work would not be possible without Steven Patrick Morrissey: "In my own strange way ... I'll always stay true to you."

Preface

Steven Patrick Morrissey was the lead singer of the 1980s British band The Smiths. Since the band's demise in 1987, Morrissey has had a successful career as a solo performer. Morrissey is a rich case study for the analysis of mediated celebrities. This book examines the ways in which Morrissey's public persona has shifted throughout his career. These changes have to do with the nature of popular cultural mediation, the status of celebrity, and Morrissey's engagement with issues of gender and desire.

Morrissey's celebrity persona, or star image, takes shape within the ongoing production of what Roland Barthes refers to as enigma, and its incompleteness is thus one of its consistent features. This star image is constructed from — and within — "streams" of information that are produced and circulate over time. The unending character of this "stream" is such that Morrissey's star image is perpetually produced and continues to evolve. The sense of the celebrity's image as incomplete leads, in turn, to an ongoing impulse, on the part of fans and observers, to find resolution. Throughout his career, Morrissey has maintained mystery around key aspects of his identity, in particular his sexuality, his feelings about England, and his relationship to pop stardom. This book explores the various elements that contribute to Morrissey's enigmatic star image: lyrical themes and critical press; music videos; live performance; musical syntax; and interviews. This work explores the interaction of these various elements and how they have given rise to ongoing speculation within fan and critical discourse, as well as the particular kinds of mystery and gender roles that arise to accompany these sorts of enigmas.

As a celebrity, Morrissey is subject to the gaze of an audience in a way that has historically been construed as objectifying and theorized within important works as feminizing. Morrissey's principal response to this objectification has been the maintenance of a constant sense of enigma. While other performers might seek clarification of their images as a means of controlling them, Morrissey's response to ongoing objectification is the ongoing production of enigma. His active control of his image is manifest through his constant transformation of that image.

Introduction

Steven Patrick Morrissey was the lead singer of the British band The Smiths. Janice Long called the band a "British institution" on the BBC Six radio program *The Dream Ticket* on 27 November 2002. The British music magazine *New Musical Express* called The Smiths "the most influential band of the last fifty years," while celebrating the magazine's 50th year of production in April 2002. Since the band's demise in 1987, Morrissey, most often referred to by last name only, has had a successful career as a solo performer. During the period from 1987 to the present, the singer's image has gone through a number of transformations, as might be expected, while a number of important characteristics have remained constant. Some of these consistencies are his vocal style, his witty lyrics, an aggressive opposition to the consumption of meat and support for the ethical treatment of animals, the engagement with images of Britishness and the meanings thereof, and a discomfort with revelation of personal details. Furthermore, Morrissey has remained constant in terms of his physical appearance; he has always dressed in a manner that shows an awareness of contemporary popular style and has featured a pompadour or bouffant-like hairstyle throughout his career. Michael Bracewell writes,

> One day there will probably be a Faculty of Morrissey Studies in more than one distinguished seat of learning. And, more than probably, Morrissey himself will make especially sure that he has nothing whatsoever to do with the proceedings of their research. And this is precisely because of Morrissey's own understanding of both the anatomy of glamour ... and, more importantly, the importance of mystery and elusiveness within his own creative spirit. For Morrissey suddenly to turn around and make himself the amiable interviewee on a thousand chat shows and as many newspaper supplements, or personally pass comment on some doctoral thesis that includes an assessment of his writing, would be nothing less than an abnegation of all that he has achieved.[1]

Bracewell stresses the importance of Morrissey's enigma in terms of "glamour" and the formulation of desire. In one of his songs, Morrissey sings that he is only partially human being, but mostly manufactured image, and the only thing that exists beneath this surface of image is, simply, more public image.[2] In another song, Morrissey suggests that he consists of two people, and that he has two faces, one that is shown in public and another that, for the sake of his fans (and the public at large), he never would show.[3] To his fans, Morrissey is a mystery, and to reveal who Morrissey is thus negates his entire project, no matter how much we as fans would like to have him revealed.

The mystery that surrounds Morrissey's celebrity persona applies also to his sexual orientation, and this mystery has been fueled by the controversies that continue to swirl around him. While it is true that many fans of The Smiths stopped listening to Morrissey after his first few solo albums, a large fan base continues to follow him with intense devotion. In particular, the singer has gained a large and vibrant audience in the Latino community in southern California and in the southwestern United States. These fans now join the Morrissey faithful in flocking to his concerts and following his every move on various Internet websites.

In Morrissey's song "Irish Blood, English Heart," first performed during his 2002 world tour, he angrily lashes out at critics for their assumption that the display of the Union Jack is a racist gesture, and he dreams of a time when England is free from the "tyranny" of the monarchy (Morrissey's use of the Union Jack was deemed a racist gesture during a concert in 1992). Although he continues to possess an "English Heart," this song suggests Morrissey's disapproval of Britain and indicates a public breaking of ties with his home country. It is important to note that the singer has lived away from Britain since the late 1990s, residing in Los Angeles and Rome. When Craig Kilborn asks him if he spends his time between London and Los Angeles, Morrissey corrects him by stating he spends his time between Los Angeles and Ireland.[4] His current home is unknown, though in a letter to *The Times* in August of that year, he signed the letter, "Morrissey, Singer, Cheshire."[5]

While nationality is an important part of Morrissey's identity, the understanding of that identity must be informed by another large and significant element, which has to do with his performance of gender. His performance of gender has remained fluid throughout his career, at times suggesting effeminacy, sensitivity and gentleness, at others evoking elements of a brutish masculinity and violence.

Morrissey is an interesting and rich case study for the analysis of mediated celebrities. As a mediated figure, his celebrity status has been an important element of his persona from early in his career. Referring to Morrissey's time with The Smiths, Julian Stringer states:

> The songs were arranged more and more as *star* vehicles. They were painstakingly written around Morrissey's voice, in order to capitalize on the public's growing fascination with his star image.... The Smiths' image was always about itself, about its own construction and reconstruction, and, in turn, this fed into the group's textual practice.[6]

Morrissey was, early on, the center of attention for The Smiths and has remained the focal point for a dedicated group of fans who followed him into a solo career in the late 1980s. This book will examine the ways in which Morrissey's public persona has shifted over some 30 years. These changes have to do with the nature of popular cultural mediation, the status of celebrity, and Morrissey's engagement with issues of gender and desire.

Themes in This Book

This book engages with the following questions and issues. How can a male celebrity maintain an audience's desire, and in doing so, how does a celebrity negotiate a sense of masculinity while under the gaze of that audience? It appears that Morrissey chooses to exert control over his star image or persona, which is subject to the gaze of the audience, by continually placing this persona in flux. This flux is achieved primarily through Morrissey's construction of an enigma that surrounds his star image. The mystery that surrounds Morrissey is not unlike that which surrounds La Zambinella from Balzac's *Sarrasine*, the story that is the object of study in Roland Barthes' book *S/Z*. As is the case with Morrissey, the draw of La Zambinella involves an enigma surrounding her that is only solved over time, through the collection of fragments of information. It is clear that Morrissey uses strategic tools, including some of those identified by Barthes, in order to create and maintain an enigmatic star image.

This work explores the particular type of star image that Morrissey conveys by analyzing various elements that construct this persona. Through a survey of critical reception, one sees how the press creates the star image and how the performer communicates a sense of identity through the press. In the early stage of his career, Morrissey, as frontman for The Smiths, had only these press reviews to contribute to his image construction. Therefore, one might observe the beginnings of a star image, and important themes are revealed through these press "clippings." These fragments provide an incomplete picture of the celebrity, while also providing common "streams" or "voices" that are consistent over time, and ultimately construct the star image. It is with an exploration of these "streams" that the book begins.

A study of Morrissey and his star image reveals a complex relationship between his masculinity, as conceived within accounts of the masculine, and his ongoing acknowledgment of the gaze of an audience. For instance, Morrissey expresses a kind of masculinity that, in ways, might not acknowledge the gaze of an audience, in the sense that this figure is presented as self-absorbed and narcissistic. On the other hand, this type of star image requires the gaze of the audience for its existence. Various masculinities engage with the gaze of an audience in interesting ways, and this book demonstrates one of their iterations.

While Laura Mulvey presents the passive figure as "feminized" by the gaze of the audience, this book demonstrates the complexities of masculinities that cannot be conceived in terms of an essentializing dichotomy between active and passive. Nevertheless, her thought has influenced much scholarship in terms of the gendered nature of media. Mulvey's influence is apparent in Susan McClary's work on the gendered character of music, discussed in detail in this book. It is also apparent in the work of Nadine Hubbs, who explores the character of the melodic line as a marker of activity and, in turn, gender. Both of these works further expand the analysis of music and gender.

There are two sides to this book, then. There is the question of how a male celebrity, in this case, Morrissey, expresses various types of masculinities under an audience's gaze. On the other hand, there is the strategy on the part of the artist to maintain the desiring of that audience, and to, in a sense, maintain that gaze. The maintenance of an enigmatic star image is one method of maintaining both the gaze of the audience and a control over the objectified star image.

The existing study of masculinities and their embeddedness in visual texts often organizes these into typologies. A figure like Morrissey does not easily fit into these typologies. For instance, Morrissey's persona is part Sonny from the television show *Miami Vice*, in terms of being an object of erotic fascination while also suggesting an air of failure (as Sonny constantly encounters difficulties in his job). He is also some of the protagonist in *Raging Bull* as described by Pam Cook, mourning the loss of a certain sense of masculinity. Morrissey presents himself often as a kind of boxer, sometimes literally as injured, as in the video for "The Boy Racer," or with a bandage over his brow during recent concerts in Europe, and sometimes with his apparent interest in the boxing world. In this way, Morrissey is Stan Hawkins' "anti-hero," self-deprecating and longing for another time past, and knowingly appropriating characteristics of Otherness.

This Otherness also indicates a certain absence, in the way that Christian Metz's "all-perceiving" audience recognizes that the mediated singer is not present with them. When the mediation is complete, all that remains of the celebrity is a trace. The analysis of Morrissey's music video for "The Boy Racer" presented in this book hints at the importance of the trace that remains once the video ends.

Such an absence is made more tangible, if you will, by the experience of a live Morrissey concert. In this context, the singer is made somewhat available to the audience, who, during the relatively short concert experience, struggles to gain an element of physical experience with the singer, either in the form of physical contact or a fragment of expensive cloth, impregnated with a particular perfume. Those of us who experience the concert in a mediated context, through video or audio recording, might experience this physicality by proxy.

Morrissey's vocal performance adds interesting color to his star image. He is perhaps expressing Otherness in his use of glottal stops, his praise of the vocal performances of past performers like Rita Pavone, and in his own invocations of Magnani and Pasolini in his song "You Have Killed Me."

While some reviewers have suggested that Morrissey's album from 2006, *Ringleader of the Tormentors*, with songs like "Dear God Please Help Me," has solved some of the major elements of his enigma, such as his sexuality, this is not the case, as can be seen in the concluding remarks of this book. Rather, his newer material has served to further fuel his complexities.

Morrissey continues to maintain a sense of mystery surrounding himself, and in turn fuels an impulse for completion of his star image, a revelation of the complete picture. That picture is, by its nature, incomplete. As Richard Dyer suggests, it is from this interaction of various elements that the star image takes shape, and this "complex totality," to use his term, does have a *chronological dimension*. That is, it changes over time. Such changes might include contradictions and even might reflect the unstable nature of the meaning of the celebrity, as suggested by David Marshall.

This book explores how various elements contribute to a star image, a construction that has been fleshed out mostly in the field of film studies, by Dyer and Marshall, and discussed by Mulvey and others. This work strives to meaningfully explore the construction of an enigmatic star image through various mediations. For instance, this work explores Morrissey's promotional videos as well as television and radio interviews. Morrissey's live performance and recorded music are also considered. Aspects of musicological analysis have been brought to this work, in discussing harmony and voice-leading in "We'll Let You Know." The musical analysis that makes up much of chapter 6 draws from Hubbs' application of the "passive" and "active" dialectic to melodic contour, where she suggests that an inactive melodic line signifies "difference." In the analysis presented here, it is argued that the supposed "inactivity" of the melodic line is, in fact, a more subtle strategy to place stress on particular lyrics, and to perhaps heighten the instability of meaning of his lyrical delivery.

Coupled with the lyrical presentation is this challenging element that is the singer's voice. Morrissey pushes the pitches that he sings, reinforcing, if you will, the instabilities suggested by the interaction between his melodic line and the accompanying music. In a way, this kind of singing shows his commonness, complete with notes out of tune and various cracks and growls. In these instances, perhaps Morrissey's voice is "overflowing its channels," as suggested by Robert Walser.

Morrissey can be seen as an expert in using various strategies in maintaining his enigma, particularly evident in his presentation in the context of live interview. In his interviews with Craig Kilborn, Jonathan Ross and Janice Long, Morrissey uses techniques that delay the revelation of truth, and at times he reverses the role of the interviewer in order to shift focus from himself. Of course, this shifting only seems to serve the enigmatic quality of his star image.

Morrissey, then, is an example of a particular type of star image, one that, while reliant on the gaze of the audience, tends to be self-engrossed. This alternate masculinity serves to complicate the conventional relationship between the audience and the celebrity. This presentation of an alternative masculinity is also somewhat unstable, in terms of the objectifying power of the gaze. In other words, the gaze is unable to fully objectify the star image shown here. In turn, it is argued that this instability of the star image maintains the desire of that audience, creating an impulse for completion or stability of that star image.

When discussing a singer, it is important to consider Barthes' thoughts on what he calls the "grain of the voice," this source of pleasure that resides, for Barthes, between music and language. It is that physical in-between from which the listener derives pleasure. While scholars like Richard Middleton and John Potter attempt to discuss the desire that is elicited by the voice, in citing intimacy, repetition, and even sheer volume, or the "reversing" power of the voice, to use Wayne Koestenbaum's term, these ways to discuss the singing voice fall short. This book should highlight the difficulties encountered when attempting to discuss the singing voice and its allure. Just as Barthes hopes to do away with the adjective in discussing such things, it remains difficult to follow through. While Barthes provides a theoretical framework with which to approach the singing voice, its practical application is difficult. It is hoped that this work highlights the need for a more robust and practical framework with which to approach the singing voice in popular music, and that this work hints at the importance and potency of that singing voice.

Two interconnected concepts run through this book. The first is the notion of enigma in relationship to star image. Morrissey's star image takes shape within the ongoing production of enigma, and its incompleteness is thus one of its consistent features. Furthermore, this star image is constructed from — and within — "streams" of information (images or facts) that are produced and circulate over time. The unending character of these "streams" is such that Morrissey's star image is perpetually produced and continues to evolve. The sense of the celebrity's image as incomplete leads, in turn, to an ongoing impulse, on the part of fans and observers, to find resolution. As Morrissey has suggested in song, even he wants what he cannot have, and he is driven absolutely insane when he cannot have it.[7] The incomplete or enigmatic celebrity should not be construed as deceptive or as willfully withholding information. Rather, the nature of celebrity in a mediated context results in a partial presentation of the celebrity's star image.

There are various tools that will facilitate the exploration of Morrissey's star image and the broader relationship between a celebrity and his or her audience. This book brings together the tools of film studies and musicology, enhancing both with notions derived from media studies and cultural studies. Musical theory and syntactical analysis are tools with which to analyze musical form and performance. Much work in media studies has dealt to a significant extent with tools of visual analysis, a key dimension of this book.

It is not the goal of this work to provide a critical judgement of Morrissey's accomplishments. This work serves not to assign undeserving status to Morrissey, but rather to bring him to a place of critical discussion, in order to be able to dismantle his complex star image. There are many other aspects of Morrissey's image that can be investigated but that will have to wait for other writings to be explored. For instance, Morrissey's songwriting process follows a certain pattern. Generally, he receives music without any words from his colleagues. It is to this music that he adds a melody line and corresponding lyrics. Ultimately, Morrissey is a poet rather than a songwriter, and some might suggest that lyrical analyses would be of the highest importance and significance. When asked about how one might get to know the truth about Morrissey, the singer states, "The truth is in the songs. So much is in the songs."[8] This project will embark on an exploration of themes located in his lyrics. Such themes are pieces or fragments that collectively contribute to the star image of this performer. It is in this context that the thematic content of Morrissey's lyrics will be explored.

It should be noted that this book is written from the perspective not only of a scholar but also of a fan. The perspective of a fan allows for certain advantages in analysis. As this work is written by a fan, it is thus informed by a greater sensitivity to the questions that persist in a figure like Morrissey, and is informed by first-hand knowledge of how this specific fan-celebrity relationship functions. The difficulty arises in how to properly and effectively express this relationship in terms that are quantitative and clear. The perspective of a fan can inject certain biases into a work, such as an overly subjective outlook on the "text" in question or an inappropriate worship or worth being applied to the figure that is the subject of critical analysis. It is the hope of the author that these instabilities are not a part of this work. Ultimately, this work benefits from the sensitivities of a fan perspective.

Morrissey is not a unique case in terms of how much of his persona is comprised of enigma, though he is one of few truly enigmatic popular musicians (for instance, Bob Dylan is an example of an enigmatic star image, especially early in his career). Furthermore, members of his fan base are fervent in their adoration of the celebrity. Thus, this case is particularly pertinent to the study of the relationship between the celebrity and the fan, and specifically to the discussion of the maintenance of desire. Morrissey's creation and maintenance of an enigmatic star image is compelling in itself, while providing a case to which other celebrities and their personae might be compared.

Chapter Outlines

The first chapter, entitled "'That's the Story of My Life': Morrissey's Career, Controversies and Comeback," explores Morrissey's career as well as briefly outlining some pertinent biographical details. While much of this book is focused on Morrissey's identity after his time with The Smiths, this chapter discusses some important events from the early years through the reception of the group's recordings in the popular press. As well, other significant elements of Morrissey's identity, such as ongoing ambiguity concerning his sexual orientation, are discussed here. This chapter serves to provide a biographical narrative against which Morrissey's changing celebrity unfolds.

It is through this biographical discourse that the complexity of Morrissey's performance of masculinity is revealed. The ambiguity of Morrissey's gender performance contributes to an overall sense of the singer as an enigma. Furthermore, the discourse that surrounds his star image continually refers to controversies that have continued to plague the singer throughout the years.

An important element of Morrissey's star image is his supposed embodiment of British nationalism, and his role as a kind of English "ambassador," even though this role has been problematized — but not discounted — by his move to Los Angeles in the late 1990s, and furthermore by his recent move to Rome (and his current "homelessness," at least in terms of public perception). This discussion deals with the various ways in which his identification with Englishness has been expressed and how Morrissey himself challenges the appropriateness of such nationalistic labels as applied to him.

The second chapter, "'The Songs That Saved Your Life': Critical Reception of the Works of Morrissey," explores much of the discourse that surrounds Morrissey's star image through a survey of critical reception in the form of album reviews. The reviews present a sampling of comments from mainstream print publications like *Rolling Stone* and *New Musical Express* and, while not exhaustive of all critical reception, provide a general sense of how both The Smiths and Morrissey were received by the press at the time. In addition to these reviews, the general themes present in Morrissey's lyrics are explored; taken together, these themes help to elucidate Morrissey's representation through his music.

The third chapter, "'Let Me Kiss You': Celebrity, Gender and Desire," explores the major theories that underlie and inform this book. This chapter outlines various writers' discussions of different types of masculinities, surveying recent writings and theoretical developments regarding these new masculinities. Morrissey, as an enigmatic figure, might be said to play in novel ways with the character of masculinity. This chapter is concerned with the ways that, while constantly offered up to the display and curiosity of his audience, Morrissey somehow remains "active." The masculinity in play is one that elicits and frustrates curiosity and, as such, remains active in interesting ways. This can be referred to as a slippery masculinity, both narcissistic and sensitive, egotistical and selfless.

One of the primary goals of this project is to explore how the sense of enigma is produced around a particular kind of celebrity. This work attempts to read the "text" of Morrissey by considering Barthes' hermeneutic code, under which

> we list the various (formal) terms by which an enigma can be distinguished, suggested, formulated, held in suspense, and finally disclosed (these terms will not always occur, they will often be repeated; they will not appear in any fixed order).[9]

Throughout his career, Morrissey has maintained mystery around key aspects of his identity: his sexuality, his feelings about England, and his relationship to pop stardom. In some cases, the mystery has arisen through contradictions in his statements. In other cases, it is because he plays quite deliberately with indirectness in his answers or statements. In yet other cases, he is simply private. This book explores the interaction of these various elements and how they have given rise to ongoing speculation within fan and critical discourse, and it explores the particular kinds of mystery and gender roles that arise to accompany these sorts of enigmas.

Definitions of celebrity as well as Laura Mulvey's gendered framework of desire and the notion of the eroticized spectacle will serve to establish the basis for the argument that Morrissey is a figure who plays with this framework. Through an exploration of various conceptions of gender as well as the complexities of Mulvey's work and its adoption and transformation, concepts of the traditionally "active" masculine figure and "passive" feminine figure in mediated works are explored. This gender dichotomy has also been applied to music, with musical syntax being labelled as "masculine" or "feminine." Finally, Barthes' "grain of the voice" is explored in considering the singing voice as a site of identity and desire. Morrissey's various mediated identities are explored in the following chapters, in terms of how identities presented through various media generate an ongoing enigma. It is argued that a celebrity is a mediated figure and thus can be explored more properly through these mediations. Studying Morrissey's identity (or identities) through the lenses of different media allows different enigmatic "units," to use Barthes' term, to present themselves. Case studies allow for a more robust star image to emerge from such an exploration.

The fourth chapter, "'The Boy Racer': Morrissey's Changing Gender Identity in Music Video," serves to discuss the complexity of Morrissey's gender performance, focusing in particular on his persona in the music video for "The Boy Racer," released in 1995. This discussion begins by considering Judith Butler's writings on gender dimorphism and performativity, and Morrissey's own gender performance and sexual identity. The discussion then turns to a survey of Morrissey's music videos, and his display of what will be termed "lack." Carol Vernallis' ideas regarding the subject of the camera and image editing in music video are then applied to Morrissey's music video for "The Boy Racer." Vernallis provides a framework in which to conduct a visual analysis closely linked to musical cues. Her approach to music video can serve to point out moments of climax and affect for the viewer.

The music video for "The Boy Racer" is presented here as a compelling visual presentation of Morrissey as injured, one of the only examples in his promotional video output of explicit injury fully disclosed to the viewer. On more than one occasion, Morrissey has brandished signs of injury, both in live concert and in mediated contexts such as video. While some writers have discussed the injury of Morrissey as aligning the singer with seedier or criminal elements and a rough sort of image, it also inserts him into a certain spectrum of cultural images and works. For instance, Mark Simpson, in his book *Saint Morrissey*, suggests that Morrissey is conveying a "ruffian" image at this point in his career.[10] In his book, *Morrissey: Scandal & Passion*, David Bret discusses Morrissey's fascination with aggression and violence during this time.[11] In terms of gender constructions of celebrity, the video presents an interesting case: Morrissey as injured *and* as object of the viewer's gaze. The mystery of his injury and his performing despite it lend him an enigmatic air. Morrissey's injury, at first sight, seems contrived to produce an association with roughness, but it is argued that its status as meaningful gesture warrants a more thorough study. This chapter attempts to begin such a work, and as such it will hopefully stimulate further study in that area.

The fifth chapter, "'At Last I Am Born': Morrissey in Live Performance," serves to identify particular characteristics of Morrissey's concert performances that add a certain element of the physical and tangible to his otherwise enigmatic presentation. Elements that are unique to Morrissey's live performance are the physical interaction with his audience, certain vocal and physical gestures, and the presence of fan Julia Riley, with whom Morrissey converses during the concerts. Furthermore, the subject of Morrissey's shirts, which he throws into the crowd, is discussed, as they are a site of connection to Morrissey's physical self. Finally, the large lettering of Morrissey's name that accompanies the 2004 tour in support of *You Are the Quarry* is discussed in terms of narcissism.

The sixth chapter is entitled "'We'll Let You Know': Inactivity and the Musical World of Morrissey." As a complex example of the male pop vocal celebrity, Morrissey seems to problematize gendered frameworks of desire by maintaining a kind of "active" power while under the gaze of the audience. Morrissey accomplishes this through the constant production of discourse, and it is possible that such a strategy can be seen within his musical production as well. The discussion begins by outlining two important musicological works that focus on Morrissey, by Nadine Hubbs and

Stan Hawkins. Hubbs' analyses provide a basis and starting point for the analysis presented in this chapter, with her notion of Morrissey's "inactivity." Hawkins' work is important in that he takes into account Morrissey's problematic gender presentation.

While both of these works deal with the music of Morrissey in a musicological context, his music has been otherwise overlooked both in musicology and in the realm of popular music studies, not unlike the music of other popular musicians. This chapter works to contribute to a greater academic discourse on Morrissey, his persona and the music that he presents. Through a musical analysis of the song "We'll Let You Know," the chapter explores how Morrissey elicits desire and delays its satisfaction. The musical analysis takes into account the melodic contour of Morrissey's vocal line and its interaction with the line played by the bass guitar, as the harmonic activity within the chordal accompaniment is relatively standard. The analysis of musical stress within Morrissey's singing further illuminates the ways in which his persona is expressed in musical form. Finally, the suggestion of Morrissey as "inactive" is explored in terms of how this might affect his star image and his performance of gender. While the musical analysis in this chapter might be difficult for those not familiar with musicological methods and language, I trust that it will help to at least demonstrate how important Morrissey's *music* is to the understanding of the *singer* Morrissey.

The song in question is chosen for analysis because of its melodic contour. While the song "We'll Let You Know" is indicative of a general stylistic trend of Morrissey's songs, there are also many examples of songs by the singer that are melodically "active." Such songs provide an argument against Hubbs' suggestions of the "inactivity" of Morrissey's singing. "We'll Let You Know," though, is a rich text on which to apply Hubbs' analysis in a more specific manner, and offers within it compelling lyrical content, which points to Morrissey's use of irony and ambiguity.

The final chapter, entitled "'The Harsh Truth of the Camera Eye': Morrissey's Enigma through Mediated Performance," discusses Morrissey's appearance on *The Late Late Show with Craig Kilborn* in September 2002. In the interview with Kilborn, Morrissey acknowledges that he is, at the time, without a record deal, but that he is taking part in a very successful world tour and that record executives in the current commercial music scene — which is full of "crashing bores"— should be executed at gunpoint.

Morrissey presents himself as a loner and a difficult character. Interestingly, Morrissey suggests in these interviews that, although he spends his days alone watching television, he is happy. He refers to the screaming fans in the audience as his "family." There exists this constant dichotomy in his presentation. During his appearance on *Friday Night with Jonathan Ross* in May 2004, Morrissey continues to present himself as difficult but comfortable; he refuses to be Jonathan Ross' friend and jokes about the death of sprouts by suffocation. Morrissey's appearance on Janice Long's radio program in December 2004 reveals little new information about himself but rather features the singer shifting the focus away from himself and onto his interviewer.

This chapter explores the enigma of Morrissey and how this enigma is constructed and maintained in these interviews, through the framework of Barthes and the tools he identifies for creating and maintaining the enigma as presented in his book, *S/Z*. Morrissey's enigmatic character, presented in conversation through media that might otherwise facilitate the revelation of personal detail, is kept intact and is further reinforced.

Finally, the concluding remarks look to more recent examples of Morrissey's artistic output. In March 2006, Morrissey released the song "You Have Killed Me," the first single from his album entitled *Ringleader of the Tormentors*. The album was recorded in Rome and was produced by Tony Visconti. It features orchestral arrangements by acclaimed film composer Ennio Morricone. Furthermore, Morrissey's move to Rome, and subsequent statements about his new home, signal new national allegiances and a new shift in his public persona. The single and its accompanying video demonstrate Morrissey's continuing strategies for the maintenance of his enigmatic character. Another song on the album, "Dear God Please Help Me," indicates the singer's continual problematization of normative frameworks of gender. This collection of songs features strategies similar to those outlined throughout this book. Morrissey continues to be controversial, entering into the public consciousness by making a statement calling for the boycott of all Canadian goods and announcing his decision to not perform in Canada because of the annual seal hunt. Finally, Morrissey evokes his earlier image of the ruffian in presenting a violent image in his 2009 album, *Years of Refusal*, and the song "It's Not Your Birthday Anymore." Morrissey's enigmatic star image continues to change and ultimately postpones the revelation of truth.

1

"That's the Story of My Life"
Morrissey's Career, Controversies and Comeback

There was little public fanfare, no admirers with gladioli or loving Latinos with the future singer's name tattooed on their arms, at the Park Hospital in Davyhulme, Manchester, on 22 May 1959, the day when Elizabeth Dwyer gave birth to Steven Patrick Morrissey. The little boy's parents were Irish immigrants to England in the 1950s, who worked at labor jobs and kept close ties with the Irish community. Morrissey was raised Catholic, an upbringing that he would later evoke when singing in the guise of a priest (in late 2004, Morrissey appeared in concert and on television wearing a priest's collar and black blazer, a costume he also sports in the promotional video for "I Have Forgiven Jesus," released around that same time). After a rather uneventful stint in primary school, he attended St. Mary's Secondary Modern, an institution in which he was subject to corporeal punishment and verbal abuse.[1] While he was not a successful student in terms of academics, he did excel in English Literature and developed a witty style that is evident in his writings to music publications praising various new bands. Morrissey wrote a letter about Sparks' album *Kimono My House* to the *New Musical Express*, dated 14 June 1974. After publishing the letter, the editor provides a response as follows:

> Conviction oozes from every sentence like the very ichor of life itself from the metal life-support systems of the Bronze Giant of Fangorak. The eyes of Mr. Morrissey gleam with a missionary zeal that shames into submission the cringing doubts of those yet unconvinced.[2]

This is a glimpse of a Morrissey unknown to the world at large, yet his wit — which would later become a staple of his lyrics — is already being recognized. It is interesting that Morrissey first attracts attention as a *consumer* rather than a *producer* of popular music. His consumption of popular music is marked by high levels of passion, which provide an interesting contrast with the somewhat passionless individual he has become.

This chapter explores Morrissey's career, both with The Smiths and as a solo artist. Morrissey's changing star image unfolds and evolves against this biographical narrative. Morrissey's sexuality and gender — or, more particularly, the complexity of Morrissey's performance of masculinity — have been important elements of the singer's persona throughout his career. This chapter's discussions explore the various ways in which his gender presentation is described within the discourse that surrounds this artist. Morrissey's ambiguities and mysteries in terms of sexuality and gender contribute to an overall sense of the singer as an enigma, a puzzle that must be solved, an incomplete persona that is revealed over time, eliciting desire for the whole.

Morrissey's ambiguity in terms of gender and sexuality, as well as his enigmatic character, continue to be contested elements of his star image, topics of discussion and debate that are continually open and unresolved. Often accompanying these discussions is the ongoing controversy regarding Morrissey's supposedly racist views. The accusation of racism, first posited by the *New Musical Express* in August 1992, is based on the singer's actions that summer and reinforced in statements made during interviews throughout the first half of the 1990s. The accusations of racism were "substantiated" by lyrical content on his 1992 album, *Your Arsenal,* and the stance might have been underlined by a change to a more aggressive musical style. The album indicates a stylistic change from more conventional "pop" to "modern rock," a more radio-friendly brand of "alternative rock."

Finally, Morrissey's associations with nationality are discussed in terms of more recent events. With his move to Los Angeles in the late 1990s, his star image is made more complex. His "inherent" Englishness is put starkly in contrast with his habitation in the United States and his appropriation by a Latino audience. Furthermore, his reappropriation of Irishness, which is his personal ancestry, challenges the appropriateness of designations of Morrissey's national identity as English.

Ambiguity in Gender and Sexuality

As can be gleaned from many of the reviews above, the ambiguity of Morrissey's sexual orientation is the focus of a discussion that began during the earlier part of his career and continued throughout the years. In April 1988, Morrissey was asked whether there is "any sex in him," to which he replied, "None whatsoever. Which in itself is quite sexy. It was never there. It goes back to being an incredibly unpopular person. No one asked."[3] While Morrissey has claimed to be above any categorization in terms of sexuality, many have continued to speculate regarding his sexual orientation. Although it is clear that Morrissey has never definitely mentioned his sexual preferences (rather, he has suggested that he has none), this fact has often been taken as evidence that he is homosexual. The "evidence" of effeminate behavior and multigendered (or non-gender-specific) lyrics points to a complex sexuality that is not of the "hetero" variety, which some feel must, invariably, point to homosexuality. Bret makes this observation in his 2004 book, although much of that work seems to attempt to expose the homosexual elements of Morrissey's persona and artistic production. Bret's book could be read as an "outing" of Morrissey as a homosexual figure.

In a now-famous article in *Rolling Stone*, James Henke interviews Morrissey and seems to make a definitive statement regarding his sexual orientation: "He goes by a single name, Morrissey. He calls himself a 'prophet for the fourth gender,' admits that he's gay but adds that he's also celibate." Henke quotes Morrissey as stating that sex, as the subject of most of his songs (according to Henke), is a motivating factor for most people, whether they are celibate or not. Henke states that "though it would appear that his [Morrissey's] is largely a homosexual viewpoint, he explains that it's really not that simple." He goes on to quote Morrissey as not abiding by the rigid definitions of the sexes, and sexuality. Morrissey states, "I don't know anybody who is absolutely, exclusively heterosexual. It limits people's potential in so many areas. I think we should slap down these barriers."[4] Morrissey adds to this in December 1984 by saying, "On the subject of sex, virtually all the American coverage we've had has been totally erroneous."[5]

Colin Snowsell analyses Morrissey's sexual ambiguity as follows:

Morrissey's refusal to construct himself as anything other than conventionally masculine — in the vein of James Dean and Elvis Presley — thus worked to counter two hegemonies. He offended the mainstream for contaminating a hallowed version of masculinity with abstinence, vegetarianism and feyness. At the same time he insulted gay subculture for refusing to either support them or assume a recognizably gay identity.[6]

In an early interview by Dave McCullough, Morrissey calls himself a "prophet for the fourth sex": "The third sex [that is, androgyny], even that has been done and it's failed."[7] Mark Simpson discusses Morrissey's label as "prophet of the fourth sex":

> Morrissey ... was intimately committed to destroying the affective world that most people inhabited, but from which he had been excluded, or had excluded himself from. His erotic terrorism consisted of nothing more than speaking the "truth" of desire — naked (if somewhat neurotic) lust unclothed by fond clichés about gender and warm prejudices about sexuality.... True to his doomed devotion to the revolutionary truth of desire, sex in Morrissey's work is almost always anticipated, frustrated, averted or disappointed rather than consummated."[8]

In terms of Morrissey's performance of gender, Simpson suggests that the singer uses subtlety, displaying what Simpson calls an *interior* androgyny, as opposed to other pop stars from the early part of his career, in the early 1980s. Simpson suggests that although Morrissey might have presented himself as subtly androgynous, this presentation "represented a rejection of tired ideas about what was unconventional." Instead, "Morrissey was really offering an exploration of *interior* androgyny, where handsomeness supplanted glamorousness."[9] "Handsomeness," then, is Morrissey's attempt at the unconventional and extraordinary, in terms of gender representation. Simpson continues:

> It was left to Morrissey to represent a "homoeroticism" which was not "camp" or "cross-dressed," "congenital" or, for that matter, "homo." It was simply *handsome*. This was the supreme subversiveness of Morrissey's erotic project — to use ordinary language and feelings to convey what were supposed to be extraordinary conditions (after all, as he has pointed out, no one talks about "heteroeroticism," instead they talk about "eroticism"). It was also the key to his artistic masterstroke: since (homo)eroticism was simultaneously universal but still beyond the pale, it offered Morrissey an entirely fresh, unadulterated and vibrant vocabulary for his depiction of human desire — and weakness.[10]

Perhaps it would be more appropriate to refer to Morrissey's project as representing simply "eroticism" rather than what Simpson calls "(homo)eroticism." As per Morrissey's own wishes, as suggested in Henke's *Rolling Stone* interview, the singer would find such a categorization of his project objectionable. By removing the prefix "homo," a complexity is reestablished in Morrissey's erotic project. Simpson's comments, though, should be read in the context of his earlier views: Morrissey performs a gender that employs an implicit androgyny (what Simpson calls an "interior androgyny"), an extraordinary category outside of "camp" or "cross-dressed." For that matter, Simpson does in fact indicate that the eroticism that Morrissey represented (or represents) was not "homo" either. Interestingly, Simpson associates this extraordinary eroticism with weakness. Simpson concludes, "When Morrissey sang about longing it would sound as if he were the first person in the world to ever speak of it." Morrissey's weakness is the openness to erotic desire and longing, and more specifically, same-sex attraction, something that Simpson suggests is, although universal, always relegated to the margins of everyday life: "Precisely because it is so universal and perfectly understandable, it had to be presented as something bizarre and exclusive [by popular musicians before Morrissey], the special sensibility of an odd, minority species."[11]

In addition to his performance of extraordinary gender, Morrissey is single, and constantly so, perhaps situating himself in opposition to normative heterosexuality or normative models of sexual or physical desire. Morrissey presents himself as a single male, one who is very private regarding details of his physical relationships, so much so that no physical relationships seem to exist. He is thus placed outside these normative frameworks. Simpson suggests that Morrissey's singleness works to strengthen his relationship with his audience:

> Crucially, Morrissey's terminal singleness meant that the fans could possess him through his work — which was full of him and his eroticism in a way that his life wasn't — reassured in the knowledge that there was no one else, no shameless groupie nor jammy live-in-lover who could possess him more fully, more authentically, than they. Morrissey's work and his public performance was, in effect, his "private life." ... Morrissey has no need of sex with people so long as he continues to have it with his audience.[12]

And, as Simpson suggests, this relationship with his audience is a crucial one, both symbiotic and monogamous. He suggests that, just as Morrissey was sustained in his younger years by a connection with "such misfit, touchingly freakish, gender ambiguous characters," the connection he has with his fans today "sustains *them* in their misfit, freakish confused years, however long they might last." In turn, this knowledge that he sustains others sustains him now. Simpson suggests that the relationship Morrissey has with his fans is particularly unique in that the "unrivalled fervour with which his fans love him is a function of their certainty that their relationship is something special, that it isn't like any other love, that this one is different because it's just *us*."[13] This is not to say that Morrissey is an "open book" to his fans. Note that Simpson is catering to the Morrissey fan with this statement by near-quoting the lyrics from The Smiths' song "Hand in Glove." It is not far-fetched to assume that a Morrissey fan would recognize the lyric immediately.

One of the more fascinating aspects of Morrissey's persona is his apparent celibacy. Though Morrissey may no longer ascribe to celibacy, Simpson suggests it defines a large part of his enigmatic character:

> Celibacy massively enhanced Morrissey's stardom by turning him into a conundrum, a puzzle which had to be solved. As a highly sexual pop star who renounced sex, he made himself the Rosetta Stone of sex itself and found himself interrogated about his "sex life" like no other pop star had ever been before.[14]

John Robertson, in his collection of Morrissey quotes, *Morrissey: In His Own Words*, suggests that Morrissey claims his celibacy as early as November 1983. In a Channel 4 documentary, *The Importance of Being Morrissey*, aired on 8 June 2003 in the United Kingdom, Morrissey claims that he is no longer celibate, although, as expected, the singer does not elaborate. Morrissey is often hidden, revealing himself only in fragments. If the discourse surrounding the singer suggests an openness toward his fans (for instance, manifested in the intimate relationship he might have with his fans), the same discourse also suggests his mystery.

The Enigma

While gender and sexuality are much discussed in the discourse surrounding Morrissey, because these elements of his persona are ambiguous and put in question, there is always a sense of mystery surrounding the singer. This sense of mystery or enigma is such an integral part of his persona that there is almost an assumption that one will never discover the true "person" behind the public persona of the singer. This has caused some to suggest that no one truly knows who Morrissey is. In the 2003 Channel 4 documentary, Noel Gallagher of the band Oasis comments, "I'd say his mother knows. He probably doesn't even know."

Morrissey's mystery is a crucial part of his star image. In a phenomenon that will be explored later in this book, many fans often clamor onstage to try to attain physical contact with Morrissey, perhaps because so little can be gleaned of the singer's real life from the discourse that surrounds him. Instead, some might feel that touching him allows one to "know" him, and in turn to be "known" by him, as if such physical contact might even supersede any revelation of the true and complete details of Morrissey's personal life.

This is not to suggest that elements of his life are not made public. Clues about Morrissey's true persona are made to circulate in a variety of media. For instance, Morrissey himself has mentioned details of his family and childhood in interviews and articles. There have been various books written that try to outline biographical details about the singer, to give the reader a glimpse into his private life. Morrissey's lyrics seem to provide the greatest insight into the singer's persona, if there can ever be a guarantee of their proper "truthful" interpretation. His televisual appearances give his audience an opportunity to match his voice with a moving picture of his physical self. The fan must create a "full" image of the celebrity by stringing these various clues and details together, by following these "streams" of information as well as speculation over time. This image continues to be produced. As new details emerge, they contribute to this image, and as these details are added to the image, it can become more intricate or begin to change. Morrissey's persona continues to evolve.

Morrissey himself seems to understand the importance of this image. The singer even admits publicly that his persona is somewhat fabricated: "If I stop at say, five in the afternoon, to do something else — then I don't think everything would be as significant, as strong as it is. I have to work at being who I am."[15] In an article that appears in *Rolling Stone*, Morrissey is quoted as follows: "I find when people and things are entirely revealed in an obvious way ... it freezes the imagination of the observer. There is nothing to probe for, nothing to dwell on or try and unravel. With The Smiths, nothing is ever open and shut."[16] The same could be said about Morrissey's own "solo" persona: with Morrissey, nothing is ever open and shut.

Morrissey as a celebrity embodies a contradictory presentation of his persona as transparent and accessible to his fans, while also being enigmatic. Johnny Rogan states that Morrissey "does not seek to break down the gap between star and audience, but to strengthen its power through the notion of possibility." In other words, Morrissey "can be seen, can be reached, can be touched ... but only for an instant."[17]

In his second biographical book on Morrissey, David Bret continues the decoding of the enigma that is Morrissey by first locating the locus of desire in a young Steven Morrissey's appropriation of personal heroes like James Dean and Oscar Wilde. Bret makes sure to describe these figures as "tormented gay or bisexual ones" while also suggesting that these were figures with which Morrissey could have "safe" relationships. Morrissey himself sheds light on such relationships: "It's easier to fall in love with images and myths. They don't answer back, they don't deceive you. There's no danger."[18] Elsewhere, Morrissey suggests, "it's better to cherish your illusions about people you admire than it is to meet them."[19] As for an autobiography of Morrissey, Bret doubts that one will ever surface, even if the singer suggests that one is in the works:

> Many believe, of course, that the closest one will ever get to Morrissey will be by listening to his songs, that certainly there will never be such a book during his lifetime because this would only defeat the objective of his very existence: Morrissey, stripped and laid bare for all to see, would no longer be of interest because it is his mystery that attracts the most.[20]

Racism

While Morrissey's enigma has worked to draw people to his star image, it is conceivable that other elements of his persona have repulsed people, or at least caused discomfort. After the demise of The Smiths in 1987, Morrissey almost immediately embarked on a solo career, which, though successful, has not been without its major controversies. One of the most enduring and striking controversies is the accusation of racism by the *New Musical Express* in 1992, after incidents at a concert on 8 August at Finsbury Park in London. Appearing on stage in a gold glittery shirt (Mark Simpson suggests that "the transformation into a ruffian was never intended to be complete or unambiguous"), he performed songs from his *Your Arsenal* album, released earlier that summer, including "The National

Front Disco."²¹ The concert featured a backdrop of a photo of a pair of suedeheads, a violent British subculture from the late 1960s and early 1970s. Following this spectacle, the *New Musical Express* published an article outlining Morrissey's apparent racism. In a new preface for the paperback edition of his book, *Morrissey & Marr: The Severed Alliance*, Rogan comments quite pointedly about the racist debate, which he felt was probably inevitable: "The *NME*'s four page dissection of "This Alarming Man" occasionally read like a prosecutor's brief rather than an impartial investigation, but it served its purpose in opening a hornet's nest of speculation." While Rogan recognizes what he calls the *fatwa*, or extreme pronouncement, against Morrissey presumably instigated by the *NME*, he was compelled to balance Morrissey's supposed infatuation with right-wing imagery with what he felt was the singer's liberalism and progressiveness. He concludes, though: "But even I was left to consider whether I had been a little too understanding in chronicling his past and present attitudes towards the Asian community. Adolescent naïvete is such a difficult thing to judge, isn't it Morrissey?"²²

When asked why he waved the Union Jack at a Madness concert, Morrissey suggests that he can no longer remember why, and that there was no plan and that it was not a statement: "No, it was not *necessarily* a statement. What happened was that the NME led the charge. They decided to get rid of me and this was their chance.... They had a board meeting and decided 'Morrissey must go.'"²³ Morrissey claims that the *New Musical Express* was dedicated to his work until they decided that they wanted to be rid of him. But perhaps the *NME* has reason for its criticisms. In its articles, the *New Musical Express* indeed cites many instances of Morrissey appropriating imagery and displaying lyrical subject matter that has been associated with racism and extreme right-wing British nationalism. Dele Fadele of the *NME* finds much of this problematic: "Is he so starved of lyrical ideas that a touch of controversy is the best way to cover-up 'writer's block'? Is he completely fed up with the liberal consensus in the more compassionate side of the media that he's resorted to baiting the right-on crowd? Is there a sizeable degree of irony at work?" At least Fadele considers other explanations for the suggested racism in Morrissey's work, but continues to suggest that Morrissey should stop such associations because of the impressionability of his fans: "Morrissey has held, and continues to hold, sway over the minds of a generation who take tips from his every utterance, try to model themselves on his sense of fashion and live their lives at least partly according to codes he's laid down with a flourish."[24] Such reasoning is simply unacceptable, as it does not take into account the intellect or free will of the audience.

In the *Village Voice*, Simon Frith comments that "as a deliberately English eccentric, Morrissey is now treading a very thin line between a wry celebration of his folk and an obstinate fantasy of the Volk. And one thing's certain, as the idea of Europe crumbles, wacky nationalism is no joke."[25]

In the same issue of *Village Voice*, Armond White feels the song "The National Front Disco" is "a tribute to the out-of-step, the insular, the misunderstood more than a paean to right-wing ideology." He continues, suggesting that the song "needs to be listened to carefully, ironically (although it can be heard as painfully obvious to the NF's bigotry). To hear it plain is to fall for the same propagandistic trap that clamped down on Britain's skinheads and left them paralyzed, Thatchered."[26]

Nevertheless, one industry insider agrees that the fault for Morrissey's racist image can be attributed solely to the singer: "All the racist stuff could have been dealt with if he'd responded immediately.... People expected things to be clarified. That didn't happen, so it grew and grew."[27] In 2001, Morrissey's response to the subject was as follows: "[The British press] accused me of everything from extreme racism to other extremes, which has always been absolute crap. And you can't really go cap in hand to people and say, Oh please accept me — I'm not racist, really. It just doesn't work. So you have to retain your dignity and step away."[28]

As suggested by the *NME*, lyrical content in a few of his songs also contributes to this belief and, as recently as 2003 in the Channel 4 television documentary, the singer has had to defend himself and deny those allegations. At least one reviewer interprets the lyrics in a different way. About "We'll Let You Know" and "The National Front Disco," Mark Coleman explains, "[These songs] peek into the sad, sick world of Britain's neo-fascist youth movement; Morrissey probes this twisted mind-set with psychological depth and deftness. Rather than preach against the general evils of racism, as most topical rockers would, he puts us inside this hopeless situation for a few revealing minutes."[29] What is perhaps striking about Morrissey's exploration of these controversial ideas is that his writing of lyrics suggesting racism was accompanied by a shift to a decidedly more aggressive musical style. The release of *Your Arsenal* signalled a marked change in Morrissey's musical career, which may have perplexed some of his longtime fans. The album also marked a change of mind for the singer. Morrissey states, "I wanted to make as physical a record as I possibly could instead of constantly being curled up in a little ball at the foot of the bed."[30] For those fans who were enamored with a previous — perhaps more cerebral — version of Morrissey, this "physical" persona might have been strange. It could be suggested that the singer's move to Los Angeles in the late 1990s, a major change in terms of Morrissey's longstanding status as a quintessentially English figure, also served to perplex some fans who identified with the singer's nationality or nationalistic elements.

Nationality, or Englishness

Morrissey's expressions of Englishness are at the forefront of his persona. But how does music itself express a specific nationality? The process of answering this question can be daunting, particularly due to the difficulty in determining how music expresses social worlds, or the details of everyday life. For instance, it is difficult to discuss, in any definitive way, how music truly expresses a particular race or region, except through the appropriation of local musics. By extension, it is difficult to discuss how a geographical nation might be expressed in music, especially considering a nation that might encompass various regional and racial distinctions. This might lead to difficulties in determining a cohesive and coherent singular national expression. Furthermore, in an age of advanced communications technologies, spatial and geographical boundaries are no longer limits that might have, in the past, served to categorize certain musics as expressing a geographical nation, by its origin or the origin of its producers. This discussion will begin by providing some examples of musics that have been explicitly identified as "national."

The notion of a "national" music has been studied in musicology, focusing primarily on Classical and Romantic period musics in Western Europe. In the 20th century, Béla Bartók, upon his immigration to the United States, brought with him the folk melodies of his native Hungary. Aaron Copland's orchestral work "Portrait of Lincoln" is now considered an intrinsically American piece of music, performed at the 2002 Super

Bowl as part of a "Tribute to America." These musics are considered "national" primarily through their melodic content, either presenting folk melodies or expressing some notion of the "local." Other musics have been labeled as "national" due to their concordance with national philosophical movements, often expressed in their composition. For instance, Beethoven's Symphony No. 5 has been analyzed for its use of Organicism, manifested in the way in which the composer develops all of his musical thematic material from a single "seed," a fragment of melody or rhythm. The opening four notes of the melody — three notes repeating at the same pitch followed by a single note at a lower pitch — serve as a basis for much of the material for the rest of the symphony; the other musical material is developed out of this single fragment. In turn, Organicism as a philosophy has been linked to German nationalism in the 1800s. Writing about Beethoven often revolves around the Germanic nature of his music and Organicism.[31] Thus, the spirit of a nation, or a national philosophy, can be expressed through musical form. Similarly, Ernest Renan suggests that a nation is built upon a "spiritual principle":

> A nation is a soul, a spiritual principle. Two things, which in truth are but one, constitute this soul or spiritual principle. One lies in the past, one in the present. One is the possession in common of a rich legacy of memories; the other is present-day consent, the desire to live together, the will to perpetuate the value of the heritage that one has received in an undivided form.... A large aggregate of men, healthy in mind and warm of heart, creates the kind of moral conscience which we call a nation.[32]

Perhaps, then, music serves as an effective signifier of national identity. This notion is not without its problems, though.

In an introduction to a journal issue dedicated to the subject of musical analysis and nationality, Richard Taruskin mentions a piece that he wrote for the *New York Times* in which he

> characterized ... what was usually viewed as nationalism in music as just the other side of the coin of German universalism, characterized the latter as a form of colonialism, and called for the deconstruction of our habitual opposition (mainstream/peripheries) thinking, with all its attendant evasions, essentialisms, double standards, and dubious prescriptions.[33]

His comments put notions of nationalism and music in a new light. What has often been labeled as nationalism in musicological circles is now redefined by Taruskin as German universalism. Countering Robert Morgan's suggestion that Skryabin was "himself not a nationalist in orientation," Taruskin writes, "Sure he was — nothing short of a Russian Messianist in fact. It's just that he didn't quote folk songs."[34] For Taruskin, nationalist characteristics in music transcend the inclusion of folk melodies. He suggests that the notion of a "national" music has no place in the present, and that the demand that composers reflect their geographic background "betrays an altogether anachronistic idea of what anybody's immediate background is in an age when all the world's music, along with the music of all history, is instantly available, electronically, to one and all.... No one has a place to stay put in anymore."[35] This lack of place seems to suggest the lack of "nation," as well as to point to the role of communications technologies in its dismantling.

In turn, one may wish to argue that popular music is nothing but "American universalism." John Covach hints at this view in his discussion of the emergence of modern popular music, in which he discusses the fundamental distinction made in American culture between two different kinds of musics. According to Covach, there is a belief that Western art music, derived from its roots in European culture, and popular music, which emerged, in his view, around 1955 with Chuck Berry as the prototypical American rock performer, are radically different.[36] For Covach, therefore, there is a fundamental distinction between the quintessentially European classical tradition and popular music as essentially American. Keith Negus suggests that the quintessentially American character of popular music was noted, and the music feared, before 1955 and the emergence of rock music. "Popular music," in this sense, was one of the cultural forms from the United States whose popularization was seen as a threat. In the early 20th century, European intellectuals noticed the one-way movement of media for entertainment from the United States, warning of "Americanization," a form of cultural imperialism.[37] Middleton suggests that by as early as the 1890s, a "growing internationalization of culture" began, manifesting itself in what Middleton calls "an emerging American hegemony." This is reflected musically in the impact of styles like ragtime and jazz, and in terms of new methods of mass production, "a drive towards 'one-way communication' in homogeneous markets." Also, Middleton describes the emergence of a new youth market after the Second World War. Unlike their parents, this generation was less concerned with established class roles and thus looked to new musical forms, most notably black

American rhythm and blues, as avenues for rebellion.[38] American music became the music of a generation. Negus discusses the "universalism" argument, which speaks of globally recognized American cultural products — like music from Michael Jackson or Madonna, to use his examples — that "serve" the global population, providing a "universal language ... which transcends cultural differences."[39] Nevertheless, there seems to remain a national character that can be expressed even in the case of popular music, and the specter of "American universalism."

Morrissey can serve as a particularly interesting example of national identities expressed in a musical context. In the introduction to a book of Morrissey photos entitled *Morrissey Shot*, Michael Bracewell points out a particularly stirring image:

> The most telling image in this book is that of Morrissey lost in thought, studying the view from a window: his expression is off-set by his black clothes; upon his lapel there is a tiny badge of Great Britain, made out of an enameled Union Jack. This is Morrissey as the solitary ambassador: a lonely, isolated figure, who carries so much invisible emotional baggage.[40]

Morrissey has often been linked to English national identity, not only because of his origins in Manchester but also because of the ways he performs. For instance, Nadine Hubbs notices Morrissey's use of perfect English diction in his singing.[41] An example of this is his proper pronunciation of the word "urinal" in his song "The Boy Racer," in which he pronounces the middle syllable as "ai." This is distinctly English pronunciation on an album that is widely distributed internationally. Also, his lyrics often make reference to various geographical locations in England: he refers to the Battersea district of London in "You're the One for Me, Fatty"; and the title of the album *Your Arsenal* provides both a play on words and might be a reference to the Arsenal football club of North London and the subway stop closest to their pitch. Also, his public display of West Ham United paraphernalia during his tour in 2000 connects him to the East London football club, leading some fans to seek out more information about the team. Bracewell describes this construction of England as follows:

> Morrissey's England was recognizable within the vision of early Auden and late Larkin ... and he shared with them an ambivalence towards the English landscape which seemed always to be mourning something lost.... [He is] the pop cultural embodiment of a century or more of English sensibility.[42]

Bracewell takes this link to nationality even further by suggesting that Morrissey is one of the *true* Brits, and "the Last English Pop Star": "His looking back to a sensibility of Englishness has been driven by a singular aesthetic and ambivalence, in which the deliquescence of national identity becomes a metaphor for personal identity." Bracewell clarifies this link between personal and national identity by suggesting that, for Morrissey, "there is a sense in which his country is in the past (as nostalgia, or memories) and as such he can have no faith in the future ... and little spiritual nourishment in the present."[43]

The substance of Morrissey's Englishness is contested, in a way, by Nabeel Zuberi, who suggests that "Morrissey's brand of Little Englandism is not simply conservative, but both regressive *and* progressive in its conflicted representations of femininity, masculinity, class, race, ethnicity, and region in relation to what becomes identifiably 'national' geography and history." Zuberi discusses these conflicts in more detail while describing an early 1990s version of Morrissey:

> A pop star in London [Morrissey] tells his audience that local language and culture are dead at the hands of American cultural imperialism while he spectacularly sells out a concert in Los Angeles; a performer known for his androgyny and Oscar Wilde obsession is abused by the macho, determinedly hetero English skins [skinheads] he seems to celebrate; and the war in Northern Ireland looms large (if offstage) as an English singer of Irish-Catholic descent wraps himself in the Union Jack.[44]

Interestingly, many still identify him as English, and perhaps as "one of the last truly British people," as he himself claims in one of his songs. Zuberi quotes Morrissey as saying, "I can't become internationalized and I don't think of the world as a place that is mine."[45] To make the case of Morrissey even more interesting, and to add to the many contradictions that surround his public persona, he moved to the United States—Los Angeles, in particular—in the late 1990s. While Morrissey's Englishness is made problematic by his move to Los Angeles, there seems to be some residue that remains with him, a sense of Englishness as being an intrinsic part of his identity. He has not stopped performing songs that reference English locality, although he has distanced himself from his English heritage, as will be explained shortly.

For Morrissey, Los Angeles is a city that he suggests is now the origin of the English language instead of London; in the song "Glamorous Glue,"

Morrissey sings, rather harshly, that London is dead.[46] More recently, he has seemingly broken ties with England while reaching out to a large Latino fan base in the United States, through songs like "Mexico" and "First of the Gang to Die," which chronicles the life (and death) of Hector, a member of a Latino street gang. There is an interesting parallel in the way that his nationality has, like his gender, also been performed in an ambiguous, and perhaps even contradictory, way. Morrissey has problematized what has been written about him in the past and continues to provide difficulties for his categorization, in terms of gender and nationality. For instance, against his previous use of perfect British pronunciation, Morrissey has chosen to speak at times with an American accent, as during his concert tour of the western United States in 2002. During an interview with Janice Long on her BBC Radio Two show in October 2002, Morrissey speaks with a slightly Irish accent. Bret explains, "The second song he performed, complementing a new speech affectation (pronouncing the word 'any' as 'annie,' Irish-style) was the sublime 'Irish Blood, English Heart'—'The components that make up my tubby little body,' he told Long."[47] Morrissey uses a distinct Irish pronunciation for the title of that song when he introduces it on Zane Lowe's BBC Radio One show in May of 2004. Morrissey continues to challenge the very utility of nationalistic labels applied to his persona and continues to generate controversies around his representation of nationalism.

Concluding Remarks

Morrissey's ambiguity with respect to gender and sexuality comes to the forefront in much of the writing about him, and a major part of his career has been overshadowed by the stigma of racism and right-wing nationalism. Furthermore, Morrissey's nationalism has become problematized in recent years by his physical move away from England, his distancing of himself from his English upbringing and his appropriation of his Irish ancestry.

In a recent interview, Jim Nelson asks Morrissey if the singer's one-time irrelevancy ever bothered him. He answers:

> I was never irrelevant to myself. And I was never irrelevant to a lot of people. And they were the people who mattered to me.... You can't let the good go to your head, because therefore you must ... believe the bad. So consequently I don't believe anything.... Which is very confusing on Thursday nights.[48]

2

"The Songs That Saved Your Life"
Critical Reception of the Works of Morrissey

This discussion begins with a survey of critical reception of his albums; these reviews contribute to the discourse that forms Morrissey's celebrity persona. It is through these reviews that various elements of the singer's star image are developed and disseminated.

Morrissey's changing star image is first glimpsed through album reviews and early interviews. The reviews and profiles provide a unique insight into the construction of his persona, because they indicate elements of Morrissey's star image already in flux, being questioned and discussed. Furthermore, the reviewers and their reviews expand and develop, as well as disseminate, a more robust star image, starting at the earliest stages of the singer's career. It is to these reviews, as well as to the themes present in Morrissey's own lyrics, that this discussion now turns.

It should be noted that this is not an exhaustive study of every Morrissey song on every album with which he has been involved. Rather, most of the studio albums by The Smiths and during Morrissey's solo career have been explored in terms of lyrical themes and topics of the songs. This study should not be considered the ultimate guide to Morrissey's writing. Of particular use is Simon Goddard's excellent *Mozipedia: The Encyclopedia of Morrissey and The Smiths*, a compendium of every Smiths and Morrissey song as well as a wealth of other relevant information. Nevertheless, this survey will serve to elucidate the themes most prevalent in Morrissey's artistic output.

The Smiths

The 10 November 1983 issue of *Rolling Stone* features a small write-up on The Smiths, in which Morrissey's musings about the popular music scene are quoted: "It's quite lifeless, faceless, synthetic. I can't think of anybody I'd cross the street to see.... Just to see modern music in its present state is like seeing a kitten dying." The author of the write-up continues by pointing out an ironic element of The Smiths' music: "Like the rest of the Smiths' music, [their first single "Hand in Glove" is] guitar-driven rock & roll, with lyrics about sex and love. As Morrissey says, 'I want to get back to affairs of the heart.'"[1] Bret notes that "the single did well in the independent charts, got nowhere in the national, but has since more than made up for this."[2] It should be noted that in early 1984, The Smiths found themselves quite successful in the independent charts: "Three of their records [occupy] the top three positions in the independent charts, and ... [they have been] voted Best New Act in the *New Musical Express* poll."[3]

The Smiths' self-titled debut album was released in February 1984. The first track begins with Mike Joyce's drums, which are quickly overtaken by Morrissey's voice. "Reel Around the Fountain," a mid-tempo ode to a strange relationship (it is unknown if the relationship is sexual or not) reveals The Smiths, musically, as a band not afraid to introduce themselves to the listener by playing beautiful and calming music and conveying quite ambivalent lyrics. In fact, the music, which can be described as comforting, lilting and lovely, seems not to coincide with the difficult — and diffident — lyrics, which describe a narrator that would, perhaps, be reluctantly happy to accept an invitation to some sort of tryst for at least 15 minutes.

A listener would be immediately and painfully aware of the difficulty of decoding Morrissey's lyrics, particularly in terms of whether they express happiness or something more sinister. The narrator might not say "no" to a tryst, or 15 minutes (or whatever) with one that, it seems, is much older, or, perhaps, one who lives a much more reserved or constrained life than normal. Rather, the narrator accepts tea and mutual admiration; this seems enough for now.

Johnny Marr's guitar line at the end of "Pretty Girls Make Graves" seems to musically foreshadow Alain Whyte's guitar line at the beginning (and throughout) Morrissey's "Hold On to Your Friends," from *Vauxhall and I* from 1994.

2. "The Songs That Saved Your Life"

One thing that seems constant in these early songs is repetition; Marr's guitar accompaniment and the work of the rhythm section seem to be a kind of recurring, meandering bed for the smooth sound of Morrissey's voice. His voice is higher here, perhaps thinner, than it is later in his career. But it is certainly his voice. One of the more striking examples of his singing on this first album is the song "Still Ill," a kind of anthem to the infidelity of the past and the suspicion of the future; the narrator decrees that life is only taking without giving anything in return, and wonders if he is whole or suffering some detriment. The encouragement is not particularly strong if one says that there are good moments in life, though they do not come around very often. Such sentiment continues in "Hand in Glove," the first single released by The Smiths, where the narrator suggests that "we" stick together, though, right at the end, he suggests that the relationship will not continue: he will probably never see the other again, because he really is unlucky.

Illness emerges again in Morrissey's lyrics for "What Difference Does It Make?" where the protagonist has been betrayed by a companion yet still feels loyalty, a fondness even, toward him or her. The illness is a result of the loss of the companion, leaving both parties alone.

The violence of the lyrics is evident in many of the songs, but most of all in the slower numbers that round out the album. For the protagonist (or is it antagonist?) in "I Don't Owe You Anything," he understands that life is not so nice, and though he is not indebted to the other, the other is certainly indebted to him, and he has come for payment. Though the narrator suggests that repayment will bring a smile, it seems unlikely.

Violence of a more heinous nature emerges in the final song, which recounts the so-called Moors murders. Between 1963 and 1965, Ian Brady and Myra Hindley murdered five people aged from 10 to 17 years, and buried four of them in the Saddleworth Moor, a moorland that is part of greater Manchester. In the song, Morrissey mentions only Hindley, who died in 2002. The song mentions three of the victims by name, 12-year-old John Kilbride (the second victim of the Moors murderers), 10-year-old Lesley Ann Downey (fourth victim), and 17-year-old Edward Evans (fifth victim). The song assumes Hindley's complete guilt; while Hindley did not actually kill the victims, she was complicit in their deaths, and the song suggests as such. For Morrissey here in the song, Manchester will forever be to blame for these murders; Manchester will be taken to account for them. Even as of 2010, the body of 12-year-old Keith Bennet (Brady and Hindley's third victim) has not been found.

The first album ends much as it begins; while the last track is explicitly haunting (in terms of the gravity of its subject matter), the first is implicitly haunting. The last track seems to point to violence that takes a life. "Reel Around the Fountain" deals with taking, shoving, pinning and mounting, a life that is perhaps given. Morrissey's wit is, for the most part, absent here, as is the beauty of his voice. It is overshadowed by violence, something that has shown itself in his more recent music.

In his four-star review of the band's self-titled album, Kurt Loder "affirms" Morrissey's "homosexuality," a position that is apparently transparent within the music: "His memories of heterosexual rejection and homosexual isolation seem too persistently painful to be dealt with obliquely." Loder continues: "Whether recalling the confusion of early heterosexual encounters ('I'm not the man you think I am') or the sometimes heartless reality of the gay scene, Morrissey lays out his life like a shoebox full of faded snapshots."[4] Loder later suggests that the album is "an intriguing curio, but not necessarily a keeper."[5]

Don Watson of the *New Musical Express* also refers to Morrissey's sexuality when reviewing The Smiths' self-titled debut album. He writes,

> Throughout the LP he plucks at the same strings of homoeroticism: "I'm not the man you think I am," he intimates coyly on "Pretty Girls Make Graves" concluding, "I've lost my faith in Womanhood"—both of which are in fact snippets open to entirely opposite interpretations.[6]

Watson comments on how Morrissey makes seemingly obvious references to specific genders, but that he does so deftly. Watson quotes Morrissey's lyrics, "'Into the depths of the criminal world I followed her...' calling up a reference to Cocteau's Orpheus films ... where Cocteau's Orpheus is left unable to look at his wife.... Morrissey ends with 'I need advice because nobody ever looks at me twice.'" Watson concludes by noting Morrissey's ability to emote "a notion of despair reflected perfectly in the lacklustre sound of his cohorts, [and] a death of the punk ideals," but in a unique way. Morrissey is distinguished by "his wit, and ... the sensitivity to deal in despair without resorting to preaching in desperation."[7] Others at the *NME* did not think the album is so extraordinary; Danny Kelly writes, "The frenziedly-awaited debut LP disappoints, thanks to elephants-ear production (grey and flat), and ludicrously overblown expectations."[8]

2. "The Songs That Saved Your Life"

Before releasing their next album, The Smiths' record label, Rough Trade, released what Johnny Rogan calls an "interim album," *Hatful of Hollow*, in November 1984: "Bringing together the John Peel and David Jensen [radio] sessions, plus selected rare flip-sides ... [the album] proved an excellent compilation and superb value for money."[9]

The Smiths starts with a somber tone, while *Hatful of Hollow* begins with a much brighter sound. The first track, entitled "William, It Was Really Nothing," focuses on relationships (like most pop songs) but without romance (unlike most pop songs). Though the life that the narrator leads is boring, it is nonetheless his, and he feels the need to live it. Morrissey's wit has finally come to the forefront. The narrator wishes to marry someone who, it seems, might wish to marry another, a fat girl who might agree to marriage, but who also requires that the ring be bought, one who does not care about a thing. Instead, the narrator will agree to marriage with William, and he can buy the ring as well. The difference between the narrator and the fat girl, though, is that the narrator cares, or so it seems.

What is particularly clear here is the gender of the narrator, who is most probably not male. The listener is confronted with a gender presentation within the narrative of the song that seems to go against the singer's own gender presentation. Ambiguity ensues.

Some tracks on this album are re-recordings of some of the tracks from *The Smiths*, these new recordings being from live radio sessions on BBC Radio One. "These Things Take Time" is a new track in the midst of the older ones. Illness is the theme again, and the narrator is simply stuck in ineptitude and will not win in the end, anyway. The narrator will be left behind (not unlike the narrator in more than one song on *The Smiths*). Wit is present, though; the narrator refuses to believe that things will not work out in this relationship (until the very end of the song, that is). In a particularly humorous moment, the narrator suggests that he never would have thought that the other would have cared, and, in fact, the other did not. But, of course, these things take time; patience will work wonders (until the very end of the song, that is).

The iconic and anthemic "How Soon Is Now?" appears here, with its cry for love, which all humans deserve. As one who has inherited a terrible shyness, the narrator wishes for companionship. Even when one goes to a club to meet others, there is the constant risk of being alone and leaving alone, which seems to be the case. The narrator ends, though, by acknowledging that too much time has passed; all his hope is gone.

"Handsome Devil" features Morrissey's voice as one element in a wall of sound, a strong voice devoid of gentleness, again hinting at violence. In the song appear whips, those deserving various sorts of treatment, swallowing and a general air of consumption. The re-recording of "Hand in Glove," which appeared on *The Smiths*, fades in (as if a continuation of the recording on the earlier album). Morrissey sounds consumed by the other members of the band, with his voice placed in the back of the mix, as if the microphone was far away from him. The song fades out, perhaps allowing the song to continue indefinitely.

The static nature of Morrissey's vocal delivery is most obvious on "Heaven Knows I'm Miserable Now," a song that features the singer returning constantly to the same pitch. The narrator sings of the constant giving of time to those that do not care for his welfare. Morrissey's static singing is punctuated by moments of singing in the higher register; his voice jumps an octave while singing the same notes as before. His tonal center remains the same. While the melodic contour of his vocal line is relatively static, the accompaniment provided by the band is upbeat and bright. It can be read as ironic that there is such a difference between the melodic contour of the vocal line and its accompaniment; it stresses ambivalence.

"This Night Has Opened My Eyes" is a particularly haunting song that deals with death and tragedy. It seems to tell of the death of a baby by drowning, presumably at the hands of its mother. The song speaks of the lies of the father of the child, and the range of emotions experienced by those involved in the narrative, emotions that are often in conflict with each other. On the one hand, the future could have held much promise for the child, and thus its death was a terrible waste. On the other hand, this baby was a real thing that would have stolen its mother's dreams. In the end, happiness and sadness are all that are left.

"Girl Afraid" focuses on a boy and girl, both wanting the other but both too afraid to do anything other than stare. The girl is suspicious of the boy's intentions, while the boy is simply being careful and thoughtful: prudence is not what is needed in this situation. She thinks that he does not notice her, while he thinks that she does not like him. This song shows ambivalence at its greatest. Nothing happened, and nothing will.

Morrissey's gentleness, something that seems to develop in his voice as his career has matured, shows itself in the last couple of songs on the album. The violence or ambivalence of *The Smiths* is replaced with a sweet melancholy, a kind of sadness devoid of the darkness of the previous release.

About *Hatful of Hollow*, Bill Black writes a more guarded review:

> Of course, we've learnt to laugh at the more salacious aspects of Morrissey's self-pity and theatrical torture — and become blase [*sic*] in the presence of [Johnny] Marr's lithe melodies — but then who can retain the shock of the new? Suffice to say, few have matched the economy and excitement of the Smiths' patented dynamics.[10]

For Black, the drummer and bass player redeem the "more salacious aspects" of the other two more prominent members of the band. Mike Joyce and Andy Rourke get the respect they deserve by being featured in a photograph on the album liner in which they are shown as equal members, standing beside the others rather than in separate photos, as in the insert that accompanies their debut. About this photo, Black comments, "It brings to the fore the maligned but magnificent rhythm section of Joyce and Rourke." He continues, "Those drums and bass just keep turning; prodding and pricking the gossamer sheen of Marr's guitar and the lacey skin of Morrissey's vocal."[11] It should be noted that at least in the liner insert of the compact disc version of the album, there are two photos of Morrissey alone, without his band-mates.[12] Furthermore, in the photos that accompany the debut album, *The Smiths*, all four members are photographed separately, with Morrissey shown in performance and Marr perhaps clapping. Joyce and Rourke, however, are pictured in a standard "portrait-like" fashion, facing the camera.[13] In the later presentation of the band, none of the performers are particularly favored. Perhaps Black appreciates the picture of the band in *Hatful of Hollow* because of its presentation of the group as unified, or as a whole, with all the members together in one photo.

Released in early 1985, The Smiths' second album is entitled *Meat Is Murder*. The first track on the album is called "The Headmaster Ritual." Here we hear the voice of Morrissey, full of richness and without much of the harshness that is certainly present in *The Smiths* and shows itself throughout *Hatful of Hollow*. While Morrissey gently and smoothly delivers his vocals, the lyrics he sings recount experiences at Manchester schools, full of violence and loneliness, causing one to abandon life, education, and to desire for home.

"Rusholme Ruffians" revisits some of the themes in the earlier Smiths albums, namely loneliness, love, violence and sexuality. The listener is treated to various characters: a boy who is the victim of a mugging; a woman who is engaged; a woman who lifts her skirt to show her legs; and a school girl who is unsuccessful in finding a companion (or so it is assumed). As the narrator recounts these players, he walks home alone, though he still believes in love. This song is a vivid account of life at the end of a country fair or carnival.

"I Want the One I Can't Have" is an example of the maturing songwriting of Johnny Marr and is a fine specimen of Morrissey's descriptive lyric writing. The narrator sings of wanting those things that the narrator does not have, including being quite impressed by a tough and rough colleague who (doubtfully) killed a police officer when he was 13 years old. It is maddening to not get what one wants, especially when it is something one cannot have. This song is a hint at how celebrity works; the maintenance of desire is required for a celebrity to survive. Morrissey understands this notion and uses it to its utmost.

In "That Joke Isn't Funny Anymore," Morrissey sings from the perspective of one who feels so very lonely and would rather end his life than continue without love. The laughter and joking at the expense of these people does not make the narrator happy; but suddenly, one who laughs at those who are lonely is (perhaps) loving the narrator. The narrator will experience what he has seen happen to other people but never first hand. While this might seem to be a happy ending, it is presented somewhat as a lament. For the narrator, happiness is not sure and all-encompassing, since happiness is such a foreign idea. Curiously, the music fades at the end of the song only to resurge and play for a few more seconds before fading a final time (a reflection of the uncertainty of this new experience of love and acceptance, perhaps).

Morrissey's wit and humor come to the forefront again with the wonderful "Nowhere Fast." The lyrics describe an individual who would happily drop his pants to the world and the Queen in order to properly convey his dissatisfaction with life. The individual, though, suggests that death would be no more appealing than life. For the narrator, the sound of a train passing by seems to be one of the saddest, perhaps because of the inability for him to be on it, to move along from the present life. All of this sentiment is wrapped in a light and humorous sound supplied by the rest of the band.

Lightness continues to be the backdrop for abject loneliness in "Well I Wonder," where the narrator is barely alive in the presence of one that he cannot have, one that barely notices him. He asks simply for consideration.

Consideration is the least of the requests in "Barbarism Begins at Home," another diatribe against violence in Manchester schools, hearkening back to the earlier track on this album, "The Headmaster Ritual." Morrissey is no longer gentle here, and neither is the accompaniment of the rest of the band; all responses by misbehaving children are met with violence.

The last track is one of The Smiths' most political, and most popular. "Meat Is Murder" has often been cited as the song that convinced many to become vegetarian. In the song, Morrissey equates heifers to human beings and suggests that animal death for the purpose of human consumption is murder ("murder" is printed in the lyric sheet in capital letters). He suggests that if one knew how animals were slaughtered, one would not consume them; he suggests that the stench of cooking flesh in the kitchen is the flavor of murder. Here, animals are not unlike the various characters that Morrissey so vividly embodies and describes in his songs; their cry is unheard. The protagonist in "Well I Wonder" is experiencing the same thing; the character in "What She Said" is also alone, unnoticed. The power in the song is not only in the sounds of cattle and chainsaws at the beginning (sounds that bring the subject matter of the song directly to the ears of the listener, who might not be used to such a close association between the two sounds) but also in the relationship that Morrissey establishes between voiceless animals and voiceless human beings, those who are lonely and outside of society. While it is unnatural to consume the flesh of animals, it is also unnatural to ignore the outcast in society (something that, for Morrissey, seems too *natural* in society, as is the consumption of meat).

In a review of *Meat Is Murder*, Tim Holmes writes about what he calls Morrissey's "curiously puritanical concept of love," suggesting that the singer is "conscious of thwarted passion and inappropriate response, yet remains oddly distant from his own self-absorption." Holmes also attempts to read into the mental state of Morrissey and his unhappiness: "The simple pleasures of others make him uncomfortable, as if these activities were the cause of his own grand existential suffering."[14] Paul Du Noyer of the *New Musical Express* has this to say about Morrissey on "Meat Is Murder":

> We afford him the sort of license that's normally only extended to children and idiots, sensing the presence of an innocence and simplicity that's been civilised out of the rest of us, and a kind of insight also. The deaf-aids, the flowers, the NHS specs, they're all the trappings of an artful vulnerability.[15]

The Queen Is Dead, released in 1986, was The Smiths' most praised album. It features a confident Morrissey singing right from the start on the title track. In fact, this is a new sort of Morrissey; he seems to have shed his diffident image in order to make fun of the Queen of England and her son (at least, through the voice of the narrator of the song). At the end, the narrator says that life is long when one is lonely. Loneliness continues as a theme in the music of The Smiths.

"Frankly, Mr. Shankly" features Morrissey's voice as modest but clear. In the song, the narrator wishes for fame though it might be detrimental in the end. The insults and wordplay that are introduced in "The Queen Is Dead" continue in "Frankly, Mr. Shankly," where the narrator calls Mr. Shankly a real nuisance, but, of course, he is speaking frankly.

Death is evoked in "I Know It's Over," featuring some of Morrissey's gentlest vocals, over an equally gentle accompaniment, until the end of the track, that is, when the narrator calls to his mother, as he is buried under the ground. "Never Had No One Ever" features Morrissey as a crooner, a style that will emerge more fully in his solo career. Here he sings of a life of 20 years alone; imagine living life in a constant state of unease. Even once the short lyrics are delivered, the music continues, repeating the musical phrases; the song fades out, again an instance where the song does not end but continues out of range of the listener, much like the life of the narrator.

Finally, a light-hearted song comes next, one in which the narrator asks another to meet at the "Cemetry Gates," for some reason misspelled. The song seems to recount a kind of gentle fight, one with Keats and Yeats on their side, while the narrator has Wilde on his (so, naturally, he is the winner). The song humorously describes plagiarism (when one produces text too good for one's talent) and then incredulity (when one produces a text for words that could only be their own). The gates of the cemetery are where the couple go on days when the sun comes out, where they are wanted, among those who no longer have a voice.

2. "The Songs That Saved Your Life"

"Bigmouth Strikes Again" is a song in which violence is humorous and perhaps not serious. The narrator was only teasing to suggest violence toward a lover, but he knows what it feels like to be burned at the stake. Perhaps his joke, violence, is his crime, and his sentence is to be burned, at least metaphorically. In fact, the narrator has no right to even be called "human," so dastardly is his crime. Morrissey continues to perform this song, though recent performances include Joan of Arc listening to a melting iPod music player rather than the Sony Walkman in the 1986 version of the song.

A love song, "The Boy with the Thorn in His Side," seems to evoke regality. This is due to the rhythm of Morrissey's vocal line, where he uses "over-dotted" rhythm, a technique that was often used in the Baroque-period French Overture, an orchestral piece performed in the courts of French royalty and aristocracy. The song explores the notion of forbidden love, a love that is not believed to be true.

Morrissey's ability to paint vivid pictures continues here with "Vicar in a Tutu," in which he describes exactly that. But this Vicar, though perhaps strange to the world at large, is simply choosing to live his life in this way. For the narrator, it is simply a lifestyle choice for the Vicar and should not be considered strange at all. The song, though, is not only about the Vicar but also about the narrator, one who is relegated to doing work on the roof of the church, something that others would simply laugh at. For the narrator, this work, and the laughter that might come because of it, is worth it for the sight of the dancing Vicar. The narrator ends the song by suggesting that he is a living sign, something that the singer also is: a rich "text" to be decoded.

"There Is a Light That Never Goes Out" is one of the most powerful, and popular, songs from this era. It speaks of unrequited love, where the narrator feels he does not belong at home but is comfortable in the presence of the other. The narrator seems to almost wish for death; death with the companion would be a pleasure. This song is anthemic; it speaks to loneliness and acceptance, as well as the fears that all of us experience in love and relationships. Morrissey's vocal delivery is particularly emotional on this track; his voice is impassioned without being harsh, and he seems to express the sentiments of the song without particular irony. It is no wonder that he still performs this song live, and that he must compete with the voices of the crowd singing the song back to him when he does so.

"Some Girls Are Bigger than Others" begins suddenly with a quick fade-in, subsequent fade-out and then perhaps a more proper fade-in. We have experienced this at the end of another Smiths song, "That Joke Isn't Funny Anymore." There it functioned to indicate the uncertainty of love; here it seems to evoke uncertainty, but due to the lyrical content of the song, it suggests playfulness as well. One the one hand, this fade-in and immediate fade-out catches the listener, surprises her and causes her to listen more intently. On the other hand, such a sonic gesture suggests that the song has always been, and that the listener is "tuning in" to a particular, important moment. The song consists of one short stanza in which the title of the song is repeated, while implicating not only girls but some girls' mothers as well. Morrissey is not writing about absolute absurdity, though; he is discussing bodily difference, a simple thing. Toward the end of the song, Morrissey delivers a set of lyrics with some sort of muted effect on his voice: he sings of pillows and dreams and an exchange of ideas. While the song is about difference, it ends on a note of commonness: we all sleep, and we all dream.

These songs move away from the general trend of the previous Smiths albums, moving away from themes of loneliness and alienation (though those sentiments do still exist here) into subject areas such as politics. Also, Morrissey's talent with humour is certainly more evident. Perhaps these are reasons why the album has gained so much critical acclaim and why it seems to have weathered time so well. It is a more mature album, even if tracks like "Vicar in a Tutu" and "Some Girls Are Bigger than Others" seem to indicate otherwise, at least upon first listen. The darkness of the earlier albums is almost universally replaced with at least a surface lightness here.

In his review of *The Queen Is Dead*, released in 1986, Mark Coleman comments on Morrissey's self-deprecation: "It's hard to imagine Morrissey poking fun at himself, but here's the same self-righteous lettucehead of *Meat Is Murder* singing a song called 'Bigmouth Strikes Again.'" Coleman makes reference to Morrissey's vegetarianism by unceremoniously referring to him as a "lettucehead." Coleman continues with the pejorative comments in mentioning other songs on the album: "As expected, Morrissey dons his misery-goat costume for 'I Know It's Over' and 'Never Had No One Ever' (except for Mom, [naturally])."[16]

Two Smiths compilations follow in 1987, *The World Won't Listen*, released in the United Kingdom, and *Louder Than Bombs*, released in

North America. The two releases are similar in that they contain many tracks only available as singles and, in the case of *Louder Than Bombs*, tracks previously available only in the United Kingdom.

"Panic" begins *The World Won't Listen*, an anthem against music that one hears on the radio, music that is absolutely irrelevant to the everyday experience of the narrator. The song features a children's choir echoing the narrator's call for the public execution of the disc jockey, a feature that foreshadows the children's choir throughout *Ringleader of the Tormentors*, released in 2007.

"Ask" seems to reflect the mood of the 1980s, where the threat of nuclear annihilation was close in people's minds. Here the narrator speaks against shyness (something that usually plagues the protagonists in Morrissey's lyrics) and encourages the object of the lyrics to ask if they want to try something new (rather than stay inside on a sunny day and write poetry to ugly foreign girls). Of course, if love will not bring the two together, the atomic bomb will.

"London" mentions a train in the second line of the song, and the music seems to evoke one, with its driving guitar accompaniment and Morrissey's forceful vocals. The song recounts the departure of a man, away from his family and girlfriend; Morrissey sings as the voice in his mind wondering if he has made the right decision to leave, an act of which his family is jealous, even if it appears that they are sad because of his decision. There is no sense, though, that the departure means freedom; rather, the departure seems to signal only uncertainty for the future, and doubt as to whether the decision to leave was the right one.

Morrissey seems to make a reference to Bob Dylan (or, at the very least, to the type of celebrity that Dylan embodies) in "Shakespeare's Sister," when he suggests that an acoustic guitar is all that is required to be a protest singer. It seems that the protagonist is wanting to go to his lover, and his mother is preventing him from doing so. Along with this external struggle, the narrator seems to struggle with suicidal thoughts.

Another of The Smiths' more enduring songs is "Shoplifters of the World Unite," in which the narrator asks the listener to learn to love them (something Morrissey does with each appearance of his star image). It seems that boredom is the reason for crime (in this case, petty theft, if one is to take the lyrics literally) and, in this case, crime does not pay; six months is the sentence.

"Asleep" is a song in which the bored of the world ask for rest—final rest—because of the lack of companionship (the theme of loneliness is present here after a time of absence in The Smiths' output). The narrator wants to sleep, to die, in order to go to a better world (though he is not altogether sure it exists). Nevertheless, he says goodbye.

"Unloveable" is Morrissey's way of identifying with the outsider in society. The narrator claims that he is unloveable, but he gives all of himself anyway. This song contains one of the most famous lyrics in the whole of The Smiths' catalogue: the narrator wears black as a reflection of his inner feelings (as an aside, Morrissey very rarely wore outfits of all black). If the narrator seems strange to the rest of the world, well, that is because he is. He is an outcast, and he knows it; if only one would get to know him, though.

"Half a Person" features the story of the life of the narrator, who lodged at the YWCA, the Young Women's Christian Association, a humorous twist on expectations. This occurred when the narrator was young, clumsy and shy, but it remains the story of his life, the recurring theme of all that transpired since. Of course, there is no way for him to actually stay at a YWCA, no matter how much he might like to.

In "Stretch Out and Wait," the narrator seems to evoke "Half a Person" with the notion of the impulses of youth, and "Shakespeare's Sister" with the requests for the small body to lay down, to go down to the death. In this case the death is actually a physical experience rather than the end of life. The song speaks of cold hands and cold blood, of awkwardness and questions of the future without answers. It is a wonderfully bleak look at the difficulties associated with physical intimacy. It informs the view fans have of Morrissey's own perceived celibacy; it is physically impossible for Morrissey to be physically involved with another, at least in the conventional sense. For Morrissey (and his fans), intimacy occurs in concert.

"You Just Haven't Earned It Yet, Baby" (a song title quoted in The Smiths' later song "Paint a Vulgar Picture," from *Strangeways, Here We Come*) describes struggle, how every move forward comes through suffering. Suffering comes in the familiar form of loneliness, longing, cruelty and rudeness. In the later song, "Paint a Vulgar Picture," this song title is cited in the lyrics; there is no mistake that that is a reference to this. That song explores stardom and the constant commodification of popular music. But great success will not come (if one thinks it great success in the context of "Paint a Vulgar Picture") until suffering passes.

"Sheila Take a Bow," from *Louder Than Bombs*, is a prime example of Morrissey's ambiguous lyric writing: it is here that he switches the narrator's gender. He first identifies himself as a boy (a gender that is naturally assigned to him by the listener) and then, only a few words later, identifies himself as a girl (and changes the gender of the subject of the song as well). This is altogether strange considering that the title of the song refers to the subject as Sheila (and this cannot easily be a boy). On the one hand, this song, with its change in gender, seems to invite both genders to find ones that they love rather than staying at home. On the other hand, this song is an excellent example of Morrissey presenting gender in flux, the male narrator identifying at once as a boy and at the next moment as a girl.

"Golden Lights" explores the nature of celebrity and its power to change, something that the narrator laments. The title refers to the displaying of the subject's name in lights, now that he has become popular; it is explained that the subject is a singer and that he has made a record and with fame has come change. The narrator (a woman) laments that she has been forgotten. This song foreshadows "You Were Good in Your Time," from 2009's *Years of Refusal*, a song that seems to explore fame that has passed. In that song, the subject is in the last moments of life and is being thanked for making the narrator(s) feel accepted. Many ascribe this sentiment to Morrissey, and so it is not a stretch to consider that this song, sung *by* Morrissey, is *about* Morrissey. While "Golden Lights" explores the change that comes from celebrity, which leads to neglect, "You Were Good in Your Time" explores the good things that come from celebrity, particularly from the perspective of fans: the investment of time and capital in celebrities by fans returns in many different ways—in this case, the investment returns in the form of belonging. Morrissey makes us feel less alone, less neglected.

In his review of *Louder Than Bombs*, Jim Farber notes Morrissey's evocation of despair as an essential part of his persona, coupled with Morrissey's more obvious use of humour. He states,

> Morrissey's sarcasm may lend him an air of self-awareness, but on another level he communicates feelings of deprivation deep enough to make those lyrical exaggerations seem absolutely literal. No small wonder, then, that audiences identify so closely with Morrissey. He speaks for the masochist in all of us.[17]

"A Rush and a Push and the Land Is Ours" opens *Strangeways, Here We Come*, The Smiths' final studio album, released in 1987. The song features Morrissey growling (while singing) for the first time in a studio context. Each time the singer begins the chorus, he sings the words with a growl, something that he continues to do in various songs in live performance.

"Death of a Disco Dancer" outlines the narrator's sceptical view of the world, where death is a particularly common occurrence. Love and peace might be something to strive for; however, they will not occur in this world. The narrator suggests that to think otherwise is a sign of ignorance.

Another of The Smiths' most enduring songs is "Girlfriend in a Coma," a title later used by Douglas Coupland as the title of his 1998 novel. In the song, the narrator is lamenting over the fact that his girlfriend is in a coma; he wonders if she will survive and wake up again. At one point, the narrator wishes not to see her but then begs to see her. The serious nature of the lyrics is greatly contrasted by the light, and playful, accompaniment by the other members of the band.

The beginning strains of "Stop Me If You Think You've Heard This One Before" are anthemic in nature, with building chords leading to the beginning of the singing. The song seems to tell the story of one who has been mistreated, and mistreating, and that nothing has changed. Morrissey's wit shows again when the narrator explains that he still loves the subject of the song, and that this has not changed, though he loves them only a bit less than he did before.

The narrator in "Last Night I Dreamt That Somebody Loved Me" laments that the dream in the title was not a reflection of reality, but simply another dream. This is a constant state for the narrator, as he admits toward the end of the song. Like this state of being, the song fades out; it also goes on.

"Unhappy Birthday" is light in its aural qualities yet dire in its lyrical character. The narrator holds nothing but ill will toward the subject of the song, because the subject is not very nice, either. Like "Girlfriend in a Coma," this song seems upbeat and light, though it seems to explore issues such as the narrator's suicide due to the subject's badness.

"Death at One's Elbow" is a dark look at desire. The narrator implores Glenn to stay home because of the narrator's love for him (or her, I suppose). Desire becomes violence toward Glenn (he is warned to stay away for his own safety), and then desire become violence toward the narrator himself. The narrator says goodbye.

2. "The Songs That Saved Your Life"

"I Won't Share You" showcases Morrissey's crooning voice, on the eve of his solo career. The song seems to be a true foreshadowing of Morrissey's success as a solo artist. It is his time to be free, to feed his drive and dream, something that the narrator cannot share with another. This song is a farewell as well. It is fitting that this song is the last on the final studio album of The Smiths.

It is important to note that the lyrics of The Smiths are devoid of much reference to religion. In all of the songs, it seems that only "The Queen Is Dead," with its admonishment to the listeners of the greed of the church, "Bigmouth Strikes Again," with its reference to Joan of Arc, and "Vicar in a Tutu," with its reference to the Vicar, explore elements of religion at all. These references are few and contrast the direct engagement with religion, and Christianity in particular, that occurs almost immediately in the solo music of Morrissey.

In their review of *Strangeways, Here We Come*, it would seem that *Rolling Stone* takes a rather negative stance regarding Morrissey, as a vocalist who "bleats" rather than sings.[18] Ascribing an instance of Morrissey's irony to almost fatal error, David Browne states that while the singer "makes the mistake of putting down record-company marketing" on the song "Paint a Vulgar Picture," the album includes a merchandising address printed on its sleeve.[19] Morrissey himself perhaps solicits negative reviews like those in *Rolling Stone*. Len Brown suggests that the album serves as an invitation for negative reviews, going so far as claiming that the album "finds Morrissey with one hoof heavily into his sarcophagus." He continues, "From the opening line of the positively raunchy 'A Rush And A Push And The Land Is Ours' ... it seems as if he's determined to give his fun 'n' money-lovin' critics as much ammo for derision as humanely possible." Brown suggests that Morrissey relishes in calling a song "Stop Me If You Think You've Heard This One Before" in the face of critics who think that all of his songs sound similar.[20]

Rolling Stone appreciates The Smiths in retrospect, as made evident in a review of the group's live album, *Rank*, released in 1988. Jim Farber's review of the live show seems to foreshadow Morrissey's future solo concert appearances.

> [The context of live performance] pushes Morrissey's depression into anger, liberating his self-pity into righteousness. Better yet, divorced from the lonely confines of home listening, the Smiths' songs in concert become the rallying

points of unity for the alienated.... In the process, the album captures the one element of the Smiths left undocumented elsewhere — their fury.[21]

With the departure of guitarist Johnny Marr in May 1987, The Smiths disbanded. The group made the split official after a few months of their status being in flux. Morrissey claims that he had no knowledge of the official demise of the band until he himself read it in the *New Musical Express*. One of the reasons for the split, cited by the article, was Johnny Marr's trip to the United States to record with the group Talking Heads. Morrissey suggests that he did not know of Marr's travels until reading about it in the *NME*, thus negating the article's claim.[22] Rogan states that it wasn't until the second week in September that Morrissey officially pronounced The Smiths dead. *Rank*, their final album, was released two weeks later.[23]

Solo Morrissey

Morrissey embarked on a solo career almost immediately. The first track on *Viva Hate*, from 1988, the accusatory (and humorous) "Alsatian Cousin," revolves around the apparent affair that the cousin is having with a scholar (complete with a leather-patches-on-the-elbows tweed blazer). The narrator of the song demands honesty, though he knows the answer, that they were lovers. This song exhibits humor in that the narrator questions whether the cousin could have done better in choosing a lover.

The fleeting and fickle nature of celebrity is the subject of "Little Man, What Now?" in which a former teen star appears on a television show a mere shadow of his former self. The narrator wonders what happened, and if the fall from frame affected the actor, concluding that he was a role model, and that the narrator looked up to him.

Like "Ask" from The Smiths' *Louder Than Bombs*, nuclear destruction makes an appearance in "Everyday Is Like Sunday," one of Morrissey's most enduring songs. The song describes a protagonist that wishes not to be where she presently is (the video features a young woman as its focus, which suggests that the protagonist is female). In the song, it would be better to have the town destroyed than for it to continue, and for the protagonist to continue living in it. If the nuclear bomb cannot bring anyone to the figure here in the song (like in "Ask"), then it should destroy her.

This song is commonly considered one of Morrissey's classics, though it is unclear why this might be. Certainly the song is beautifully written and creates a rich, if not melancholy, atmosphere. Morrissey's subdued performance is particularly apt, though perhaps it lacks emotional intensity, something that subsequent — and recent — live performances have provided.

A song that is often cited as being an example of Morrissey's racist agenda, "Bengali in Platforms" describes the plight of an immigrant who wishes to be included in Western culture. Unfortunately, his style is just not right; it is no longer in style to wear platform shoes. The narrator's response is that it would be almost impossible to fit in: it is difficult even if you are Western to begin with. His advice to the Bengali is to stop trying.

In "Angel, Angel, Down We Go Together," the narrator seems to be speaking to a figure from whom much is taken without getting anything in return; the song suggests a kind of celebrity figure, one who is taken advantage of but who will ultimately be cast aside. The narrator assures them, though, that he will remain with the subject; he loves "Angel" more than life itself. On the one hand, the narrator pleads that "Angel" not take her (his?) life, while also suggesting that he loves her more than life. Thus, they are destined to go down together.

"Late Night, Maudlin Street" features a beautiful vocal performance by Morrissey. The lyrics are among the most rich and prolific of his catalogue. The song drips with regret of lost opportunities and tragedy. The narrator is leaving a house on Maudlin Street in which much of his life has taken place. It seems that the house was also occupied by his love, someone who has since left. The song is full of rich images: of the narrator being driven home after missing a bus; of the narrator and his love sneaking through a park; and being without clothes and not wanting to steal a pair of pants from a laundry line. The song contains moments of self-deprecation (where the narrator suggests that, while he cannot help but laugh when seeing his love naked, the world looks at him naked and gags), but also moments of terrible regret and loss (where the narrator is sorry for hurting his love because of taking pills, or when they took his love away by police car from Maudlin Street). In the end, the narrator is still in love and hopes that his love is somewhere singing.

"Suedehead" recounts a sexual encounter: the narrator describes the constant returning of a previous lover, though her or his return makes things awkward for him. Though the experience was a good one, the narrator is sorry about it, and sorry to have the lover return repeatedly. When the subject of the song tried to read the narrator's diary, there was nothing but blank pages; the narrator wrote nothing of their relationship.

"Break Up the Family" recounts the choice of the narrator to grow up, to leave his friends behind, and thus "break up the family." In doing so, he admits that he is glad to leave his youth, and darker times, behind, along with his friends, and he does not feel any regret in doing so. For now he is in love, and for the first time.

The narrator in the song "Hairdresser on Fire" suggests that if the hairdresser would include him in their diary (if an empty page be found), then his life would be transformed. In other words, to be the object of desire for the hairdresser (or at least an object of attention worthy of mention in a diary) would be a life-changing experience for the narrator. The image of a hairdresser that is so busy as to be "on fire" is humorous. The humor seems to be accentuated by the range of sounds that Morrissey produces throughout the song, including growls, groans and hisses.

The narrator in "The Ordinary Boys" sings of those ordinary people that would hang around and do nothing but be cruel to the subject of the song. The narrator sings to her, suggesting that her being alone, and her being different, is something good. The ordinary people feel that they are so lucky, though ultimately their foolish lives are empty.

"I Don't Mind If You Forget Me" is a raucous response to those that reject and forget the narrator. He states, without regret, that he does not mind being forgotten, and in a way rejection from a fool is the worst sort of rejection that one might experience. Like in "Break Up the Family," the narrator says goodbye and moves on, having learned from the experience, perhaps happy to grow up.

"Dial-A-Cliché" explores personal authenticity: the narrator sings of someone who forcefully requests that he change his ways. The narrator wonders who the real person is beneath the clichés that are constantly spouted. At the end, the narrator proclaims (though this might just be another cliché) that he has tried to follow the suggestions but is now in pain. This song seems to be a diatribe against prescriptive authority, that is also the subject of the last track on the album, "Margaret on the Guillotine," an ironically gentle song that calls for the death of then–British

Prime Minister Margaret Thatcher, complete with a much-noted sound of a guillotine blade smashing down at the very end of the song.

Morrissey's first solo album, *Viva Hate*, is approached with a favorable but cautious review in *Rolling Stone*. Mark Coleman suggests that the album is simply an extension of The Smiths' musical output: "Morrissey has paid his former band mates a perverse sort of tribute, when you think about it: he's nearly equaled them on his own. Nearly."[24]

A joint end-of-year review of both *Rank* and *Viva Hate* paints the latter as "a day without sunshine"; the reviewer concludes, "Morrissey wears his heart on his sleeve just as plainly on *Viva Hate*; at their best, as on *Rank*, the Smiths always made you feel as though he'd given you that heart to hold."[25]

Conversely, in his review of Morrissey's first video compilation, *Hulmerist*, Jim Farber recognizes the singer's strategy of "distance." He suggests that the video portrays constant desperation: "Missed connections are the whole point. Nearly all the clips feature alienated fans trying to reach Morrissey or the performer himself trying to reach his idols — all of whom are dead."[26]

Released in November 1990, *Bona Drag* is a compilation of singles that were released since *Viva Hate* in 1988. The first song, "Piccadilly Palare," features the narrator engaging in palare, a spoken slang that had been used by the homosexual subculture, a practice that has faded since the 1960s. This song has often been used by fans as a mark of Morrissey's own homosexuality, though the singer has never made a statement indicating, for certain, his sexual orientation. For the narrator, the palare spoken by him and his companions was nothing but slang, and silly in any case. Such a stance seems to criticize the use of the language, and to make less serious its use in the song. From another perspective, the narrator is simply saying this in order to further obfuscate his own position. Of course, in both of these cases, it is impossible to deduce Morrissey's own feelings for the language and, by extension, his position in terms of the subculture that uses palare. It is not a stretch to suggest that Morrissey is feeling some sympathy for palare and all that it connotes. As Morrissey's lyrics have shown, he is often conveying the view of the downtrodden, the lonely and the minority. It is quite possible that the same is going on here with his use of palare; it need not be argued that this is an external indication of his own homosexuality.

"November Spawned a Monster" recounts the life of a girl who is so physically deformed that she is unloveable (at least in the conventional way that pop songs construct love). Furthermore, she is unable to walk; she calls out to Jesus for relief from gossip and pity. The narrator seems to wish for the girl's death; in death, in Jesus' own domain, the "monster" from the song's title could finally walk and purchase her own clothes. Even in death, though, Morrissey makes sure to write that she will not be beautiful or well-off. Through the healing of death, she will be free.

In "The Last of the Famous International Playboys," Morrissey describes a protagonist who is fascinated with crime; this person is now himself imprisoned for murder. This song explores the nature of celebrity as well; the song suggests that mediation — that is, the exhibition of criminals through the news media — creates celebrity. In this mediated context, the narrator suggests that he himself wants stardom; crime is one way for him to achieve it.

"Ouija Board, Ouija Board" recounts the story of the ever-so-lonely narrator who wishes to contact a dear friend who has since died through the use of the titular board game. The song is a sort-of joke, though; the narrator (presumably called Steven, because of the response from the board) is told, ultimately, to leave the dead alone. The narrator will need to live his life alone; the dead do not want anything to do with him. It can be assumed here that the narrator is Morrissey himself, as the board identifies him as Steven.

"He Knows I'd Love to See Him" is an interesting song in that the title is somewhat misleading. The lyric suggests that the narrator desires not simply to see the subject of the song, but to see the subject of the song happy (or as close as possible to happiness). This is a theme that is revisited in "I Just Want to See the Boy Happy" from *Ringleader of the Tormentors*. In the song from *Bona Drag*, the narrator is known by the police, who suggest that he is a radical, but one who wants to affect change in the world by remaining unemployed, thus not becoming a full member of society.

Morrissey evokes God again in "Yes, I Am Blind," in which the narrator calls for God to intervene in the current situation, if God exists and if God cares. This invocation of God is sung twice by Morrissey, while its lyric is curiously omitted in the lyric sheet that accompanies *Bona Drag*. In the song, the narrator also warns that Christians want to kill the subject;

while this might not be a literal statement, it does cast a negative light on Christians, something that was perhaps hinted at in the past but is now affirmed. Morrissey's own harsh Catholic upbringing could contribute to this; his Catholicism is something that he continues to hold on to, though it is unknown to what extent he practices the faith of his childhood.

Christianity appears again in "Lucky Lisp," where Jesus and the Saints are mentioned. The title seems to refer to the subject's speaking talent. It seems his fame, his talent and the adoration of those that hear him were all created by Jesus just for him. It is a curious song, much more religious than one might think.

The last track, "Disappointed," again explores the subject of celebrity, at least at its end. The narrator (it is not a stretch to suggest that it is Morrissey) states that this will be his last song ever; a crowd seems to cheer at this suggestion. The narrator then states that he has changed his mind; immediately, the crowd groans. This is a prime example of Morrissey's self-deprecation; he ends the song by thanking the audience and wishing them a good night.

Stuart Maconie calls *Bona Drag* "an album that Morrissey himself seems spectacularly unconcerned about and is quite unashamedly a stop-gap. It's also terrific."[27] Morrissey's second album is a collection of singles and includes a couple of tracks from *Viva Hate*. *Bona Drag* was re-released in September 2010 to commemorate the 20th anniversary of its original release. The re-release was overseen by Morrissey (thus giving it a certain sense of credibility) and includes new artwork and tracks not included on the original release.

Kill Uncle was released in 1991. The first track, "Our Frank," has the narrator complaining about deep conversations and wishing that he could stop thinking about things all the time. He wishes not to think about things so bleakly as well.

"Asian Rut" tells the tale of an Asian boy who attempts to avenge the killing of his friend. Unfortunately, he is outnumbered and fails (it is unclear whether he dies as well). Toward the end of the song, the narrator speaks in the first person, commenting that he is just passing through, trying to make it to more civilized environs, but doubting that he will ever get there.

"Sing Your Life" is an encouragement for the subject of the song (perhaps the listener) to express themselves in song. For the narrator, singing in this way is different from rhyming words together, and because life is short, one should begin singing immediately. This song can be read as a sort-of call to unity between the singer and the listener; our pointless lives will end, but we have wonderful singing voices. Let us sing truth. Because of its assumed encouragement to the listener, this song is an anomaly in Morrissey's catalogue.

"Mute Witness" is far from an anthemic song like "Sing Your Life." In "Mute Witness" the listener is introduced to a mute woman who is trying to recount, unsuccessfully, something that she saw the night prior. She leaves by taxi without successfully communicating what she saw. This song is an example of Morrissey's excellent ability to tell stories; we feel for the woman as she is unable to communicate. Morrissey is, again, writing about those that lack something; the mute witness cannot communicate or participate in any sort of normal relationship. And what exactly did she see? Morrissey creates an enigma, a mirror of his own star image.

In "King Leer" the narrator is again unable to find companionship with the subject of the song. Rather, the subject's boyfriend has foiled every attempt with cruelty. Morrissey is writing from the perspective of the inept, the unloved and the abused. Even when the subject gushes over a small dog, she returns it to the narrator after becoming bored. Even with access, success does not come. That same girlfriend might be the subject of "Driving Your Girlfriend Home." In this song, the girlfriend is questioning how she came to end up with that particular boy. Of course, the narrator does not have an answer and simply drops her off after politely shaking her hand.

In "Will Never Marry," from *Bona Drag*, Morrissey writes from the perspective of one who will live their life alone. This theme continues in the song "(I'm) The End of the Family Line," from *Kill Uncle*. This song explores issues that surround Morrissey himself: celibacy, loneliness and the notion of being unloveable. The narrator (Morrissey?) works against nature itself by not reproducing like those that came before him. He is the end of the line and is thus spared the need to say goodbye. Interestingly, the song fades out and then returns suddenly with the chorus again. Here, the narrator seems reluctant to simply fade out, though he is the last in his lineage.

The last song on the album is "There's a Place in Hell for Me and My Friends," a theme that is revisited in songs like "Satan Rejected My

Soul" from *Maladjusted* and "One Day Goodbye Will Be Farewell" from *Years of Refusal*. In this song, the narrator wishes that he and his friends will not be a bother after they pass on, as they have been in life. It is a curious song in that it suggests both hostility and bitterness (the narrator will be in hell with his friends, and thus will never be alone — which suggests a certain hostility toward those friends) and sorrow and contrition (he forgave, and hopefully forgiveness will come in exchange for the lack of bother). The song ends with Morrissey expressing three tenses in one phrase: he suggests that if he wanted to mourn (the past tense), he will (in the future) because he is able (the present tense). Perhaps he is evoking a sense of eternity here. Furthermore, the vocals are accompanied by a subdued piano, a bass, some strings and light percussion appearing only in the last few moments; while the arrangement is peaceful, the lyrics are not, lending an air of awkwardness to the song.

Rachel Felder's review of Morrissey's third solo album, *Kill Uncle*, is encapsulated in her last sentence: "Ironically, disappointment is an integral component of Morrissey's work — it should, however, derive from the mood of each song's lyrics instead of from listener's reactions."[28] Such reviews are easily forgotten, it seems, with the release of Morrissey's fourth solo album, *Your Arsenal*, in 1992.

Your Arsenal begins with a much more aggressive guitar-based sound, an aural characteristic that has become a staple of Morrissey's music. "You're Gonna Need Someone on Your Side" features the narrator offering his support to the subject of the song, only to have his support so easily taken. The song seems to illustrate the need to be supportive of those who need it, and thus the song might be read positively. The aggression of the band, though, lends the song an air of irony; perhaps there is some advantage-taking that is occurring here.

Such a negative air seems to continue in the next song. "Glamourous Glue" speaks of all people being liars and a world in which respectable men, and women that are the object of affection, are nowhere to be found. Furthermore, it is no time to dream about anything. Even the English language must languish in Los Angeles, as London has failed to protect and produce it. All this diatribe is the result of the narrator being in love, knowing that he will ultimately walk away empty-handed.

Songs like "We'll Let You Know" and "The National Front Disco" thrust Morrissey in the spotlight because of their controversial subject matter: football hooliganism and racism, respectively. In "The National Front Disco," a boy named David has decided to attend the National Front Disco, which is assumed to be a party or gathering of the National Front, a right-wing nationalist organization. This move has been met with despair by his friends and family, who claim that they have lost him. It seems, though, that David has a score to settle. If one properly reads the lyrics to this song, it is clear that Morrissey is not praising David's stance. In fact, the lyrics suggest that David is truly lost. Like Morrissey, though, David has lost his sense of an ideal home country; this is perhaps what Morrissey is sympathizing with in this song, rather than any racist ideology of the National Front. This song, along with "Glamourous Glue," seems to eulogize (albeit indirectly) an England that no longer exists.

"Certain People I Know" is much lighter in tone than the first half of the album, employing turns of phrase that evoke an earlier Morrissey. This song does suggest violence, when the narrator swings a (pool) cue and hits someone in the eye, and others break their necks without being able to fix them. Of course, these certain people laugh at danger. In all, though, the narrator feels that these certain people are terrible.

"We Hate It When Our Friends Become Successful" seems to come from Morrissey's own subject position. The narrator bemoans the clothes and music video of friends, commenting that they really are humorous. Darkness emerges again, though, when the narrator suggests that destruction is his aim, and then laughs about it. After all, it should have been his songs (Morrissey's?) that were successful; they have all the right ingredients to be so. In order to reinforce the narrator's voice as Morrissey's own, he asks the listener to listen to this very song in order to judge whether it should be successful.

Morrissey writes lyrics that are scathing and tender at the same time. "You're the One for Me, Fatty" has the narrator pledging his undying love to a larger person (it is assumed) and promising to move out of her way should he be in it.

The darkness returns with "Seasick, Yet Still Docked," a meandering song describing a life far from what the narrator wanted. The narrator is unable to be close to his loved one; there is no way for him to reach the other, nor does he have the ability — like a beast, he is devoid of charm. The narrator is self-deprecating here, though not in a particularly endearing way. Finally, the narrator sneers at the reaction of the other, passing him by; after all, his love is nothing if not obvious to the point of painfulness. Bitterness (not bittersweetness) is the theme of this song.

Such a feeling is completely absent in the next track, "I Know It's Gonna Happen Someday," where the narrator encourages the subject, and the listener, that "it" will happen some day. What this "it" is isn't obvious, but perhaps it is that one will find love. Interestingly, the narrator begins the song by addressing the subject with an amorous salutation and begging the subject to be patient. If this love is between the singer and the listener (which is suggested by the salutation at the start of the song), it will never come to fruition. It cannot.

The final track on the album is called "Tomorrow." It speaks of an instance of unrequited love to which the narrator would like to have some resolution. He asks for the subject to hold him before tomorrow comes, a day that will bring him pain. He makes sure to promise not to tell anyone. He asks the subject to tell him that they love him, even if they do not mean it. Tomorrow will be a terrible, fearful change, and lies will help him through it.

About *Your Arsenal*, Mark Coleman in *Rolling Stone* comments: "Mope no more.... *Your Arsenal* is the most direct — and outwardly directed — statement he's made since disbanding the Smiths. Buoyed by the conversational grace of his lyric writing, Morrissey rides high atop this album's rip-roaring guitar ride."[29] The album marks a change of musical style as well as band members for Morrissey. This album is considered a clear marker of Morrissey's shift from a more mainstream "pop" styling to one of "modern rock." Many of the songs have also been considered lyrically controversial, especially in terms of right-wing nationalism and racism. This album also features a new group of musicians who have largely remained with him since its release. This group includes guitarists Alain Whyte and Martin "Boz" Boorer, and bassist Gary Day. Both Whyte and Boorer have written the music for almost all of Morrissey's output since 1992, and although Whyte has not toured with Morrissey since 2004, or recorded with Morrissey on his most recent albums, he remains the singer's most prolific songwriter. The contribution of this musical group is evident right from the start of the recording.

As mentioned above, the opening strains of *Your Arsenal* feature distorted guitars, which are not widely used on the previous albums, if used at all. This new musical style, as alluded to by Simpson, injected a more aggressive energy into his performances.

After the disaster of the previous year's anaemic *Kill Uncle* for which he received a richly deserved critical pasting, Stretford's rebel with a bookcase seemed to turn from the aesthete interested in rough lads into a rough lad interested in aestheticism (and rough lads).[30]

A certain "break" can be seen not only if one examines Morrissey's music from the early 1990s but also if one compares the album art for *Kill Uncle* and other albums from before 1991 with *Your Arsenal*. Except for the cover of *Viva Hate*, which features a black-and-white close-up of Morrissey, the other albums feature Morrissey's body in various poses. *Bona Drag* takes its cover image from the promotional video for "November Spawned a Monster," while *Kill Uncle* features Morrissey with arms outstretched and hair styled high. *Your Arsenal* features a different image altogether. Morrissey is presented in concert with his shirt completely open, exposing his chest and abdomen. The image presented here is not one of the gaunt sickly Morrissey, but a stockier, perhaps more muscular singer.

If *Your Arsenal* might be considered a musical change for Morrissey, his 1994 release, *Vauxhall and I*, is a further change, though perhaps keeping the emotional vitality of the earlier release. *Vauxhall and I* features a gentler Morrissey, though the concerts from this period, if the video *Introducing Morrissey* is any indication, illustrate the raucous nature of these songs as performed live, something that is only hinted at in the recorded music.

The first track of the album, "Now My Heart Is Full," begins with Morrissey's voice and a very limited pad accompaniment. Morrissey cites actors and poets' poetry. It seems that Morrissey is placing himself within the pantheon of these figures while expressing sheer joy in particularly poetic ways. The lyrics here are marked with a greater abstractness, if not a greater complexity. It seems that there is yet again a shift from his earlier work here, that is, an easiness with disjointed images and words, a style that is foreshadowed in songs like "Late Night, Maudlin Street," but that finds its true manifestation in "Now My Heart Is Full."

"Billy Budd," a memorable song that opens the *Introducing Morrissey* concert video, suggests the close relationship between the narrator and "Billy," a relationship that costs the narrator a job in town. The narrator goes to such extents as to suggest that he would lose his limbs in order for "Billy" to be free. This is in the face of jeering laughter from their peers and 12 years of dismay, the length of time that he and "Billy" have been together.

The loyalty evoked in "Billy Budd" is reinforced in "Hold On to Your Friends," in which the narrator encourages the subject to remember the worth of loyal companions. The narrator also raises concern that the subject only contacts him when he is depressed. When filled with happiness, his friends are of no consequence. Thus, the narrator warns the subject to make sure to foster the relationships with his friends; their assistance might be needed in the future. Alain Whyte borrows heavily from Johnny Marr's guitar work at the very end of "Pretty Girls Make Graves" for the main theme played on the guitar throughout the song.

"The More You Ignore Me, the Closer I Get" describes the tenacity of the narrator, who will not back down. The narrator suggests that the subject will not be able to resist any intrusion by the narrator, including intrusions into the mind. The song foreshadows Morrissey's (and Marr's) legal battle with Mike Joyce in 1996 over royalty payments: Morrissey sings about high court judges and bad debts.

"Why Don't You Find Out for Yourself" seems to discuss the pitfalls of celebrity and the number of interested parties that demand ownership of the profits of celebrity. The narrator expresses feelings of bitterness, knowing that there are those who seek to profit at the expense of the subject, but the narrator will allow such things to happen, since the subject will not listen to advice in any case. While the narrator has made mistakes, the subject has done nothing to defend him, and so the narrator wishes him ill. This is simply the state of things: those who have control over things will take yet more. It is not a stretch to consider this song a commentary on the state of the recording industry circa 1993.

Morrissey expresses the feelings of those that are marginal in "I Am Hated for Loving," a gentle (some might say passive) reminder of the singer's isolation. He suggests that he does not belong, a state of being that is punctuated by violence in the form of a pelting of bricks. In the end, the narrator is his own person, surrendered to solitude, as there seems to be no other choice.

"Lifeguard Sleeping, Girl Drowning" features Morrissey singing *softly*, a feat impossible without the aid of microphones. Truly, Morrissey is a crooner here. The song recounts the drowning of a swimmer (a woman who is attempting to get the attention of the lifeguard) while the lifeguard sleeps (as he has had a very busy day). While the premise is tragic, it is made that much more so by the suggestion that the drowned woman will be missed by no one, that she is nothing. The theme of beaches (and tragedy) continues with "The Lazy Sunbathers," a song that lambastes an apathetic public in the face of war, where exploding children are also nothing but bothers for those that are more interested in their own leisure.

The final track on the album, and the final track on the *Introducing Morrissey* concert video, is entitled "Speedway." It speaks of the narrator's own self-deprecation to the extreme; he is willing to be destroyed rather than be disloyal to another. Of all the things that have been said of the singer — those lies and rumors — not all of them are false. In the end, though, the singer moves the spotlight away from himself and professes his undying loyalty to the other. In this way, the spotlight does not move very far; in the display of his loyalty, he is the one that will suffer destruction, and he wants everyone to know it. Nevertheless, he will not waver, even if it means his death. This is one of Morrissey's most emotional songs, and a fitting end to the *Introducing Morrissey* video.

Unlike his live album *Beethoven Was Deaf*, released in May 1993, *Vauxhall and I* received widespread critical acclaim. Steven Volk talks about the album as being "among the most emotionally powerful of Morrissey's career": "Morrissey has been exploring the relationship between pop and angst since his days with the Smiths, but *Vauxhall and I* is a particularly full expression of his talent."[31] In the October 2005 issue of *GQ* in Britain, Adrian Deevoy asks Morrissey whether he feels it ironic that *Vauxhall and I* is recognized as "something of a masterpiece." Morrissey answers,

> If you were to remove the "something of" from that sentence, then yes. But you could have fooled me. It's never mentioned by anyone. There are weekly lists of the 2,000 Most Potent Albums In The History Of Music which I scan avidly, and it has never appeared.[32]

About the compilation *World of Morrissey*, released in 1995, Paul Evans describes what he calls "Morrissey's keynote, a passionate ambiguity that is riveting and disturbing." Evans suggests that, while Morrissey's fans are not as numerous as those which followed The Smiths, they make up with fervency what they lack in numbers. Evan continues,

> An expert tease enamored of masks and artifice, Morrissey whets their fascination by constructing songs that are all about vulnerability — his thematic range (failure, loss, betrayal, secrecy) is determinedly narrow — but he hides as much as he reveals. Morrissey confesses, but in code.[33]

2. "The Songs That Saved Your Life"

Southpaw Gammar, released in 1995, furthers the stylistic transformation begun with *Your Arsenal* in 1992. On the liner notes, the 10 songs are listed on a simple orange background, with no lyrics, save a portion of the first track, "The Teachers Are Afraid of the Pupils." Also devoid from the packaging is any photo of the singer. This is the first solo release by Morrissey to not feature his face on the cover. Another striking characteristic of this album is the framing of the album by tracks that are over 10 minutes long.

"The Teachers Are Afraid of the Pupils" is an epic track, well over 10 minutes long, that begins with a Shostakovich sample taken from his Symphony No. 5 in D minor. The looped sample of 20th-century art music lends the piece an epic, and serious, quality. From that beginning (and the continued playing of that portion of the Shostakovich symphony), the song is a dense diatribe against teachers who humiliate their students. The sheer hostility that is expressed through this song is frightening; though the lyrics are delivered in Morrissey's gentle tone, the message conveyed is one of a terrifying threat of violence.

"Reader Meet Author" expresses the difference between reader and author. In this case, an author (and a cowardly one at that) is of a different culture and class from the subject of his writings. This is a problem for the narrator of the song, who suggests that the author would leave the world that he is writing about because of fear. The narrator of the song might refer to the sad voice of Morrissey himself toward the end of the song as a kind of catalyst for imaginations on the lives of those less fortunate, and as the influence of deceptive writing on the part of the author.

"The Operation" begins with an almost two-and-a-half minute drum solo before Morrissey's voice enters the front of the mix, singing about a two-faced subject. The narrator was in love with the fickle subject of the song, but is now not, along with most all others, who seem to loathe the individual just as much. The individual has permanently changed, unable even to listen to advice, as if having undergone some sort of operation.

"Dagenham Dave" seems a paean to a character loved by all, one not afraid of women (at one point, Dave advertises his women by name, Karen and then Sharon, on his car windshield). He is described as a kind of dreamer, but he has a secret that the singer will not divulge (it seems that Dave, for risk of self-combustion by the fires of passion, would love to touch *someone*). It is assumed that that someone is not Karen or Sharon;

the promotional video for the song suggests that it is Morrissey himself, as Dave pastes the name "Moz" after Karen and Sharon on his car windshield.

Morrissey writes about how criticism can be one's worst enemy in "Do Your Best and Don't Worry," a song that seems to encourage its listener that failure is inevitable if standards are so high. If one were to compare best days and worst days, it seems that worst days would win out in the end. Thus, sings Morrissey, don't worry.

"Best Friend on the Payroll" describes a relationship in which the narrator is making many accommodations for a friend, though the accommodations should not be made. For instance, though the narrator owns the house, he must turn down his music. In the end, the narrator concludes that the relationship will not work. Of course, the song is a humorous, if not true, note on the difficulty of mixing work and pleasure.

The album concludes with another 10-minute epic, "Southpaw." The song describes the loneliness of a boy who is abandoned by his friends. As a result, the boy runs to his mother, a characteristic that seems to follow the boy as he grows into a man. The narrator of the song announces, though, that the man's dream girl is alone, as the man has chosen his own dream girl, his mother. Morrissey again chooses to describe loneliness as an unending state of life, especially for those abandoned, never able to reconnect.

Al Weisel calls *Southpaw Grammar* Morrissey's "most powerful solo outing to date.... Together they [Morrissey, band and producer] have constructed an aural landscape of raucous, barreling guitars that makes Morrissey's oh-so-familiar themes sound almost fresh."[34] However, such positive reviews are in the minority when this album is considered. David Quantick of *Melody Maker* writes: "Every song here is crushed under the weight of loud guitars and mind-numbing overdubs.... In the end, there is no reason why anyone who already owns a record made by Morrissey—or, more particularly, The Smiths—should even want to hear this record, let alone buy it."[35]

Starting with an Anthony Newley sample from the 1955 film *Cockleshell Heroes*, the song "Maladjusted" opens the album of the same name, released in 1997. Here, a confident Morrissey sings what seem to be fragments of lyrics that paint a picture of an England filled with drives on Parkside and lights on Fulham Road. The lyrics describe the nights of a young woman, it seems, who reflects on her own untrustworthiness. Morrissey is singing from the perspective of the female gender, at least in a portion of the song, which is something he has not done explicitly since his output with The Smiths.

The confidence expressed in the song "Maladjusted" is continued in "Alma Matters," where the narrator maintains that it is his life to destroy any way that he might wish, no matter what others might think. "Alma Matters" in that Alma means something to someone, somewhere, though it is unclear what exactly Alma means. What is clear here is that any opinion concerning the narrator's life has no bearing on that life, which is unequivocally his own.

"Ambitious Outsiders" announces the return of the violent voice to the work of Morrissey. In the song, the narrator(s) warn the listeners to lock their doors, as he (they) are going to target the children in order to keep the population down. Like any threatening force, the narrator warns the listener to not underestimate him.

The violent narrative voice of "Ambitious Outsiders" gives way to a more pathetic voice in "Trouble Loves Me," a song that describes a narrator unable to escape the grip of trouble. The narrator longs to be held, consoled, by a love, but seems always to find himself in trouble of some kind. Morrissey returns, though, to the kind of disjointed — though incredibly rich — writing showcased in "Maladjusted" and "Late Night, Maudlin Street."

"Papa Jack" addresses nostalgia, describing Jack as one who wishes for younger days in which he had a rapport with the younger generation. Unfortunately, at that time, Jack had no time for those young people. The song addresses the misuse of time and opportunity, where the subject, Jack, is now grieving his past. This is yet another lament for the vitality of celebrity that has faded over time. For Morrissey, celebrity is a fickle thing, one that quickly fades.

"Ammunition" is a song of acceptance. The narrator sings of traveling down roads toward an inevitable cliff, but he sings also of not dwelling on the impending failure. He suggests that he has always been; it is others that he has been missing. He concludes the song by accepting his state and offering that he has no time for revenge. Thus, he does not need any ammunition. In any case, he will not use it.

Curiously, mediation is the topic of the song "Wide to Receive." Such subject matter seems to be ironic in a song with a title so evocative of the physical, bringing to mind the notion of being in the open ready to receive the ball in American football, or, more fittingly here, having legs spread to receive a sexual physical response. In contrast to such physical evocations, the song mentions downloading, unlocking and processing, terms that suggest mediation of some sort, removed from the realm of the physical. Modern technologies, rather than people, are the tools for such activity.

"Roy's Keen" gets its title as a play on Roy Keane, former captain of the Manchester United football club. Roy is a window cleaner who seems to be in love with a person who watches him wash windows. The song uses spatial language to describe the Roy's ladder as a planet, Roy as a star, and the narrator as a satellite (the one that just "circles around," perhaps). The narrator first sings to one that Roy is romancing and then sings to Roy himself, suggesting that the love that Roy is looking for is at the foot of his ladder. Roy, though keen, is not keen enough to notice; the narrator's love, then, will remain unrequited.

"He Cried" describes the power of words; the song describes the response of the subject after letting another know that he needed them and, assumedly, receiving a negative response in return. The subject, with a deadened soul, is barely alive. The narrator of the song suggests that he also is in such a position, unable to live without emotion, but also denied after expressing his need for another.

Morrissey's personal anger and bitterness is expressed in "Sorrow Will Come in the End," a song thoroughly imbued with violence and ill wishes. The song is a clear response to the lawsuit brought upon Morrissey and Marr by Mike Joyce, which Joyce won. Morrissey calls the win "legalized theft."

More religious themes are featured in "Satan Rejected My Soul," a song that predicts the afterlife for the narrator and his associates. After death, the narrator knows that his place is not with God, and he is so much lower than Satan himself (after all, Satan would not want to be dragged down by him). So, with the rejection of both God and Satan, the narrator offers himself to the subject or listener of the song. Perhaps this is an invitation to the fans themselves to take Morrissey's soul, all that he is, his very essence. Of course, this is an easy offer, especially when there is no real transaction taking place; the listeners experience Morrissey's soul at a distance, captured in sound recording, but separated by time and space. He invites the listener to pull him into their personal space, while in reality it is only a false "presence," one that points ultimately to Morrissey's absence. But one must take what one can.

Surprisingly, *Rolling Stone* provides a positive review for perhaps Morrissey's most hated album, *Maladjusted*, in which Matt Hendrickson gives it three and a half stars (between "good" and "excellent"): "Despite his predictability, *Maladjusted* is Morrissey's strongest musical effort since his 1988 solo debut."[36] The suggestion that this album is the "most hated" is not easily supported, but many fans acknowledge the album as coming short in comparison to his other works. A review in *Spin* conveys a broadly different viewpoint: "It musn't be pretty being Morrissey. His glory days as the reigning Hero of Sad Young Things are behind him (Kurt [Cobain of Nirvana] took that crown), but the poor dear doesn't seem able to play any other role." The reviewer basically disregards Morrissey and this album as irrelevant: "Beyond the remnants of his rabid cult, Morrissey hasn't mattered for nearly a decade."[37]

Writing for *The Guardian* newspaper, Jude Rogers does not have kind words for the re-releases of *Southpaw Grammar* and *Maladjusted* in 2009. She writes, "I didn't expect to be getting the two lumpen albums that preceded Morrissey's seven-year exile from all matters musical." She continues, "So Morrissey has taken it into his own hands to rewrite his past. He does this not only by flagging up these albums as lost masterpieces, but by changing the order of the tracks and the CD sleeves." She concludes that Morrissey has made a misstep by making his "worst albums worse, and then [by asking] people to buy them all over again."[38]

In 1996, The Smiths drummer Mike Joyce successfully sued Morrissey and Marr for an increase of royalties, a ruling with which Morrissey continues to be displeased. After *Maladjusted*, due to a record company buyout, Morrissey was left without a record deal, a state in which he remained until 2003. During that time, Morrissey embarked on two successful world tours and appeared on American television.

From 1997 to 2004, Morrissey did not release any albums, and, while he toured, he did not have a recording contract. In May 2004, Morrissey returned with *You Are the Quarry*, a collection of new songs, ushering in a new era in his solo career.

"America Is Not the World," a diatribe against America, opens this album, a song in which Americans are not just nor equal, and where Americans are compared with pigs and gluttons who eat beef. Nevertheless, the narrator loves them, not unlike a Savior loving the world. The biblical evocation of the lyric is not a stretch: the narrator implores America to touch him with their hands, to hear with their ears, and to understand that he is with them.

Morrissey's own sense of citizenship and nationality is expressed in "Irish Blood, English Heart," a song in which he distances himself from the intrinsic Englishness of his past. Here, Morrissey explicitly acknowledges his Irish ancestry while expressing his struggles with Englishness as it is now. Another diatribe, this time against the monarchy, closes the song, a cry against English partisan politics. When once he wrote against Thatcherism and the conservative government of the 1980s, he now calls for nonpartisanship.

Religion reemerges in "I Have Forgiven Jesus," a beautiful song that expresses the narrator's frustration with the desires he has been given and the inability he has to convey such desires. In the song, the narrator addresses Jesus directly; while he has forgiven Jesus, he wonders if God's son hates him. It is Jesus who is at fault for making him this way. One cannot help but think that the songs on this album are more personal, more real, closer to the "real" Morrissey, than some of the songs in the past. In the music video for this song, Morrissey walks along a deserted street dressed as a priest, evoking his own Roman Catholic upbringing. The costume in the video personalizes the song, suggesting that Morrissey himself is in some privileged position, able to absolve Christ himself of sin that he committed toward Morrissey. This might sound like narcissism or egotism of the utmost degree; instead, it comes across as a serious lament, and we sympathize with the singer.

"Come Back to Camden" begins with the narrator describing his loneliness; he wishes to express himself when he realizes that he is alone. The narrator is alone, despairing in his solitude, living in squalor (or so it would seem), but constantly longing for companionship. And so the narrator calls out to the subject of the song to return to Camden, and thus return things to a state of goodness. The topics of loneliness and heartbreak are essential in the work of Morrissey.

Themes of resistance and stubbornness are the essence of "I'm Not Sorry," a song in which the narrator returns (not unlike Morrissey himself after his seven-year hiatus from recording), noticing that the world still goes on. The narrator suggests that the pressure remains because he still enjoys what he is doing. The subject matter of the song seems to likely parallel Morrissey's own feelings at this point in his career: with his return, the pressure to perform well is great, not least because he is invested in his performance himself. Of course, the lyrics also turn to love; the narrator suggests that he is going to choose whom he would like to be with rather than just choose anyone. He makes a startling admission, though: the right woman for him never came along. He immediately suggests that, in any case, such a woman never existed.

One of the themes of *You Are the Quarry* is a resistance to mainstream culture. Morrissey chooses to embark on diatribes against American pride in the global context, Christianity (and Christ himself), and against the popular music industry and its participants. In "The World Is Full of Crashing Bores," the narrator separates himself from conventional pop stars who are afraid to show that they are capable of a trace of intellectual thought. He is not one of these, and though his fans might not understand how he is situated within the realm of pop stardom, they are still willing to love him.

Anger and bitterness are expressed in "How Can Anybody Possibly Know How I Feel," a song in which the narrator conveys his anger at being slandered and defaced. While he is angered by this, he also contributes to his self-effacement by suggesting that those who would come on his side in order to defend him are those that do not truly know him. Finally, he lashes out at those in authority, an authority made manifest in a uniform. He would never be as rude as those in authority, even though he might be sick (it seems that he is "Still Ill" after all of these years).

After the termination of his recording contract in 1997, Morrissey moved to Los Angeles. "First of the Gang to Die" seems to draw its inspiration from Latino culture in California, recounting the story of Hector, the first of the gang (the Pretty Petty Thieves) to die. Not only was Hector a thief, but he was also a charming thief, stealing the hearts of those around him, as well as their money.

Self-effacement continues in "Let Me Kiss You," a song in which the narrator asks the subject of the song to kiss him, while picturing someone she would actually like to kiss. Though the subject is not physically attracted to the narrator of the song, the narrator still loves her.

"All the Lazy Dykes" recounts the struggles of a woman who is a regular wife, but who is actually a lesbian. The narrator (assumedly her lover) encourages her to begin her life of freedom, for her to be herself among those who share her desires. This is one of Morrissey's more controversial songs, in his prominent use of an often derogatory term for "lesbian."

In "I Like You" the narrator states that he and his companion (the one who he likes) are both eccentric; the sickness of "Still Ill" and "How Can Anybody Possibly Know How I Feel" has spread, it seems. The one is allowed to speak to the narrator in the ways that he or she does simply because he or she is liked by the narrator. They are of one mind, a mind that is slightly off, that does not work the way that those in authority or in the mainstream does.

Morrissey returns to the theme of celebrity with "You Know I Couldn't Last," in which he expresses his own misgivings regarding the machine that is the recording industry. Ironically, in his first album after a substantial break, he expresses his inability to continue. The pressures of commercial success, as well as the critical onslaught that comes with the release of recordings, seems too much for the narrator, and so he wishes to return home. After all, there is no way that he could last (we all know this). This is due to his sickness, his inability to be a "crashing bore," a member of the mainstream.

While *You Are the Quarry* has proved to be one of his most commercially successful works, not all critics receive it as favorably as his fans do. Calling Morrissey ridiculous, Michael White writes, "[He is] a disconnected, bitter coot making observations that are either self-evident or drawn from pure egocentricity. And where his songs were once communal anthems for misfits everywhere, his writing is now so coldly inward-gazing that it excludes the interests of everyone but Morrissey."[39] White gives the album a score of one out of five.

James Hunter of *Rolling Stone* finds that the new album has Morrissey returning in fine form. He states, "The album, like Morrissey's tenor, never stops defining and reinventing itself. The world, as Morrissey leaps to declare in one song, continues to be full of crashing bores. But *You Are the Quarry* is a triumph of maladjusted vitality."[40] Hunter gives the album three and a half stars.

The tour in support of *You Are the Quarry* is the source for *Live at Earls Court*, a concert recording released in 2005. Michael Idov praises the release with a rating of 7.8 out of 10. He writes, "The moment it captures is indeed somewhat phenomenal. It certainly bears documenting.... He is a pre-rock crooner commanding Beatle-level hysteria; a smooth, urbane party host backed onstage by anonymous young chord-bashers."[41]

Ringleader of the Tormentors, the second of Morrissey's "new" albums, released in 2006, opens with a noisy "I Will See You in Far Off Places." The song is an exploration of the purpose of human life and holds to the hope that companions will be together one day again. It points to the difficulty of true compatibility between two people, able to be in physical proximity to each other, yet unable to truly bond. The narrator of the song commends the subject to God and the United States; through the protection of one or the other, the two will meet again.

"The Youngest Was the Most Loved" describes the raising of a young boy who turned out to be a killer, though he was raised in a sheltered environment. The song points to the difficulty in determining the trajectory of others; though the boy was shy, and though he was most loved and raised protected from the eyes of the world, he still ended up being a killer. The song illustrates the repeated adage in Morrissey's work that there is truly no such thing as normal.

The narrator in "In the Future When All's Well" is stuck playing not the game of nostalgia but the game of looking forward to better times, when all is well. The narrator calls to a mysterious figure known only as "Lee" to defend him in the future. Perhaps, as the narrator is not currently being defended, he will be in the future when things are better. Of course, looking forward to better times inevitably leads to looking forward to death, which is the final perspective offered by the narrator.

"The Father Who Must Be Killed" recounts the story of a murderous step-child, whose father (curiously, printed with a capital "F" in the lyric sheet) deserved his end due to his petty swipes and general disdain for the step-child. The narrator, perhaps an inner voice, implores the step-child to murder her father with a knife. After fatally wounding the father, and after the father apologizes to the step-child, the step-child takes her own life. Like the sentiments expressed in "Satan Rejected My Soul," the step-child remarks that no one will meet her in the afterlife.

Death, the ultimate future in life, is the subject again in "Life Is a Pigsty," an epic song in the vein of "The Teachers Are Afraid of the Pupils" and "Southpaw." The narrator confesses that he lives only for the subject and will continue to do so even in the face of abuse and injury. He begs the subject to stop time, and to stop pain, because he is now falling in love, even at the end of his life. The song might seem to some as an ultimate statement of the futility of life. But the narrator states that even though life is terrible and unfair, he has fallen in love. Obviously, for the narrator, this makes life worthwhile. This is why he begs for the pain to stop, for time itself to stop.

In "I'll Never Be Anybody's Hero Now" the narrator's love is dead (it seems that, despite the futile begging featured in "Life Is a Pigsty," time did not stop for them). That person also thought highly of the narrator, but now that they have passed on, the narrator must concede to the truth conveyed in the title of the song. And with that passing, the narrator is now alone from his love but also from others in his circle. Those who should naturally respond to his suffering instead treat him as a ghost.

Death comes again in "On the Streets I Ran," a song in which the narrator begs God not to take his life (he asks that God take the lives of people from Pittsburgh instead). But the narrator also asks God to bring him to where he belongs, though it is unclear where this might be. Referring again to the theme of sickness, or the notion of not fitting in, the narrator's image in the mirror seems to speak to him, reminding him that this has been his project: turning his awkwardness, his inability to fit with the mainstream, his sickness, into popular (and later unpopular) song.

The narrator is at prayer again in "I Just Want to See the Boy Happy." In the last throes of his life, he begs God to bring happiness to "the boy" by returning his true love to him. This song revisits the theme of *Bona Drag*'s "He Know's I'd Love to See Him" almost exactly.

"At Last I Am Born" is a triumphant end to an album dominated by notions of death and lamentations toward God. The narrator, in the past before his "new birth," would pang after love that was not forthcoming, thought that time only made pain stronger, had many reasons for sorrow, and experienced much guilt because of physical desire. Now that he has been reborn, all of these things are in the past. They no longer affect him. It is unclear whether a religious experience has truly occurred or from where this rebirth comes.

Regarding *Ringleader of the Tormentors*, Alex Needham at the *NME* found "Morrissey not only in wonderful voice, but more flamboyant and alive than at any time in his solo career." Note the use of the word "solo," differentiating the singer's later career from that of The Smiths. About the tracks "Life Is a Pigsty" and "Dear God Please Help Me," Needham writes,

> These are the key tracks; the ones which push the Morrissey sound and which hit home the hardest. Elsewhere, Moz retreats into the patent jangly pop which seems to be his "default" setting (although nothing descends to the "will this do?" levels of his disastrous 1997 album "*Maladjusted*.")[42]

Ross Raihala calls the album a "potentially polarizing mash note," adding the following: "While lust has been a key theme of his work ... it's always been the tortured, unrequited type. What are we to think now that the ringleader of the tormented virgins has finally gotten himself laid?"[43] This will be further explored later in this book.

With the release of 2008's *Greatest Hits*, Mark Beaumont calls Morrissey "the Blingleader of the Compilors," noting that he has released five compilation albums among eight studio albums at this point in his career.[44] Stephen Thomas Erlewine calls the compilation "rather pointless but harmless," but concludes that "if that kind of hodgepodge is what you're looking for, well, you've now got it."[45]

The common theme of sickness is most often represented in Morrissey's music as being "off," not living up to the expectations of society at large, and not being accepted by it, rather than meaning physical or mental sickness. In the opening song from 2009's *Years of Refusal*, Morrissey sings of physical and mental sickness. In "Something Is Squeezing My Skull" the narrator describes life as going well, in that he can forget both his past and his present — perhaps not the optimal way of carrying on. In any case, the narrator expresses his disenchantment with the spate of drugs that he must consume, including Diazepam and Temazepam, both anti-anxiety drugs. He wishes to be relieved of these things and confronts the subject of the song, who swore to stop giving these drugs to him. Of course, the source of his anxiety is the fact that the world and modern times are devoid of any sort of love.

Death, one of the themes in *Ringleader of the Tormentors*, returns in "Mama Lay Softly on the Riverbed," which is a lament from a child to his dead mother (who presumably took her own life). The narrator expresses difficulties that occur in life, coming mostly from those in authority, either dressed in uniform or dressed in suits, both authority figures and all seemingly wanting money. The song concludes with the child deciding to join his mother in death.

"Black Cloud" introduces the theme of unrequited love yet again. Here the narrator laments the idea that, though he make every effort to woo the one that he loves, he will never have him or her, who he calls "Black Cloud." Such sentiments regarding unrequited love continue in "I'm Throwing My Arms around Paris." The narrator has decided that he will embrace the city of Paris, as only unfeeling and inanimate buildings and architecture are open to his advances. His true love will not accept him, as has been made very clear.

Though his love is constantly unrequited, the narrator still suggests that "All You Need Is Me," which is the title of one of Morrissey's singles from the album. The narrator conveys his belief that all the subject needs is him, though the subject does nothing but complain about the narrator. After all, the narrator will be missed when he is gone. It is as if Morrissey, the singer, is making the suggestion that he is the reason for his listeners' existence, and though he is imperfect and the bane of jokes, he will be sorely missed.

"When Last I Spoke to Carol" deals once again with death, this time with the death of Carol, a young woman (if the lyrics are literal, born in 1975). The song conveys a kind of hopeless gloom, with the narrator expressing his lack of love for her while she was alive. The narrator concludes that no one will come to one's rescue; we die alone, perhaps. This song is peculiar in its use of brass instruments, an unusual accompaniment in Morrissey's output.

"One Day Goodbye Will Be Farewell" brings to the forefront death, and the afterlife, again. Here the narrator sings that he desires to go to hell after death, obviously a place where he would not be accepted (if "Satan Rejected My Soul" is any indication, though "There's a Place in Hell for Me and My Friends"). The song begins as a warning not to take advantage of those that one might love, as they will be gone forever one day. This song describes the fickleness of love and beauty and the cruelty of time.

In fact, the cruelty of time is illustrated at the death of the narrator in "You Were Good in Your Time," a song that could easily be about Morrissey himself. He made his audience, with their deformities and abnormalities, feel less alone and less abnormal. Morrissey sings from the perspective of his audience, describing the words that his audience gives him and, ultimately, describing his own death.

In "Sorry Doesn't Help," Morrissey writes of the meaninglessness of apology; in the song, the narrator rejects contriteness. For the narrator, it is too late for apologies; forgiveness will not come. He has been wronged, and there is no reversing those wrongs. Instead, the song ends without any resolution of the relationship and leads into the next with its theme of total independence. Morrissey is expressing a break here and a move to unequivocal control of his own destiny at the end of his latest album. In "I'm OK by Myself," the narrator expresses his ability to go on without the support of others, a sentiment that has rarely been conveyed in his songs prior to this. While Morrissey has written about needing others, his love being unrequited, various laments toward and diatribes against God, and while he has addressed the idea of being his own person, he has not often expressed the notion that he needs no other. In this song, the narrator, paranoid of those who claim to support him, suggests that he is all right without their help or companionship. He speaks against notions of benevolence, philosophy and morality; Morrissey is singing of a deeper degree of independence, of spirit as well as of body.

About *Years of Refusal*, Ben Ratliff writes, "'Years of Refusal' feels vibrant as an art of words and images; it's somehow weaker as music." He suggests, though, that Morrissey is ultimately honest with this release: "There it is [in the lyrics]: romantic possibility, paranoia, weariness and practicality, in the order that they naturally occur to him." He concludes, "Stand and marvel: it's a great system."[46] Anthony Thornton gives the album an 8 out of 10, writing, "Morrissey is feeling mortality like never before but will — thankfully — not go quietly.... Or without a well-aimed witticism. So, Morrissey, may you continue to rage against the dying of the light that previously never went out. You'd be so much less interesting otherwise."[47] Joe Gross, writing for *Spin*, triumphantly states that the "Mayor of Mope is back for another term." He sums up Morrissey at this stage of his career as follows: "Ever since *You Are the Quarry* in '04, our man from Manchester has been weirdly unstoppable, making vital music, throwing exhaustively energetic live shows, and honing in on 50 as well as or better than any rocker this side of Neil Young."[48]

Another compilation released in 2009, *Swords*, was met with mixed reviews. Evie Nagy writes that "plenty of the 18 tracks follow classic Moz formulas, putting wistful lyrics against melodic optimism. But the songs also show the artist's continued creative stretch," adding that the album "is a welcome catalog addition."[49] Writing for the BBC, Nadine McBay thinks that Morrissey should know better: "Not that there's been a fatal lack of quality control.... It's more that Swords largely sounds like what it is: an off-cuts album from someone who shouldn't be content with the plodding mediocrity of the likes of [the song] I Knew I Was Next."[50]

Concluding Remarks

Many of the reviews discussed here are concerned with Morrissey's lyrics and his status as a moping performer, representing the dejected and depressed; the reviewers often compare newer works with previous works by either The Smiths or, more specifically, Morrissey's first couple of solo albums. If his new output differs too much from these previous works, the reviewers then suggest that the music is simply a decoy to disguise lax lyrics and a lax attitude toward those dejected and depressed members of his fan base. White's suggestion that *You Are the Quarry* "excludes the interests of everyone but Morrissey" and *Spin* magazine's declaration that "Morrissey hasn't mattered for nearly a decade" illustrate how the singer's relevance and authenticity are often called into question.[51]

As for lyrical themes present in his music, Morrissey constantly covers themes of loneliness, depression and unrequited love, as well as being marginal, what Morrissey calls a "sickness" in his lyrics. These are all stereotypical themes in the music of The Smiths and Morrissey. But his music also plays with notions of death, religion and the afterlife, as well as the fleeting nature of youth and fame. Morrissey's lyrics are peppered with wit and clever wordplay, but they often display harsh violence as well. What is clear in his lyrics is ambiguity; the listener knows little of the true man behind the lyrics, except for his views on these various issues. What is made known throughout his catalogue of lyrics is that Morrissey is his own person; he has created himself, and he is in control of himself. The fact that we are unable to see who he really is through his lyrics is part of his project.

3

"Let Me Kiss You"
Celebrity, Gender and Desire

How, as performers of music, do celebrities negotiate various gender categories and limits? This chapter is concerned with the ways in which celebrity personae assume their particular form in the performance of music. As will be made evident in this chapter, the relationship of music to gendered identities is a controversial area within several bodies of scholarship. Music is variously considered as the most traditionally feminine of artistic fields and as a privileged arena for the performance of traditional masculinities. This chapter works through the key theoretical areas relevant to the analysis of gender, celebrity and audio-visual media. Some of these areas include the gendered character of music and the relationship between the voice and desire. The discussion continues with an exploration of the celebrity and his or her star image. Laura Mulvey's writing on spectacle and the eroticized image of woman in classical narrative types of films is explored. The discussion then turns to how the question of celebrity and performer persona has been reformulated in relation to gender. This chapter concludes with a review of writings on various masculinities, emerging primarily from the field of film studies. These various arguments and viewpoints must inform any discussion of Morrissey, in terms of his celebrity star image, and certainly form a foundation for the analyses in this book.

All of these notions must inform any discussion of Morrissey, and certainly inform what follows in this book. It is through these theoretical lenses, of the gendered frameworks of music, of the gendered nature of spectatorship and of the changing face of masculinity (or, more appropriately, the emergence of masculinities) that one can begin to understand the relationship that audiences — and fans — have with a figure like Morrissey.

Gender and Music

The relationship of music to gender is hotly contested in the sense that competing accounts of this relationship circulate within scholarly literature. One set of issues that emerges from the literature is the idea of music as physical and personal. A competing set of issues has taken shape around the idea of music as an abstract system. A variety of secondary issues have emerged in the analysis of music's relationship to gender. First, there is the stereotyping of certain kinds of performance as gendered. For example, singing is stereotypically considered "feminine." Second, there is the sociological question of access to music and how that access is organized along gender lines. Third, the gendered character of music has been analyzed in relation to the gendered investments in knowledges about music — in the gendered status of connoisseurship, for example. Finally, music has been considered gendered in terms of its consumption. These competing views on music and its relationship to gender make the link between the two difficult to establish. It is to these competing views that this discussion now turns.

In their article "Music and Sexuality," first published in 1978, Simon Frith and Angela McRobbie suggest that popular music — and in particular rock music — is gendered in its performance. Frith and McRobbie posit the assumption that the rhythm of rock music is a direct expression of sexuality:

> If rock's lyrics mostly follow the rules of romance, its musical elements, its sounds and rhythms, draw on other conventions of sexual representation, and rock is highly charged emotionally even when its direct concern is nonsexual.[1]

It should be noted that they argue against any notion that rock music expresses some sort of "natural" sexuality, but rather suggest that it constructs a certain sexuality. They wish to "describe rock's representations of masculinity and femininity and consider the contradictions involved in these representations." Frith and McRobbie emphasize a binary division of musical forms, between "cock rock" and "teenybop." They explain,

> Cock rock shows are explicitly about male sexual performance (which may explain why so few girls go to them — the musicians are acting out a sexual iconography which in many ways is unfamiliar, frightening, and distasteful to girls who are educated into understanding sex as something nice, soft, loving, and private).[2]

In contrast, Frith and McRobbie talk about "teenybop," pop music aimed toward young girls: "The teenybop idol's image is based on self-pity, vulnerability, and need.... It is less physical music than cock rock, drawing on older romantic conventions."[3]

Frith and McRobbie's "teenybop" performer is reminiscent of the crooner of the late 1920s. Allison McCracken suggests that Rudy Vallee, a singer who became a national idol in the United States, "offered his audiences a singing lover, one who was sophisticated, romantic, vulnerable, and, most important, accessible to them in their home." McCracken points out that, at the time, masculinity was defined by "physical vigor and muscularity," as opposed to the disembodied and artificially amplified voice that was broadcast on the radio.[4] In using a microphone, the performer was thus able to convey a more intimate tone than previously available in live performance. McCracken states that in crooning songs, "traditional gender roles are redefined, and women are given more agency in romance. Although men still desire women, it's the crooners who are portrayed as passive and their girls as aggressive."[5] As an example of an early crooner, Rudy Vallee seemingly strayed too far from normative gender expectations, resulting in a crisis of masculinity. Alternately, Bing Crosby's image was renegotiated by both radio and Hollywood to allow him to become the next star crooner:

> Crosby's crooner did not offer an alternative masculinity, as previous crooners had done, but sought instead to legitimize crooning by connecting it to traditional notions of white masculinity: a good work ethic, patriarchy, religious belief, white supremacy, and contained emotions.[6]

Therefore, for the crooner to be successful, he had to conform to conventional notions of masculinity rather than present an alternative masculinity. These associations naturalized the break from singing as a physical exercise.

Discussing male performance in the indie rock scene in Liverpool, England, Sarah Cohen presents an example that challenges the dichotomy put forward by Frith and McRobbie, and the "masculinist" nature of popular music. Like the crooner, Cohen suggests that the male participants of this music scene embrace and encourage an alternate type of masculinity, which includes notions of "male freedom and domination, but also ... powerlessness and constraint." She writes:

> The music of Liverpool's indie rock scene is thus not naturally or essentially male as if its musicians were born to create music in a particularly male way, or as if musical sounds and lyrics directly reflected biological male characteristics, despite popular beliefs to the contrary (hence notions of women's or men's music). The music does, however, contribute to the continual process through which categories of men, male and masculine are produced, contested and redefined, and rock and pop have typically involved exploration of both behaviour and ideas concerning gender and sexuality. The Liverpool scene reflects and reinforces conventional gender relations and masculinities, but it also offers, within certain constraints, the possibility to explore alternative male behaviour and identities that challenge or subvert existing conventions.[7]

While Cohen denies that "musical sounds directly reflect male characteristics," she acknowledges that the music does reinforce certain gendered practices. Against the convention presented by Frith and McRobbie, male behavior within this rock music scene includes a vulnerability: "Being on stage in public is in some ways a vulnerable and exposed position that often involves performance of music and lyrics of a private and personal nature." Cohen concludes, "All of this indicates how complex the production of rock as male can be, involving multiple, diverse and contradictory masculinities, and male power that is ambiguous and precarious."[8]

When discussing the relation between gender and music, there is a question of access, often in terms of the engagement with technology. For instance, vocal music carries with it an overt sense of the physical and personal. In opposition to the external and technological, the instrument directly involved in music-making is the body itself, thus making vocal music particularly corporeal. In much of the musicological writing on the voice, singing is considered feminine. The main reason for such a distinction is the opposition between the male artist as performer and instrumentalist and the female artist as singer. Barbara Bradby reinforces the notion of women as vocal performers, relegating the instrumental performance to men.

> If women have had an acknowledged role in rock and pop, it has been as performers, even though this has been mainly limited to vocal rather than instrumental performance, and has been circumscribed by ideologies that do not generally allow women's performances to be "authentic" in the way men's are.[9]

Bradby also points out that women have been equated with sexuality and the body, while men have been equated with technology and language.[10] McCracken states that the crooner was marked as different because of his lack of musicianship as defined by those who accompanied him: "A man who did 'nothing' but croon into a microphone in the natural, easy fashion of these singers could potentially undermine the standards of masculinity established by a band's hard-working, professionally trained musicians."[11] It should be noted that with the recent success of women in all areas of popular music performance, including rock, this "division of labour" has been blurred.

Popular music is gendered along lines of knowledge. Diane Railton suggests that various writers have, in the past, focused on the idea that rock culture is "masculine in terms of band membership and production, its lyrical content, and its political agenda. Women [are] marginalised by being denied a mind and reduced to their bodies ... incapable of handling the intellectual sophistication of the music."[12] While Railton is referring here to the music culture of the 1970s, she maintains that such categories remain strong. Frith and McRobbie reinforce this "division of knowledge" while touching on the notion of a gendered consumption of popular music, suggesting that female pop consumers are less concerned with the technical performance or syntax of the music as opposed to discriminating male rock consumers. The authors suggest that "teenybop" places less emphasis on live performance than on posters and television appearances, although they do concede that there are always overlaps and contradictions between the two groups. Even so, "the problems facing a woman seeking to enter the rock world as a participant are clear. A girl is supposed to be an individual listener, she is not encouraged to develop the skills and knowledge to become a performer."[13] Her job is to listen, and perhaps to watch, to desire and to swoon. There are problems, though, with such a dichotomy: if "teenybop" is about "self-pity, vulnerability, and need," what can be said, then, of Morrissey, a singer that is considered vulnerable, and, as will be argued later, in need, within a serious rock context? Furthermore, unlike the "teenybop" audience suggested by Frith and McRobbie, it is evident that Morrissey's audience is not exclusively female. Actually, it seems that his audience contains many more male members than female.

Commenting on music as gendered in terms of consumption, Railton, in her article on the carnivalesque aspect of pop music, acknowledges the construction of the role for women as popular music consumers. She argues,

> Just as this music is perhaps the only form of popular music to have a predominantly female audience, the threat that it poses is the threat of the feminine, and of female encroachment into what is still predominantly a male, and masculine, world.[14]

Women are also relegated to roles of "supporting, encouraging and facilitating music activity," rather than actually making or performing the music.[15] Mavis Bayton suggests that "women have been music consumers rather than music producers: the main role for women is that of fan."[16]

Gender and Western Tonality

There is also the question of whether the very structure of Western tonal music is gendered. While Cohen might want to suggest that the mechanics of the music cannot be read as masculine or feminine, musicologist Susan McClary, writing about Art Music, identifies such gender labels within the syntax of the music itself. Although one might be hesitant to look at "Absolute Music," or any other form of what is commonly known as classical music, when one is discussing popular pop or rock styles, it is no secret that these different genres utilize similar harmonic and melodic syntax in the West. McClary is concerned with so-called "Absolute Music," a label that refers to orchestral music without explicit narrative, in the form of text or vocal performance, which emerged from German Romanticism. Drawing from Stuart Hall, McClary states that "signification extends far beyond the surface in instrumental music: its formal conventions — often held to be neutral with respect to meaning — are likewise socially encoded."[17]

In her analysis, McClary identifies two narrative schema, tonality and sonata, of which the former is directly applicable to popular music. She defines her usage of the term as follows:

> I am referring here to tonality, not in the broad sense of pitch-centeredness (which would include most of Western music), but in the more specific sense of the grammatical and structural syntax of eighteenth- and nineteenth-century European musics.... On both local and global levels, tonality is intensely teleological; it works through the simple mechanism of suggesting a particular

pitch for purposes of release, but then withholding that pitch while continuing to imply (through a particular brand of harmonic syntax) that the goal is nearly within reach. The surface of the tonal piece thus alternates between carefully sustained tension or protracted longing and periodic moments of relief.[18]

McClary sums up her theory by stating, "The schema thus outlines a kind of narrative based on identity and certainty on the one hand, and difference and excitement (with at least the illusion of risk) on the other." Thus, she goes on to argue that such a syntax reinforces a notion of tonality as natural. Furthermore, the "beginning" tonality has consequently been labeled as "masculine," while the different tonality has been referred to as "feminine."[19] Therefore, McClary suggests that the very teleological nature of Western music points to notions of difference: the harmonic progression of this music is goal-oriented, with the goal being some kind of harmonic resolution, a "return" after a tonal "departure." Music which uses this schema places masculinity as a starting and ending point, while relegating femininity to a marginal place. While it can easily be acknowledged that current popular music generally follows such a schema of tonality, McClary's point is that the syntax of 19th-century "Absolute Music" reflects a particular cultural ideal. The notion that this cultural ideal still exists in the same form as it did in 19th-century German Romanticism is more difficult to ponder. Her insights, though, do show the possibility of labeling music in terms of gender.

McClary clarifies and expands her exploration of the gendered nature of traditional music theory in her book, *Feminine Endings: Music, Gender, and Sexuality*. She begins by discussing the binary of the "masculine" and "feminine" cadence, or musical ending. Citing an accepted definition of these cadences, McClary concludes, "The 'feminine' is weak, abnormal, and subjective; the 'masculine' strong, normal, and objective." In another example, the "feminine" is viewed not only as weak but also as a sign of excess. Furthermore, the binary of masculine/feminine has been mapped onto that of major and minor quality since the 18th century and as recently as the composer Arnold Schoenberg in the 20th century. Interestingly, Schoenberg strove to resist such trappings, longing instead for an "asexual" musical discourse, "no longer driven by the attraction and revulsion between major and minor."[20]

McClary's primary argument is that tonality in music "with its process of instilling expectations and subsequently withholding promised fulfillment until climax — is the principle musical means during the period from 1600 and 1900 for arousing and channeling desire."[21] For instance, McClary explains,

> [German composer Richard] Wagner's music relies heavily on the traditional semiotics of desire available in the musical styles he inherited, and listeners understand his music in part because they too have learned the codes (the minor sixths demanding resolution, the agony of the tritone, the expectation that a dominant-seventh chord will proceed to its tonic, and so on) upon which his metaphors depend.[22]

While McClary uses technical musicological language to describe these examples of the "semiotics of desire," her intent is clear. Wagner, working in the 19th century, used this syntax, and although musical language is not timeless, its legacy remains. This legacy informs "pop" music, since most of its syntax relies on traditional Western tonality and harmony.

For example, Lori Burns presents an interesting analysis of text/music relations to consider the gender constructions inherent in musical discourse and, in this case, popular music discourse. In her analysis of a cover of Joanie Sommer's "Johnny Get Angry" by k. d. lang, Burns not only looks at musical syntax in terms of gender but also focuses on the text that lang sings, and the relationship between these two elements. By studying also the text of the song, Burns is able to not only identify gendered portions of musical syntax but also explore what lang does with these codes and conventions, and how her text and delivery interact with these conventions. Like McClary, Burns believes that "tonal harmonic function carries with it a code of predictable idioms and relationships." She shows how "harmonic implications are denied or realized" within the structure of the song.[23] Burns explains, "By playing on the 'weaker' versus the 'stronger' features in the original song's musical discourse, she exposes the imbalance of power ascribed to women and men in patriarchal society."[24]

The Gendered Character of Music as a Discipline

While McClary and Burns discuss the delineation of masculinity and femininity in the semiotics of music, other scholars point out that music itself can be labelled as feminine. In discussing various forms of difference within music, including those related to style, genre and nationality, John Shepherd questions the definition of music itself. He states,

> It is questionable, for example, whether there *are* "classical," "popular," "folk," and "traditional" musics. It seems more likely that there are *discourses* constructed around concrete musical practices, and that those discourses group such practices into categories that render the music amenable to various forms of social, political, and economic control.[25]

He continues by clarifying that this does not render music as "universal," or affecting listeners in the same way everywhere in the world. Rather, Shepherd states, "The meanings invested in it are not consistent but contested." He tries to distinguish how sound evokes meaning in a different way than language, outlining sound's ability to imitate and thus "refer" to other sounds, the way sound can be homologous in meaning to certain "non-sound" phenomena, and finally that "sound can act as a purely arbitrary means of signification in relation to the phenomenon evoked."[26] The first two "potentials," to use Shepherd's term, provide the basis for the generation of meaning in music, while the third is an element of language. The break of sound from the homologous meaning of language has led to the creation of massive social structures, argues Shepherd, which in turn leads to balances and imbalances of power.[27] Furthermore,

> Sound is shaped and shaping, structured and structuring. In connecting these aspects of the external and internal physical worlds it can act, homologously and symbolically, as a code, a concrete ground and pathway, for the evocation of the relationships between the inner and outer social worlds.
>
> Because music can enter, grip, and position us symbolically, it can act powerfully to structure and mediate individual awareness as the ultimate seat of social and cultural reproduction.[28]

Shepherd concludes that music as a whole is coded as feminine, as sensual and seductive artifice, and is thus marginalized in a capitalist society. He explains, "Music has been categorized as an unimportant mode of human expression — unimportant, that is, to processes regarded as central to the continued life of society." While being considered less important than other cultural processes, music is powerful in terms of its ability to reproduce societal norms. Shepherd explains,

> Through the appeal of various genres to individual and collective realities, music serves to reproduce the life of capitalism, yet this very function is implicitly denied through the ways in which music is understood and institutionalized in various cultural and educational processes. In this sense music occupies con-

tradictory positions in the social structures of industrial capitalism that are parallel to those of women: music reaffirms the flux and concreteness of the social world at the same time that, through its categorization and packaging, it denies them.[29]

Thus, music is marginalized by its "feminine" character, yet maintains the power to reproduce norms in society.

Like Shepherd at the beginning of this section, Suzanne Cusick questions the definition of music. She provides an unexpected answer by suggesting that music can be construed as a sexual act. She explains,

> If sex is free of the association with reproduction enforced by the so-called phallic economy (and it is, remember, exactly so for people called homosexual, as it has become in the last thirty years for people called heterosexual who practice contraception), if it is then *only* (only!) a means of negotiating power and intimacy through the circulation of pleasure, what's to prevent music from *being* sex, and thus an ancient, half-sanctioned form of escape from the constraints of the phallic economy?[30]

Cusick suggests that music is both a giver of pleasure (to the listener in performance) and a receiver of pleasure (she cites the example of performing an organ piece, describing the use of her hands to coax musical climaxes and events). While she focuses on what she deems a "lesbian" relationship with music, in which one can escape the power relationships inherent within what she calls the phallic economy, her discussion does shed light on the esoteric and sensual nature of music and performance as pleasure. Music as sex, or as "a means of negotiating power and intimacy," is another element in discussing issues of performance and mastery.

This intimacy is hinted at in Elizabeth Wood's notion of "sapphonics." She suggests that sapphonics is a rubric that "has overtones and resonances in and beyond voice production and hidden vestibules of the body." This notion allows for the exploration of what she calls "lesbian possibility," and "a range of erotic and emotional relationships among women who sing and women who listen." She explains, "I stage an imaginary intimacy between voices: theirs singing, being heard; mine listening and, with other listeners writing, being read."[31] While her discussion focuses on the female voice (and, in particular, the "lesbian" voice), this concept can be applied to the male voice in terms of pleasure and intimacy in performance. Interestingly, Wood discusses the female *falsetto* voice, or a high voice that would not "naturally" reside in the vocalist's range, as "a transvestic enigma, belonging to neither male nor female as constructed—a synthesis, not a split." The falsetto voice provides a challenge to conventional categories of gender and sexuality by suggesting their fluidity and transferability. She continues:

> The extreme range in one female voice from richly dark deep chest tones to a piercingly clear high falsetto, and its defective break at crossing register borders produces ... a merging rather than splitting ... an acceptance and integration of male and female.[32]

The use of falsetto in the male voice is even more pronounced. While singing out of the normal range is unnatural in both males and females, the expectation of a low voice from a male makes the use of falsetto striking. Accepting the above commentary regarding the falsetto voice, it therefore embodies a certain power for its user in terms of freedom from or transgression of established gender codes. It seems that this experience of power and mystery is particularly dramatic for the listener. Wood explains,

> For the listener, the Sapphonic voice is a destabilizing agent of fantasy and desire. The woman [or man] with this voice, this capacity to embody and traverse a range of sonic possibilities and overflow sonic boundaries, may vocalize inadmissible sexualities and a thrilling readiness to go beyond so-called natural limits, an erotics of risk and defiance, a desire for desire itself.[33]

The Voice and Desire

Morrissey's voice can be difficult to describe. It is an open voice, not nasal or sneered, at least by my ears. It is a smooth voice, not gravelly or rough. It is a soft voice, one that needs a microphone (it is a crooner's voice). He has a restrained voice, always held at bay, it seems. It is marked by a wide vibrato, that vibrating that the singing voice does as it sustains. His voice is not operatic (perhaps because of the lack of power behind it). His voice can have trouble staying on pitch, though this is only really evident in live performance. In some of his softer songs, one can hear his body in the voice, in particular, his breath and his lungs. The listener can hear the breath in his throat in these softer songs. In most of his songs, though, the listener can hear his mouth, his teeth (he has a bit of a lisp, it seems); his English accent is prevalent in all he sings. Some people I know have described his voice as too whiney for their tastes. Some people say he is too glum.

One person told me that once she saw a picture of Morrissey, her experience of listening was ruined. For her, Morrissey's voice was the totality of the experience. The image of Morrissey "ruined" the voice (too much information, perhaps?). This was never the case with me: I was first introduced to Morrissey's voice in The Smiths, singing "Frankly, Mr. Shankly." My memory of my first engagement with Morrissey was when my wife, then simply a colleague, was recounting the lyrics to a "humorous" song about a "Mr. Shankly," as we were walking along a downtown Toronto street in 1998. For me, it was his voice that enthralled me, captured me on first listen. But later seeing his image did not destroy that experience. For me, the image of Morrissey made the voice richer; his voice pointed to his physical image. His voice was a marker of his presence; he was (is) physically present even though he was not (is not) really physically present.

The voice is where I meet Morrissey. Ben Ratliff writes about Morrissey as follows: "He's always known what he wants to sing about.... He also knows how he wants to sing it. (In a pop-operatic tenor, straining against the limitations of his melodic imagination.)"[34]

When one hears a singing voice, whether recorded or in concert, one is often captivated by that sound and drawn into a different world created or expanded by the sound to which one listens. The sound recording, or live performance, might consist of a singing voice along with other sounds, including the instruments that serve to accompany it. These sounds also contribute to the building of this "world" into which the listener is drawn. Apart from the singing voice, and beyond these accompanying "voices" (or instruments), there are other "voices" to which one also listens. One can try to describe a voice and write out what the voice sings, but ultimately those elements that draw the listener to that "world" lay beyond that singing voice, beyond the surface of the sound. These elements are what might elicit the listener's desire; they keep the listener enthralled in this new "world," and they urge the listener to return. What are these other "voices"?

In fact, there is, as Barthes would say, a "weaving of voices" that in turn produces the text: "Alongside each utterance, one might say that off-stage voices can be heard."[35] These off-stage voices come from life and culture, the greater discourse of society. When one hears a singing voice, whether live or recorded, one might know very little of the singer, her or his circumstances, origin, or appearance. The "voices" that lay beyond the sound are expanded or illuminated in other media, through visual and aural texts. These other "voices" may be glimpsed through these other texts as "streams" that serve to elicit desire from the listener, as, ultimately, elements that cannot be separated from the singing voice. The "streams" weave together to make the celebrity known to the listener. A celebrity, the being behind the singing voice, might be veiled in mystery. While the listener might be able to engage with a mediated version of the person, the real being behind a celebrity — or any mediate figure, for that matter — is not available to the listener. This enigmatic figure continues to be desirable if he or she is still unknowable; it is arguable that if all that can be known about a celebrity is discovered, he or she is no longer interesting. Thus, if these "weaved" voices are unidentifiable, or constantly evading identification, then desire for the figure at the center of the "text," the celebrity, is maintained.

Jacques Lacan describes this desire for the unattained (or unattainable) in his discussion of metonymy and metaphor. Lacan suggests that human instinct is "eternally stretching towards the *desire for something else*." This "something else" is ultimately unattainable and unidentifiable. Lacan explains, "There is no other way of conceiving the indestructibility of unconscious desire — in the absence of a need which, when forbidden satisfaction, does not sicken and die, even if it means the destruction of the organism itself."[36] Here, Lacan is discussing the quest for the Other, which lies in the unconscious. This Other is the ultimate signifier of everything the subject is not, as well as what the subject does not have. The discovery of the Other is of utmost importance to social identity. Lacan makes a distinction and refers to a lowercase "other," which refers to any object of desire in reality, which may just be a cover for the true object of desire residing in the unconscious.

There are two parts to these underlying voices to which the listener is drawn. There are those elements of the celebrity that are able to be identified in some way, such as biographical facts or physical attributes. There are also some aspects that evade identification, that elicit desire. These elements constitute, in part, what Roland Barthes calls the "grain of the voice."

The "Grain of the Voice"

Barthes refers to such desiring when he discusses the "impossible account of an individual thrill that I constantly experience in listening to singing."³⁷ He attempts to give materiality to this thrill in terms of what he calls the "grain of the voice." For Barthes, this "grain" does not only refer to the timbre or tone of the voice: "The *signifiance* it opens cannot be better defined, indeed, than by the very friction between the music and something else," that is, language.³⁸ Between these two communicators of meaning — music and language — there emerges, for Barthes, *signifiance* within the "grain" of the voice. On one hand, the "grain" refers to the physicality of the voice, pointing not to any sort of meaning but rather to the present physical body. On the other hand, *signifiance* suggests a continuing process of some kind. In his "Translator's Note" to Barthes' text, Stephen Heath sheds some light on the term: "*Signifiance is a process* in the course of which the 'subject' of the text, escaping the logic of the *ego-cogito* [a sense of self constructed through thought] and engaging in other logics ... struggles with meaning and is deconstructed ('lost')."³⁹ Thus, within and perhaps through singing, the subject of the "text" is in the process of losing this subjectivity. Barthes continues:

> The "grain" is the body in the voice as it sings, the hand as it writes, the limb as it performs. If I perceive the "grain" in a piece of music and accord this "grain" a theoretical value (the emergence of the text in the work), I inevitably set up a new scheme of evaluation which will certainly be individual — I am determined to listen to my relation with the body of the man or woman singing or playing and that relation is erotic — but in no way "subjective" (it is not the psychological "subject" in me who is listening; the climactic pleasure hoped for is not going to reinforce — to express — that subject but, on the contrary, to lose it).⁴⁰

Therefore, according to Barthes, the relationship between the singer and the listener could be thought of as erotic, as sexual. Furthermore, the listener also loses his or her subjectivity along with the "subject" of the text. There is a pleasure associated with such a loss, and Barthes attempts to clarify this pleasure which comes with the reading of a text:

> It's not a question of "contemplating" the text, or even of "projecting" oneself, of "participating" in it; if the text is an "object," it is in a purely psychoanalytical sense: caught up in a dialectic of desire, and — to be more precise — perversion.... The "pleasure of the text," to my mind, refers to something entirely unknown to aesthetics, particularly literary aesthetics, which is: bliss, a mode of vanishing, of annulment of the subject.⁴¹

Barthes expresses the difficulty in articulating this pleasure, as there is no word in French — Barthes' language of writing — which encompasses both the concepts of "pleasure" and "bliss," and also the complexity of its effects. He writes:

> Why say "pleasure of the text" and not "bliss of the text"? Because in the textual practice there is a gamut of dispersions of the subject, which may go from consistence (when there is contentment, plenitude, satisfaction, pleasure in the proper sense) to loss (when there is annulment, fading, bliss).[42]

Although Barthes recognizes that a framework of desire is in place when one reads some kind of text, he suggests that such a framework only exists for a moment: the text is an "'object' only long enough to put the 'subject' into question."[43] It is in the reading of the text that the subject ultimately loses him- or herself, and thus experiences this pleasure. If "reading" can be replaced by "listening" and "text" by a "singing voice," then these ideas of desire and pleasure can be applied to music, which Barthes does freely.

Barthes discusses the meaning that can be drawn from the voice:

> The voice, in relation to silence, is like writing (in the graphic sense) on blank paper. Listening to the voice inaugurates the relation to the Other: the voice by which we recognize others (like writing on an envelope) indicates to us their way of being, their joy or their pain, their condition; it bears an image of their body and, beyond, a whole psychology (as when we speak of a warm voice, a white voice, etc.).[44]

Therefore the voice works in two ways for the listener: it allows him or her to identify the user of the voice, and also to thrill the listener. Part of the thrill is in the loss of the subject, but also in the subject's constitution.

Barthes refers to an "imaginary" in music that serves to "reassure, to constitute the subject hearing it (would it be that music is dangerous — the old Platonic idea? that music is an access to *jouissance*, to loss, as numerous ethnographic and popular examples would tend to show?) and this imaginary immediately comes to language with the adjective." Thus there is a difficulty in discussing music in a satisfactory way. Instead of changing the language by which one talks about music, Barthes wishes to "change the musical object itself, as it presents itself to discourse." When Barthes talks about the "grain" of the voice, he is referring to the "very precise space ... of *the encounter between a language and a voice*."[45] He states:

> What is listened to here and there (chiefly in the field of art, whose function is often utopian) is not the advent of a signified, object of a recognition or of a deciphering, but the very dispersion, the *shimmering* of signifiers, ceaselessly restored to a listening which ceaselessly produces new ones without ever arrest-

ing their meaning: this phenomenon of meaning is called *signifying* [*signifiance*], as distinct from signification.[46]

There is an attempt on the part of the listener to "stabilize" or "decipher" the voice, but there is also a willingness to become "destabilized" by it, or to lose one's subjectivity within it. About the voice, Barthes says:

> But what interests me the most in the voice, to begin with, is that this very cultural object is, in a certain way, an absent object (much more absent than the body, which is represented in a thousand ways by mass culture): we rarely listen to a voice *en soi*, in itself, we listen to what it says. The voice has the very status of language, an object thought to be graspable only through what it transmits; however, just as we are now learning, thanks to the notion of the "text," to read the linguistic material itself, we must in the same way learn to listen to the voice's text, its meaning, everything in the voice which overflows meaning.[47]

Therefore, for Barthes, meaning can come from the voice itself, and not only from what it communicates through language. Therefore, it is this meaning that might also be desired by the listener. One becomes engulfed by the voice in search for this meaning, to further gain knowledge of the physical producer of the voice.

Popular music scholar Richard Middleton recognizes the importance of Barthes and the "grain of the voice" as a way to talk about musical pleasure within a semiological framework, but wishes to include melodic and timbral elements of music in such a discussion. In response to both Barthes and the work of Frith and McRobbie, Middleton states:

> Recognizing the erotic importance of the voice helps to avoid a misleading overemphasis on instrumental rhythm as the sole or predominant locus of musical sexuality; at the same time it reinforces the point that the ranking of genres and styles in terms of erotic quanta is equally misleading: what is important, rather, is the *forms* in which desires are revealed and pleasures made available.[48]

John Potter holds similar sentiments in discussing the singing voice as a site of desire, not because of musical style or rhythm, but rather because of intimacy in delivery: the pop vocal delivery affords the singer the opportunity to "retain the simplicity of speech but modify it by musical phrasing." He continues:

> The shapes thus produced have their own micro-cosmic elements of tension and release. The poetry, in other words, is in the mode of delivery, as much as in the text itself. This is very sophisticated post-composing which draws the

listener in — a sort of rhetorical reversal of the accepted idea that the singer must project.[49]

Potter suggests that this new way of thinking about the voice reduces the significance of gender. Like Potter, Middleton wishes to find new sites of musical pleasure, taking into account the voice. He suggests:

> There is no need to limit *jouissance* in music to a level somehow beyond structure, to an assertion of materiality against form.... To the extent that repetition is defined, precisely, as carrying predictability to the limit, it becomes possible to link repetition not (not only?) with the *plaisir* of signification (the most obvious extrapolation from Barthes) but (but also?) with the possibility of *jouissance*.[50]

Middleton thus finds a site of desire in the repetitiveness of music, apart from simply the delivery of the singing voice. Wayne Koestenbaum also suggests that repetition elicits desire, but is speaking, rather, of the repetition of recordings as reminders of special musical moments. He explains:

> How loudly do you play your opera? Loud enough to hurt the ear? In the opera house, I distinguish between two kinds of sound: the baritone, mezzo, and bass, in whose presence I remain Subject, knowing the heard voice as Object; and the soprano and tenor, which, as they ascend in volume and pitch, become Subject, incapable of remaining the distant Object. Thus opera interrupts and reverses our ground. I can't remain separate from the tenor or soprano at the height of their ranges, because high notes enter my ear, assault, make a demand.... Moments of being pierced, being surrounded by sound, being called, are worth collecting.[51]

Koestenbaum's point can be transferred from opera to popular music, not necessarily on the basis of pitch but certainly of volume. Popular music is often touted as music to be listened to loudly; concerts are often deafening and recordings are played back at high volume. The music thus surrounds the listener, "reversing" his or her "ground." Koestenbaum describes the desire that results from this reversal:

> And so the opera queen keeps lists. Experiences are accreted, because none can be exhaustively explained. If, once, you could describe the summons a voice sends out, maybe you could stop listening, stop looking to opera for satisfaction and consummation.[52]

One needs only to replace the term "opera queen" with "fan," and "opera" with some kind of celebrity discourse, such as popular music. Koestenbaum is suggesting that his desire requires a continual cataloguing of experience in terms of that musical style, a listing that takes into account not only the actual hearing of the voice but also attendance at a particular performance and other information. "The purpose of a list is not to refine or browbeat, but to include, and to move toward a future moment when accumulation stops and the list-keeper can cull, recollect, and rest on the prior amplitude."[53] It is unclear, though, if this future moment ever comes. Perhaps celebrity itself will not allow such a moment to come about.

The Incomplete Celebrity

In considering the status of celebrity, one must take up the question of the celebrity's completeness, of the closure of identity. Each mediation of the celebrity is necessarily incomplete, giving the consumer or audience a "stream" that is only partial and may even contradict previous elements of the celebrity's star image. These continual clues to the complete identity of the celebrity constantly postpone a connection to the truth of the actual person. The complete image of the celebrity is pursued along this "stream" or series of clues. As is explored below, the pursuit of the complete image of the celebrity raises issues relating to desire and spectacle, and it involves, in particular, a gendered framework of desire.

It is argued here that the notion of an eroticized celebrity persona poses a problem for a male celebrity. The problem can be solved by the constant production of uncertainties with regard to the celebrity's identity. If a celebrity is a slippery figure, he or she cannot be fully subject to the gaze of the audience, and thus deflects what Laura Mulvey argues are the eroticizing effects of the audience's gaze. Her ideas are further discussed later in this chapter. Therefore, if a celebrity is able to deflect those effects, such a celebrity is, in a sense, active. If, as Laura Mulvey argues below, the act of eroticization as spectacle can be considered in terms of gender, with the "masculine" gaze "feminizing" the one who is subject to that gaze, then such a power to deflect the eroticizing effect of the gaze might be considered "masculinist." The constant evasion of any fixing of the celebrity star image might render the celebrity as active against the passifying effect of the audience's gaze.

Another result of this constant production of uncertainties in a celebrity persona is the sense of mystery and the unknown. Barthes discusses the unknown in terms of the enigma, or the embodiment of a mystery. He analyzes such parts of that which are deemed enigmatic by utilizing what he calls the hermeneutic code. Barthes explains:

> Let us designate as *hermeneutic code* ... all the units [of the text] whose function it is to articulate in various ways a question, its response, and the variety of chance events which can either formulate the question or delay its answer; or even, constitute an enigma and lead to its solution.[54]

These clues are pieces of a puzzle, hopefully leading to an answer that may not always be completely provided. According to Barthes, the reader desires these items that he or she does not have or know about.

Celebrity and Star Image

In recent academic writing on celebrity, there has been much interest in what has been called the "star image." The star image of a celebrity refers to an interaction between various elements of a celebrity. These elements include the discourse that might surround a celebrity away from, or in conjunction with, his or her performance. This includes the biography of the performer, as known publicly and as constructed in narrative form. Also, these elements include the roles with which a performer is associated, which have certain continuities and discontinuities between them. Finally, the celebrity can be thought of as a performer as part of a certain kind of tradition, which he or she both embodies and transforms. It is in the interaction between these different parts of celebrity that a star image takes form. A performer's audience comes into contact with this star image, the public persona of the celebrity, informed by these various elements.

John Ellis states that a star is "a performer in a particular medium whose figure enters into subsidiary forms of circulation, and then feeds back into future performances."[55] In the construction of a star image, bodies of discourse — those elements that enter into subsidiary forms of circulation — emerge on the margins of actual performance. These might include biographical or media texts, which Richard Dyer calls "publicity." Publicity refers to texts "distinct from promotion in that it is not, or does not appear to be, *deliberate* image-making. It is 'what the press finds out,' what the star lets slip in an interview." Dyer states:

> The importance of publicity is that, in its apparent or actual escape from the image that Hollywood is trying to promote, it seems more "authentic." It is thus often taken to give a privileged access to the real person of the star. It is also the place where one can read tensions between the star-as-person and her/his image, tensions which at another level become themselves crucial to the image.[56]

Richard deCordova, in a study of the emergence of the cinematic "star system" in America, discusses the difference between a film personality and a star. He states, "The star is characterized by a fairly thoroughgoing articulation of the paradigm professional life/private life. With the emergence of the star, the question of the player's existence outside his/her work in films entered discourse."[57] Barry King suggests that "it is the extrafilmic discourse that has the greatest impact on the public's knowledge of the star." He continues,

> The moment of the star image is, in fact, the moment of a proprietorial claim to such effects as though they were a property of the star as a person, a claim which subsists not particularly in what is represented on screen, but in the subsidiary literature where the image is rendered as a 'real life' property of its bearer, the actor as star.[58]

A blurring between the actor and star occurs. King suggests that this is when the actor becomes a part of the star system.

The roles with which a performer is associated also contribute to this star image. For Dyer, the film as a star vehicle, one built around a specific star image, contributes to a "continuity of iconography" across which one can discern how a celebrity carries him- or herself.[59] Dyer notes, though, that there might be cases in which the films of a celebrity might be lesser elements of his or her image.

Another element that contributes to the construction of the star image is a "continuity" of "the professional experience of the actor." DeCordova writes:

> Insofar as this knowledge related to the actor's previous film experience it worked to establish the intertextual space between films.... However, this knowledge often referred to the actor's stage experience and can be seen as a continuation of the discourse on acting.[60]

Dyer comments on how these elements and various media texts come together to constitute the celebrity's star image:

> It is misleading to think of the texts combining cumulatively into a sum total that constitutes the image, or alternatively simply as being moments in a star's

image's career that appear one after the other—although those emphases are important. The image is a *complex totality* and it does have a *chronological dimension*. What we need to understand that totality in its temporality is the concept of a *structured polysemy*.

By *polysemy* is meant the multiple but finite meaning and effects that a star image signifies.... This polysemy is *structured*. In some cases, the various elements of signification may *reinforce* one another.... In other cases, the elements may be to some degree *in opposition or contradiction*, in which case the star's image is characterised by attempts to negotiate, reconcile or mask the difference between the elements, or else simply hold them in tension.[61]

Dyer uses the term "star's image's career" to stress that he is referring to the celebrity not as a real person but as a media text. Dyer continues, "Images also have a *temporal dimension*. Structured polysemy does not imply stasis; images develop or change over time."[62] Dyer discusses how a star phenomenon works ideologically. He states that "in the early period, stars were gods and goddesses, heroes, models—embodiments of *ideal* ways of behaving." After the emergence of cinema with sound, "stars are identification figures, people like you and me—embodiments of *typical* ways of behaving."[63] P. David Marshall suggests that the celebrity is the "epitome of the individual for identification and idealization in society." Furthermore, "the celebrity is a commodity, and therefore expresses a form of valorization of the individual and personality that is coherent with capitalism and the associated consumer culture." Here Marshall is exploring how a celebrity is created not only by the culture industries but also by "the audience's reading of dominant cultural representations."[64] Thus, for Marshall, the celebrity represents a "site for processes of hegemony."[65]

Like Dyer, Marshall acknowledges the complex nature of the star image and the celebrity persona, suggesting that there are a variety of factors that contribute to its formation. He lists the various factors as follows:

- The collective/audience conceptualization of the celebrity;
- the categorical types of individuality that are expressed through the celebrity;
- the cultural industries' construction of the celebrity;
- the relative commodity status of the celebrity;
- the form of cultural legitimation that the celebrity, singly or as part of an entire system, may represent; and
- the unstable nature of the meaning of the celebrity—the processual

and dynamic changeability of the individual celebrity and the entire system of celebrity.⁶⁶

Marshall suggests that celebrities are "given greater presence and a wider scope of activity and agency than those who make up the rest of the population." A celebrity is deemed successful and valorized in some way, and is afforded a discursive power: "Within society, the celebrity is a voice above others, a voice that is channeled into the media systems as being legitimately significant." Marshall continues by pointing out that the celebrity is an ambiguous figure because the valorization and status that accompany the title are achieved without any obvious labor: "The sign of a celebrity is ridiculed and derided because it represents the center of false value." Marshall defines the celebrity as such:

> In its simultaneous embodiment of media construction, audience construction, and the real, living, and breathing human being, the celebrity sign negotiates the competing and contradictory definitions of its own significance. The cementing character of this negotiation is the basic and essential authenticity that a "real" person is housed in a sign construction. In a cultural sense, the celebrity is one form of resolution of the role and position of the individual and his or her potential in modern society. The power of the celebrity, then, is to represent the active construction of identity in the social world.⁶⁷

The celebrity's weakness is its reliance upon an audience for its existence. If this audience does not exist, the celebrity's status is weakened.

As a public figure, Marshall suggests that a celebrity might become objectified as an idealized representation of the individual. Furthermore, Marshall suggests that the celebrity can be seen as a representation of the potential of the individual, although this potential is achieved without obvious labor. Dyer suggests that the celebrity is a model, perhaps no longer for ideal ways of behaving, but for typical ways of behaving. This objectification as type means that the celebrity is, in a sense, being passive; the figure is a "type" and ultimately a passive object to which the active audience looks.

The Gendered Character of Celebrity and Desire

As a figure that is the object of the gaze of his or her audience, a celebrity is placed within a framework constructed in terms of gender.

3. "Let Me Kiss You" 99

The celebrity as a figure who is looked at provides pleasure; the celebrity as an eroticized spectacle is "feminized." This concept is developed in an influential article by Laura Mulvey, "Visual Pleasure and Narrative Cinema," from which many film scholars have drawn. Mulvey's arguments revolve around the notion of the image of woman in narrative film being eroticized as spectacle, as the passive object of a gaze, while the man is considered active, and the one doing the gazing. Furthermore, Mulvey suggests that patriarchal society has structured the form of classical narrative film. She points out that, paradoxically, this phallocentrism relies on women to give it meaning: "It is her lack that produces the phallus as a symbolic presence, it is her desire to make good the lack that the phallus signifies."[68]

Mulvey's argument draws on Freud and his association between scopophilia, one of the possible pleasures afforded by cinema, and the "taking [of] other people as subjects, subjecting them to a controlling and curious gaze."[69] In her discussion, scopophilia is essentially active. In contrast, the one who is being looked at is passive: "In their traditional exhibitionist role women are simultaneously looked at and displayed, with their appearance coded for strong visual and erotic impact so that they can be said to connote *to-be-looked-at-ness*."[70] Furthermore, "the male figure cannot bear the burden of sexual objectification.... Hence the split between the spectacle and narrative supports the man's role as the active one of forwarding the story, making things happen."[71] The male actor is defended from the feminizing gaze of the audience by becoming the active supporter of the narrative of the film.

Mulvey's article, with its now-famous conceptualization of the active/male gaze and the passive/female object, has been used extensively in the analysis not only of film but also of visual texts in general. As is demonstrated by Dyer's comments below, many have found Mulvey's view too rigid and totalizing. The limits of her view are particularly evident when one considers the male celebrity, or the male mediated figure, who is not involved in narrative progression or support. It should be noted that Mulvey is talking about characters within films and does not consider celebrities *per se*, and thus gives little recognition of the extratextual information that enters into the reading of these figures.

For instance, Dyer discusses the male pin-up model not as a passive object, as Mulvey's model might suggest, but rather as an object with the *potential* for action. Dyer adds:

> The model prepares her- or himself to be looked at, the artist or photographer constructs the image to be looked at; and, on the other hand, the image that the viewer looks at is not summoned up by his or her act of looking but in collaboration with those who have put the image there.[72]

Dyer problematizes the active male/passive female dichotomy put forth by Mulvey, suggesting that "constructed" media disempower the viewer. Dyer does state, though, that "it remains the case that images of men must disavow this element of passivity [presumably inherent in the pin-up] if they are to be kept in line with dominant ideas of masculinity-as-activity."[73] Mulvey's framework has served as the basis for many analyses of film and has also been appropriated by scholars outside of film studies. For example, as was discussed earlier, the active male/passive female model has been applied in the field of musicology as a way to problematize gendered constructions in musical syntax.

Mulvey's argument, by which she suggests the feminization of the mediated figure as subject to the viewer's gaze, poses a problem in terms of the mediated male subject not involved in narrative action, such as a popular music celebrity. Mulvey's influential article can serve not only as a basis but also as a point of departure for this present work.

Various Masculinities

A number of scholars have built on Mulvey's work, offering a typology of masculinities to be found in film or televisual texts. These include masculinities whose meaning is dependent upon the gaze of female characters within the diegesis. Within this typology one may find, as well, masculinity that functions as the object of erotic fascination for spectators. In more problematic cases, one may find images of a lost masculinity, or of passive, narcissistic and sensitive masculinities. Finally, there are versions of masculinity that emphasize the constructed character of masculine identities through a foregrounding of those processes (such as shopping or dressing) through which masculinity is "put on."

Discussing F. W. Murnau's *The Last Laugh*, Stephan Schindler suggests that the film reinforces "the characteristics of the masculinities constructed therein, that is, a man is a man when he acquires a body armour (uniform/money), when he excludes women from his world, and when he receives the recognition women refuse him in homoerotic and homosocial relationships."[74] In a move that may seem to produce an alternate model of masculinity, the female gaze is actually required for the construction of masculinity in the film. Schindler comments,

> Although the porter reassures himself of his external image by peering numerous times into mirrors, there is a certain anxiety inherent in all these scenes because the essence of his appearance is to-be-looked-at. The gaze of women is indispensable to sovereign masculinity, and the doorman's imaginary identity depends on women's recognition in particular.[75]

The author points out, though, that the female gaze also destroys the porter's sense of masculinity.

Scott Benjamin King discusses the representation of masculinity in the television show *Miami Vice*. He suggests that the show is extraordinary because of its use of looks:

> After years of female display designed for the (male) viewer, the man is now in the televisual showcase. Sonny's status as a clothes hanger is defined not only by the programme (with its lingering shots of him in full body, in close up) but by the hype and the critiques that follow *Vice* wherever it goes. Within the definitions of patriarchal culture, Sonny is "feminized" by his objectification; the cultural gender confusion over the prominence of a *male* model manifests itself physically in Sonny's trademark stubble, which serves to remind us that this pretty displayed human is, counter to our expectations, a man.[76]

Here is a presentation of a different sort of masculinity, both of the protagonist Sonny as an active man in the sense of fighting crime and racing around Miami, and of a man who is invariably looked at and on display. The problematic nature of Sonny's masculinity is further compounded by the difficulties he encounters in the performing of his job. King points out that there are many instances in the show when criminals get away: "Sonny, in his failure at work, is thus humiliated along strictly masculine definitions.... He is unable to maintain mastery over his work, a part of his character that defines his cultural masculinity."[77] The male is presented as a beautiful consumer image, which King suggests is a position traditionally reserved for women, while also having difficulty in his work which defines him as a man. King concludes:

> Sonny may be feminized by his position, but his character is by no means feminine, a positive affirmation of traits associated with women. Like his stubble, his almost hyper-masculine characteristics (silence, emotionlessness, violence, etc.) reassure us that this suffering, punished human being is male and that

the tenets of masculinity are not too much in danger. Sonny's macho stance and his affirmation of the masculine gender role, however, do not undermine the gender contradiction that the blatantly displayed Sonny Crockett embodies.[78]

King does not delve into what effect such a masculine contradiction might have on the viewer, or whether the image is ultimately effective at all. While reinforcing traditional masculinity through the use of hyper-masculine characteristics, Sonny's character also problematizes the notion of the ideal man by making him an object to be looked at, and an object that is a failure at work. What kind of man, therefore, is he?

Is it possible that, as Pam Cook suggests, this problematic notion of masculinity is presented so that one can mourn its loss? In her article, "Masculinity in Crisis? [Tragedy and Identification in *Raging Bull*]," Cook states:

> *Raging Bull*, like its predecessors in the boxing genre, presents the powerful male body as an object of desire and identification, but moving towards the loss of male power. This loss activates the desire to call it up once more: we mourn the loss, so the founding image of male power, the phallus, is centred yet again. The place for desire which the tragedy promises to open up — the celebration of the overthrow of the phallus — is closed off in the search for the lost object.[79]

For Cook, the film raises the question of whether there exist alternatives to conventional masculinity and what these alternatives might entail. Perhaps this is the case with Sonny in *Miami Vice*; the viewer is called to mourn for the loss of masculine virility, or at least cry for its reinstatement to its previous position of primacy. Therefore, according to Cook, although the film raises "crucial questions of desire," it is "far from progressive, bypassing the questions of female desire, denying the value of many of the changes that have taken place in the area of sexual politics, retreating into retrograde romanticism and anti-intellectualism."[80]

Jeffrey A. Brown discusses the star image of Gary Cooper and its problematic representation of masculinity. Cooper represents an interesting paradox in the fact that he was considered the ideal man, a perfect image of masculinity, but also as an object to be looked at. Brown suggests that the juxtaposition of traditional masculinity and the feminization of the male as an object reveal the true project of Hollywood filmmaking. He explains,

> The objectification of Cooper allows us to glimpse Hollywood's practice of both looking at the male as a sexual ideal, a role model for identification, and denying the obvious invitation of that look. The imperative of masculine eroti-

cism, to care about one's appearance but not appear to care, is reinforced by the very *careful* presentation of Cooper as an object to be looked at and the diagetic denial of that look. Cooper's diversity of roles, and his dual image as rugged and "pretty," reinforced by his womanizing personal life, all work to expose the objectified nature of cinematic ideals of masculinity.[81]

Much like Murnau's protagonist in *The Last Laugh*, the feminine gaze is required here to reinforce masculinity. A man must care about his appearance, but *carefully*.

Rachel Adams, in her analysis of the film *Copland*, discusses the shift in the representation of masculinity in films during the 1990s. She argues that a new "gentler and more physically expansive" masculinity, portrayed by "less conventionally manly stars ... [challenges] the primacy of the hard-boiled action hero." She states,

> This shift is nowhere more dramatically emphasized than in the vertiginous transformation of Sylvester Stallone, the crown prince of action cinema, into the stoop shouldered, paunchy Freddy Heflin in James Mangold's 1997 *Copland*.[82]

The author points out that most media coverage around the release of the film suggests the emergence of a hybrid action/drama film, as well as a new image of masculinity. Adams is quick to point out that the media failed to recognize the link between the film's racialized landscape and the racial politics of the Clinton Administration. This is one of the main thrusts of her analysis. Stallone's character no longer looks good: "The camera zooms in on the swelling guts and rounded backsides of protagonists who are depicted not as idealized, statuesque figures but as appropriately proportioned to their very average surroundings." Adams suggests that the placing of Stallone in such a role conjures up images of all the action heroes he depicted previously, and therefore, the film can be read as a critique of the action genre. In a scene that was shown only to preview audiences, Stallone turns over on a bed to reveal a protruding belly; this scene caused such a negative response that it was omitted from the final cut of the film. "The response of preview audiences is evidence that Freddy is shadowed by the complex of meanings that are sutured to the celebrity persona of 'Stallone.'"[83] She states that although the film showcases an unlikely hero, his masculinity is fully restored through his search for justice. Adams concludes:

> While it upholds a form of masculinity quite different from that of the hard-bodied action hero, *Copland* is nonetheless heavily invested in masculine hero-

ics. The bodies of women and people of color that are so emphatically contained by the film's spacial geography are not liberated by this conclusion.... Thus rather than shifting its focus away from masculine primacy, *Copland* tells us something of the suppleness and variability of white masculinity, which has the ability to expand and contract, grow hard or soft, while remaining the focus of narrative attention.... New forms of masculinity are not necessarily harbingers of more progressive social change."[84]

This does not bode well for new forms of masculinity. How far does a new form of masculinity need to stray from the traditional Hollywood presentation to suggest progressive change? Is there such a possibility of presentation in a form and society that are ingrained with patriarchal values?

Rey Chow suggests that a new form of masculinity can show what must be overcome for a society to undergo social change. Chow discusses a film by Chen Kaige, *King of the Children*, which presents a narcissistic masculinity, manifesting itself in the protagonist of the film, a self-absorbed, passive character. Although the film presents an alternative masculinity, it does so while excluding "woman and the physical reality she represents." Chow explains:

> Chen's film offers a fantastic kind of hope — the hope to rewrite culture without woman and all the limitations she embodies, limitations that are inherent to the processes of cultural, as well as biological, reproduction.... As such ... it partakes of a narcissistic avoidance of the politics of sexuality and of gendered sociality that we would, in spite of the passive "feminine" form it takes, call masculine.[85]

Chen's version of a narcissistic masculinity — a masculinity that bypasses the presence of women — presents itself not as a positive option for social change, but rather as a catalyst for the self-examination of present forms of masculinity within a society: "This masculinity is the sign of a vast transindividual oppression whose undoing must become the collective undertaking for all of us who have a claim to modern Chinese culture."[86] Where does this leave presentations of masculinity that differ from ideal presentations as given to the viewer of Hollywood films? Is there no redeeming factor in these divergent presentations except as reminders of the oppression of present forms of masculinity?

What many of these models of masculinity lack, as narcissistic, as object or as failure, is the presence of *sensitivity*. Discussing the star image of French actor Gérard Depardieu, Ginette Vincendeau suggests that sensitivity is built into his version of masculinity:

> While in many ways Depardieu represents a traditional vision of aggressive French machismo ... one of the most common descriptions of his screen image as well as his behaviour as a performer ... is that of his "femininity": "a fragile man, with a flaw in his personality, a very feminine character in the end."[87]

Vincendeau points out that Depardieu exhibits elements of a more sensitive form of masculinity, incorporating characteristics such as gentleness and nurturing. Still, this "feminine" masculinity, if one could refer to it as such, functions to reinforce a sense of masculinity through the increase of desire: "Depardieu's stake in repeatedly emphasizing his 'femininity' is that it gives him a surplus of sexiness; his sexual identity is somewhat beyond that of a mere heterosexual man though he is, also, unambiguously that."[88]

There have been other conceptualizations of masculinity that have surfaced in disciplines other than film study. For instance, Sean Nixon discusses the notion of the "new man" in British men's fashion in the 1980s. He suggests that rather than referring to Mulvey's conceptualization of the active male and passive female in the analysis of visual texts, such as fashion trends and print advertisements, one should apply Foucault's notion of the "technologies of the self." These technologies refer to a subjectivity as a set of practices, techniques, behaviors and beliefs; Foucault's idea allows one to "conceptualize the articulation of individuals with particular representations as a performance; a performance in which the formal positions of subjectivity are inhabited through specific practices or techniques." Nixon explains:

> In conceptualizing the way the formal positions inscribed within the regime of "new man" representations might have been inhabited by men, Foucault's comments, then, direct us towards a specific set of practices or techniques of the self. A number of techniques of care, consumption and leisure seem to me pivotal in this respect. The practices of grooming and dressing and the activity of shopping represent practices through which the attributes and characteristics of masculinity coded in relation to the "new man" imagery might be operationalized as an historical identity.[89]

While Nixon is referring to a specific historical — and perhaps national — notion of masculinity, the suggestion of looking at practices and techniques of the self offers a new angle for analyzing masculinity. Nixon makes another interesting point which has not been adequately made by the writers in the field of film studies outlined above. Again drawing from Foucault, Nixon points out that subjectivities can be made up of multiple notions of masculinity. He explains,

In Foucault's terms, not only is there not one singular, totalizing version of masculinity, but the masculinity of individual men is itself (potentially) plural. In other words, individual men might be addressed by a range of discursive masculine identifications: as fathers, union officials, Englishmen, northerners, consumers of clothing, as taxpayers, and so on. Lived masculinities, then, are crucially determined by both the co-articulation of these discursive positions and the tensions and fractures between them. Much of the work of identity involves the organization of a more or less coherent sense of self through these identifications and a handling of the various disjunctures that might exist between them.[90]

Furthermore, the appropriation of particular masculinities is controlled by what Foucault calls "social hegemonies," or by "common attributes and characteristics or recurrent positionalities" across multiple discourses.[91] Therefore, Nixon suggests that although there exist multiple notions of masculinity, there also exist those notions that are stronger than others and that thus control what sort of masculinities manifest themselves in a subjectivity. While this is certainly not a groundbreaking suggestion in the realm of cultural studies — and even in terms of what is presently being discussed as a search for new models of gender — the notion of an over-riding masculinity defined by techniques of the self can be very useful in identifying those masculinities that lie outside of it.

The conception of social hegemonies and their controlling of manifest masculinities is a thread that implicitly runs through the film studies literature; most of the writers discuss a particular form of masculinity that flourishes in Hollywood film. It seems that many of the writers look to Mulvey's discussions of the male gaze for clues regarding the construction of masculinity.

Concluding Remarks

This chapter explores the key theoretical areas relevant to the analysis of gender, celebrity and audio-visual media, and ultimately, the analysis of Morrissey's star image. Frith and McRobbie's work, though perhaps problematic, provides a basis for the notion of the consumption of music as gendered, as well as providing examples of gendered characteristics of the pop musician's constructed star image. Their view must be updated to take into account musicians who, as Cohen's discussions of the Liverpool music scene illustrate, portray vulnerability or constraint within a serious rock context. Railton and Bradby continue by characterizing the voice and the act of singing as "feminine," as opposed to the act of playing a musical instrument. Susan McClary discusses in detail the gendered character of musical syntax, and what she calls a "semiotics of desire." Shepherd furthers this by considering the discipline of music itself as marginal in a capitalist society, placed below other cultural processes. Cusick and Wood illustrate the relations between the singing voice, power and desire, pointing to the concept of the "grain of the voice," formulated by Roland Barthes.

Koestenbaum links the singing voice as a site of pleasure to the fan who desires to catalogue experiences with that voice so as to work toward a future when the accumulation can stop. Barthes identifies tools that can help to gain insight into the nature of desire from the realm of textual semiotics. He sees texts and their conveyance of knowledge in an incomplete way as a means of eliciting desire from the reader. Clues and questions within the text formulate an enigma that begs for resolution and thus propels the reader forward in the text in order to gain more information, which may or may not come. Barthes' hermeneutic code is well suited for a study of the enigma.

Such a conceptualization of the relationship between the fan and the celebrity suggests the notion of the celebrity's incomplete star image. Dyer, deCordova, King and Marshall outline how a star image is constructed and how one functions in society, and how this star image is placed within a framework of desire. Laura Mulvey's writing on spectacle and the eroticized image of woman in classical narrative types of films further contributes to the understanding of the relationship between an audience and a celebrity. Mulvey outlines the active/masculine and passive/feminine dichotomy, and the "feminization" of the object of a gaze. How the question of celebrity and performer persona has been reformulated in relation to gender is demonstrated through a survey of writings on various masculinities present in visual media.

Morrissey, as a celebrity and a persona that can be (and is) eroticized as spectacle, is an interesting case in the negotiation of various gender categories and limits. For many, Morrissey's voice is the site of engagement with his celebrity persona. It is through the voice that his persona is often first defined, albeit in an incomplete manner. This incompleteness is paired with the maintenance of an enigmatic character; in other words, there exists the continual production of discourse surrounding his star image.

Therefore, Morrissey can be read as an active mediated figure, imbued with a "masculinist" power, able to deflect the feminizing effects of being eroticized as spectacle.

The following chapters explore how Morrissey's incomplete celebrity persona is presented in various media. Morrissey's complexity of gender performance is particularly evident in his promotional music videos. The discussion that follows addresses Morrissey's music videos, and his display of what is termed "lack," often manifest in signs of injury. In live performance, Morrissey adds certain tangible elements to his otherwise enigmatic star image, including a kind of physicality. The discourse surrounding Morrissey is colored by the inclusion of public figures like Julia Riley, a fan who attends almost every live concert. These particularities are present only in Morrissey's live performance.

The continual production of discourse surrounding the singer's star image can also be seen within his musical production. Nadine Hubbs' notion of "inactivity" and the gendered character of musical contour provides a basis for the analysis that is presented later in this book. A musical analysis details how Morrissey's music seems to elicit desire and delay its satisfaction. The suggestion of Morrissey as "inactive" is explored in terms of how this might affect his star image and his performance of gender. Finally, there is an exploration of how Morrissey's enigmatic character is constructed and maintained through appearances on television and radio. The maintenance of an enigmatic character imbues a certain sense of instability to Morrissey, which allows him to remain active while being rendered passive by the eroticizing gaze of the audience. As Pat Reid suggests, "For a man who has spent much of his life in the spotlight, Morrissey is really only ever glimpsed in silhouette."[92] It is to this silhouette that this study now turns.

4

"The Boy Racer"
Morrissey's Changing Gender Identity in Music Video

Morrissey has often been written about in terms of gender and sexuality. For instance, Pat Reid's book *Outlines: Morrissey* focuses on the singer's enigmatic sexuality. The *Outlines* series, of which Reid's book is a part, is dedicated to "chronicling the lives of some of the most exceptional gay and lesbian artists of the last century."[1] Mark Simpson's *Saint Morrissey* discusses at length Morrissey's performance of masculinity and his discomfort with traditional gender roles. Nadine Hubbs' article "Music of the 'Fourth Gender': Morrissey and the Sexual Politics of Melodic Contour" analyzes Morrissey's music in terms of gender and, in particular, passivity. Melinda Hsu's master's thesis, "Celibate Cries: Queer Reading of Morrissey's Sexual Persona" (California State University, Fresno, 1996), discusses Morrissey's use of camp gestures and identifies a "queer eroticism" in his ambiguous lyrics. Also, Taina Viitamäki wrote an article on Morrissey's "Fourth Gender."[2] The singer has been a constant object of discussion regarding his own appropriation of gender roles and sexual orientation. This chapter begins with a discussion of Judith Butler's ideas regarding gender dimorphism and performativity, and Morrissey's own sexual identity. The discussion continues with a survey of Morrissey's past music videos and the characteristics of what might be called "lack" that are therein present. The discussion then turns to what is ultimately the complexity of Morrissey's performance of gender, focusing in particular upon his persona in the music video for "The Boy Racer," released in 1995. There are various paths upon which to embark when considering this music video, gender being the most obvious in this context. Perceived injury is also a striking element within this video, and consideration is given to the transmission of music video on television, which introduces issues of spectatorship and desire in the light of Morrissey's persona.

Morrissey is enacting multiple sexualities, presenting contradictory stereotypes of gender. He is what might be called an ambiguous masculine figure. Appropriating such a persona involves going against the heteronormative project. This project, according to Judith Butler, dictates how one is gendered and, in turn, how one must act.

In her book *Bodies That Matter: On the Discursive Limits of "Sex,"* Butler discusses gender performativity and the subject. She explains:

> If I were to argue that genders are performative, that could mean that I thought that one woke in the morning, perused the closet or some more open space for the gender of choice, donned that gender for the day, and then restored the garment to its place at night. Such a willful and instrumental subject, one who decides *on* its gender, is clearly not its gender from the start and fails to realize that its existence is already decided *by* gender. Certainly, such a theory would restore a figure of a choosing subject — humanist — at the center of a project whose emphasis on construction seems to be quite opposed to such a notion.[3]

Butler suggests that "gender is part of what decides the subject" and thus questions the agency of the subject in terms of gender practices. One of Butler's arguments is that gender is performed, but more importantly that this "performativity must be understood not as a singular or deliberate 'act,' but rather as the reiterative and citational practice by which discourse produces the effects that it names."[4] Furthermore, those involved in this performativity do not recognize the discourse as the producer: "It conceals or dissimulates the conventions of which it is a repetition."[5]

More recently, she writes,

> If gender is a kind of a doing, an incessant activity performed, in part, without one's knowing and without one's willing, it is not for that reason automatic or mechanical. On the contrary, it is a practice of improvisation within a scene of constraint. Moreover, one does not "do" one's gender alone. One is always "doing" with or for another, even if the other is only imaginary.[6]

She continues by linking desire with the gender that is performed: "The social norms that constitute our existence carry desires that do not originate with our individual personhood." She concludes, "To the extent that desire is implicated in social norms, it is bound up with the question of power and with the problem of who qualifies as the recognizably human and who does not."[7] She discusses gender in this way as well: "In the examples of those abjected beings who do not appear properly gendered; it is their very humanness that comes into question."[8] Therefore, Butler links gender not only to discourse and hegemonic heterosexuality but also to desire. It follows that if one is rendered inhuman if one is not properly gendered, then one is also rendered inhuman if one does not properly desire. This leads to the labelling of asexuality as inhuman.

Butler raises an interesting problem in *Undoing Gender* in a discussion regarding the case of David Reimer, "a man born a man, castrated by the medical establishment, feminized by the psychiatric world, and then enabled to return to who he is." Butler explains:

> The point is to try to imagine a world in which individuals with mixed genital attributes might be accepted and loved without having to transform them into a more socially coherent or normative version of gender. In this sense, the intersex movement has sought to question why society maintains the ideal of gender dimorphism when a significant percentage of children are chromosomally various, and a continuum exists between male and female that suggests the arbitrariness and falsity of the gender dimorphism as a prerequisite of human development.[9]

It seems that Western society dictates that gender dimorphism is required for human development and humanness. If one is a product of multiple viewpoints, in terms of appropriation of various sexualities, a cyborg subject if you will, then one is not human or a member of the human community.

Donna Haraway introduces the concept of the "cyborg" in her very influential article, entitled "A Manifestation for Cyborgs: Science, Technology, and Socialist Feminism in the 1980s." For Haraway, the cyborg is not a man or a woman, but an ungendered and incomplete subject: "The cyborg is resolutely committed to partiality, irony, intimacy, and perversity. It is oppositional, utopian, and completely without innocence." She states,

> The cyborg is a creature in a post-gender world; it has no truck [deal or association] with bisexuality, pre–Oedipal symbiosis, unalienated labor, or other seductions to organic wholeness through a final appropriation of all the powers of the parts into a higher unity.[10]

Haraway describes the cyborg and its world in terms that might be familiar when discussing Morrissey. She writes, "A cyborg world might be about lived social and bodily realities in which people are not afraid of their joint kinship with animals and ... not afraid of permanently partial identities and contradictory standpoints."[11] She identifies a "cyborg identity" as a "potent subjectivity synthesized from fusions of outsider identities."[12] While Haraway is mainly suggesting that "outsider identities" are primarily female and related to marginal race and class categories, her ideas can also be applied to gender dimorphism as discussed by Butler: "To be other is to be multiple, without clear boundary, frayed, insubstantial."[13]

Morrissey's "Asexuality"

Morrissey has often been linked to what is commonly termed (in discourses around Morrissey) "asexuality," or being without sexual feelings or associations. Simpson dedicates a chapter to Morrissey's being "above sexuality." When a report was released in *The Journal of Sex Research* in August 2004, and *New Scientist* in October 2004, that suggested that 1 in 100 adults were "asexual" or "have absolutely no interest in sex," Morrissey's name was immediately attached in both weblogs and at the main Morrissey fan website, *Morrissey-Solo*.[14] It should be noted that the discourse does not strictly suggest that Morrissey is *without* sexuality, but rather that he is *above* sexual desire and categories of sexuality and gender. Pat Reid makes some interesting comments regarding Morrissey's sexuality in terms of homosexuality. He states,

> These days, it seems Morrissey is only a gay icon to straight men.
> Well, a certain type of straight man, at any rate. When Suede emerged as natural successors to The Smiths in the early '90s, frontman Brett Anderson made the oft-quoted announcement that he considered himself to be a "bisexual man who has never had a homosexual experience," expressing something which, although much-ridiculed, was in fact keenly felt by a sizeable proportion of his — and Morrissey's — audiences.[15]

Reid continues, "This is where Morrissey's true power resides. Like all real pop stars, he has the ability to make you fall in love with him."[16] Reid's comments point to Morrissey's complexity of sexuality, or at least the complexity of sexuality that surrounds his persona and the engagement of some of his fans. Reid also points to the ability of Morrissey to elicit desire from fans.

Another term that has often appeared in discussions and popular writings about Morrissey is "fourth gender," seemingly synonymous with asexuality. Both Hubbs and Viitamäki mention the "fourth gender" nature of Morrissey's gender performance. James Henke's article "Oscar! Oscar! Great

Britain Goes Wilde for the 'Fourth-Gender' Smiths" (in *Rolling Stone* 423 [7 June 1984]) seems to be the originating source for this label as applied to Morrissey. These labels have been placed on Morrissey due to his public dissatisfaction with traditional categories of gender and his suggestion that they are simply limiting. In September 1983, Morrissey stated, "I can't recognize gender. I want to produce music that transcends boundaries."[17] As of January 1984, Morrissey's gender project was as follows:

> You couldn't have a world free from sex, that would be impossible. I'd like to cleanse the world of sexual stereotypes, though, because they can be extremely dangerous. It would be quite easy to do if you had control over the media and the images it presents.[18]

It is presumed that Morrissey has some control over certain media and their images, especially when they surround his music and performance. He would have some say as to how his image is conveyed through media such as his promotional music videos. It is to these videos that this discussion now turns.

Video Survey

A striking characteristic emerges when one considers the whole of Morrissey's promotional music video output. Morrissey is often presented as injured in some way. To injure is to harm or impair, and thus to weaken or damage. An injury implies the need for healing and also indicates the vulnerability of the subject and its susceptibility. It is with this perspective that one can approach the imagery presented in Morrissey's music videos. From his time with The Smiths onward, Morrissey often displays elements of injury or, at the very least, need or lack. The following survey maps out where these elements appear. This mapping helps to delineate musical and visual changes to the Morrissey persona, like his appropriation of more masculine traits at a certain point in his career. While displaying characteristics of traditional masculinity, Morrissey has employed certain elements that might be considered conventionally feminine, or that denote physical weakness or vulnerability.

In one of Morrissey's first video appearances in 1984, in the promotional video for "This Charming Man," the singer is presented dancing on a covering of flowers, wearing an open button-up shirt and what appear to be costume jewelry and pearls around his neck. He is also waving a bouquet of flowers in his hand while singing. In a televised performance of "What Difference Does It Make?" also from 1984, Morrissey is shown wearing similar jewelry and a shirt, while also wearing a broach and glasses. Interestingly, it seems that his glasses are not part of a costume; throughout his career, while on stage, he has most often worn contact lenses. In the televised performance of "Heaven Knows I'm Miserable Now" (from 1984), Morrissey is wearing, in addition to a broach on his blazer and jewelry hanging from his belt, a hearing aid. While also wearing glasses, he has flowers coming out of his back pants pocket. In the video for "Stop Me If You Think You've Heard This One Before," from 1987 before the breakup of The Smiths, there is a roving pack of imitators following after Morrissey, all riding bicycles and wearing glasses similar to those of the singer; this video showcases the cult of Morrissey, with fans wanting to identify outwardly with the singer. Throughout these videos with The Smiths, Morrissey is often dancing in a very fluid manner, waving his arms about and sometimes flailing; such gestures seem to evoke traditional notions of femininity in terms of their fluidity and unreservedness. Furthermore, Morrissey is wearing jewelry most often worn by women, as well as being in the possession of flowers, elements that are traditionally coded as feminine.

Such feminine gestures continue in Morrissey's solo career, at least for a time. In the promotional video for "November Spawned a Monster" from his 1990 collection of singles, *Bona Drag*, Morrissey is featured in a desert setting, wearing a pair of low-riding black jeans and a black see-through zipper shirt. Throughout the video, his shirt is zippered open, revealing much of his bare chest, while he flails about and moves his hips dramatically. While some of his movements might be traditionally coded as feminine, his presentation also evokes a sense of weakness. As Morrissey's upper torso is often bare, the viewer notices how gaunt he is. Interestingly, his thinness is greatly contrasted with the size of his hair in this video, which is styled very high off his head. As is often the case with Morrissey's hairstyle, the hair on the sides of his head is shaved. This may seem to be a trivial matter, but the result is, in fact, quite striking visually. Most interesting is his use of a somewhat more modern and subtle hearing aid in some of the shots, perhaps referencing his days with The Smiths. In this video, the hearing aid is a subtle feature that may not be noticed upon a single viewing. Hubbs suggests:

The hearing aid, one might observe, is not standard issue in studly rock-star accessorizing; still, Morrissey's wearing it was an exercise in semiotic power. "In the midst of all the glamour, light, and shallow veneer of pop," he has said, it was "a symbol that spoke for downtrodden and lonely people."[19]

While physical weakness and vulnerability have often been associated with the feminine (as opposed to the physically and emotionally strong masculine), Morrissey continues a kind of "display of weakness" in his later videos, in the form of cuts and bruises, while also presenting himself as a much more masculine figure. For an example of this dichotomy, one needs only to remember McClarey's distinctions of the "weak, abnormal and subjective" "feminine" cadence as opposed to the "strong, normal and objective" "masculine" cadence.

In the "November Spawned a Monster" video, Morrissey also wears a bandage over his left nipple. It is unclear what kind of violence may have befallen the singer, but the image conveyed by the injury is certainly sexually charged, evoking notions of sexual violence and corporeal sensitivity. Instances of perceived body mutilation or injury continue in Morrissey's later videos. For instance, Morrissey also sports a bandage over an eye in the video for "Our Frank" from his 1991 release, *Kill Uncle*, which features the singer doing nothing but posing and singing in front of a black background. In the video for "The More You Ignore Me, The Closer I Get" (from *Vauxhall and I*, released in 1994), Morrissey is visibly hurt, displaying a scratch or cut under his left eye, an injury that is unexplained in the context of the video. The video for "Dagenham Dave" from *Southpaw Grammar* (1995) features Morrissey in a stylish suit and unbuttoned shirt, but he is also noticeably more rugged. He no longer possesses such sullen features; his face has filled out, and his body seems to be more full and substantial. This is probably due to simple aging, but it does give Morrissey a sense of further masculinity. In this video, Morrissey also has an abrasion on his right cheek. As has been mentioned earlier, the facial damage suggests both weakness as well as aggression; it is unclear as to whether the singer was the instigator of the conflict or simply a victim. In one scene, Morrissey is shown breaking up a pool game by striking the balls while walking by, which could be read as an act of aggression. The pool-playing heterosexual couple is featured in the rest of the video; the male is somewhat infatuated with Morrissey, which ultimately aggravates the female.

From the same album, the video for "The Boy Racer" is perhaps the most striking in terms of injury. Morrissey has an abrasion around his right eye, a scratch or cut under his left eye and a cut across the bridge of his nose; these injuries are not present during certain shots of the video, particularly immediately prior to having his vehicle pulled over by a police officer. Nevertheless, the narrative of the video does not contribute significantly to the cause of these injuries. An injured Morrissey is also presented in the live concert video *Introducing Morrissey*, from 1996, in which he has an abrasion on his face and a very noticeable gash on the back of his hand, as if he was involved in a brawl of some kind. While these various injuries may be easily attributed to the amount of abuse that Morrissey goes through during a live concert, with a large number of fans running onto the stage and violently embracing him, often knocking him down in the process, it is interesting that similar wounds appear on the performer in studio videos, without the help of a live audience. Wounds are also displayed on Morrissey's upper forearm, in the form of cuts or scratches, on the cover for the *Introducing Morrissey* concert video. A photo from the same photo session provides the cover for the 2001 collection, *The Best of Morrissey*.

In these later videos, while his movements are somewhat fluid, as a whole his physical presentation seems to coincide more with traditional masculinity; he is more filled out, less gaunt, with hair more subdued and less visible jewelry. In his newer videos from the album *You Are the Quarry*, Morrissey has left injury behind but perhaps has not stopped displaying lack or need. In the video for "I Have Forgiven Jesus," Morrissey is dressed in a priest's collar and black blazer and pants.

Lack

Contemplating what Morrissey is lacking, Simon Reynolds and Joy Press discuss melancholy and its place in the singer's life and image. The authors draw on Julia Kristeva's conception of melancholy as "'the most archaic expression of a non-symbolisable, unnameable narcissistic wound'— in other words, the loss of the mother. To this breed of self-obsessed melancholic, 'sadness is in reality the only object'— a phantasmic object that he cherishes."[20] Reynolds and Press discuss Morrissey's confession to Adrien Deevoy in 1992 of taking the drug Ecstasy, after which he "looked in the mirror and saw somebody very, very attractive."[21] Reynolds and Press continue:

> The idea of Morrissey taking Ecstasy to bond more closely with himself conforms so closely to the profile of his pathology it's preposterous — beyond self-parody. But more perturbing is the fact that he restaged the primal scene that creates identity: the mirror phase, in which the infant recognises the existence of the Other (usually the Mother). Instead of the Other, Morrissey saw only himself, which is never enough. Failure to pass through the mirror phase properly leads to an inability to form object-relations. And for the melancholic, as we saw, there is no object, only an indefinable sense of lack.[22]

Reynolds and Press put Morrissey in the "Mother's Boy/Soft Male" category, suggesting that he, and performers like him, possess certain "feminine" attributes like limpness, the penchant for sanctuary and the pastoral, and laziness. They end their discussion with questions rather than conclusions:

> What to make of the mother's boy? Is he truly androgynous? Are his passivity, his apparent acceptance and affirmation of castration, his womb-nostalgia, the marks of a female-identified masculinity, or has the "soft male" simply taken the soft option? Are these dandies, slackers, playboys and would-be playthings merely a partial, unfulfilled version of what a true New Man should be? Above all, amongst all the "Boys Keep Swinging" fun 'n' games, the feminisation and effeminacy, where do women fit in?[23]

In fact, as will be seen in the analysis of the music video, women do not fit in at all. Morrissey and the women have no contact with each other in the video. It is only the "boy racer" who picks up the women, while Morrissey is stopped by the police and removed from the car.

As for Morrissey's aspirations to become what Reynolds and Press call "a true New Man," the transformational process could be linked chronologically with the release of music that was more aggressive, achieved by Morrissey surrounding himself with new musicians, with some of whom he has remained. While he did not necessarily completely reinvent his persona, as, for example, David Bowie has, he did evolve both musically and in terms of his visual persona, showing both a stereotypically aggressive masculinity, signs of injury and a more aggressive musical style.

The music during the opening moments of Morrissey's 1992 release, *Your Arsenal*, is decidedly aggressive in relation to the more melodic music of The Smiths. The appropriation of distorted guitars and an overall driving rhythm provided by the drums and bass guitar suggest a more aggressive musical approach. As Simpson suggests, this aggression translates into the concert experience, with fans violently trying to approach the singer. Nevertheless, Morrissey continues to allow fans to embrace him and often tackle him on the stage while he is performing. In an interview from 2001, Morrissey states, "Lots of people make the stage and it can seem very violent and over the top, but it's not really. It's always a kind of gentle ballet."[24] While such an activity affirms Morrissey's messianic status, unselfishly giving of himself for the fans' benefit even though it may be detrimental to his health, it also suggests that he can in fact take the physical abuse. It is very rare that Morrissey backs away or cowers from the aggressive advance of a fan; if this does occur, it is usually because Morrissey has just been tackled or knocked down by several people to the extent that he has stopped singing. It should be noted that Morrissey does have bodyguards that are present at these concerts. Obviously, they allow the activity to occur, while also keeping a close eye on Morrissey's well-being. Also, at least during his tour in 2000, Morrissey has displayed, both in his clothing and concert merchandise, support for the West Ham United football club. Based in east London, West Ham was originally the Thames Iron Works company team, and, in the 1980s, had a reputation for aggression and an association with organized hooliganism.[25]

This change is also evident in Linder Sterling's book of photographs documenting the *Kill Uncle* world tour in 1991 entitled *Morrissey Shot*, from which the cover of *Your Arsenal* originates. In the collection are images of Morrissey that could easily be read as very much masculine, while other images seem somewhat feminine. The book shows that this tour was a site of transformation, in terms of both Morrissey's persona and gender performance. The individual pictures in the collection show the complexity of his performance of gender at various moments, often displaying contradictory stereotypes of gender. Such a contradiction is made very clear in one particular set of photos from San Diego, taken on 30 May 1991.[26] One photo features a shirtless Morrissey, presumably enjoying the sunshine. He is standing up against a large fence, his arms stretched over his head, hanging onto a top bar of the fence. His head is relaxing on his raised arm, his eyes, only slightly open, looking away from the camera directly in front of him. This image also evokes the crucified Christ, a figure in the throes of weakness, defeat and suffering. In the next photo, featured on the following page in Sterling's book, the camera captures

Morrissey from below, still shirtless, looking at the sun or sky, with his arms up and his hands clasped at the back of his neck. In contrast to the previous image, Morrissey is shown here in much the same way as a male model would be presented. What this shot effectively does, which the first fails to do, is capture the texture of Morrissey's musculature, however slight, while the other stresses his gauntness. By shooting from below, the picture captures the shadows made by Morrissey's body contour, thus drawing attention to his abdominal and pectoral muscles. Of course, Morrissey is obviously not a body builder and does not come close to exhibiting the musculature of a world-class body sculptor. The display of Morrissey's musculature is a hyper-masculine image in relation to Morrissey's general presentation previous to 1991 and in contrast to the previous photo. In the previous photo, Morrissey's torso is stretched by the reaching of his arms above his head, and the shot is taken from directly in front of the singer. Therefore, there is no shadow created or musculature evident from this angle. The second image could be read as a strong masculine one, often used for male models and so forth. The first image suggests inactivity; it is essentially a photo of Morrissey waiting. If one takes into consideration Richard Dyer's analysis of male pin-up models, in which the *potential* for action must be present to deflect the feminizing gaze of the viewer, there is no apparent potential for action present in the first photograph. Morrissey's musculature in the second photograph would at least point to the ability of Morrissey for some kind of action. As will be seen with the music video for "The Boy Racer," even if the ability or potential for action is afforded Morrissey, certain factors will keep him from action. It should be noted that the photographs do not show Morrissey being active — he is in a relaxed position — but it could be that he is active in terms of putting himself on display.

The Video for "The Boy Racer"

The video, directed by James O'Brien, opens with images of Marshall stacks (guitar amplifiers), a drum set and a guitar, complete with strobe lighting evoking a sense of a rock concert. The viewer is then introduced to the "boy racer," a man who gets into his car and speeds off into the night. Morrissey is then shown singing, dressed in an untucked white button-up shirt — of course, with some buttons undone — contrasted with the band, who are primarily dressed in black and aggressively playing their instruments. The lyrics deal with anger and jealousy toward the "boy racer," but also admiration. Morrissey sings that the "boy racer" has many positive characteristics, that he is rich, good-natured and is successful with women. To this, Morrissey responds that he is jealous. He affirms the worth of the "boy racer" as someone to be admired, admitting that he has watched him.[27] The "boy racer" continues to drive around while the band continues to perform. Then there is a scene during which two male police officers pull over a vehicle, presumably for speeding, from which Morrissey emerges. Morrissey continues his diatribe against the "boy racer," accusing him of thinking that he owns the streets, that he speeds and never gets stopped by police. Unfortunately, when Morrissey speeds, he does in fact get pulled over.

The "boy racer," even by his very title, is a masculine figure, perhaps embodying an ideal masculinity; Morrissey even hints at an expression of male sexual pride when he suggests that the "boy racer" has the world in his hands as he stands to urinate. The video goes on to feature the "boy racer" successfully picking up two young girls after a short conversation, "convincing" them to join him. There has been the suggestion that the "boy racer" is driving around the city with a passenger who is never seen, and that the driver is successful in picking up the girls because they realize whom the passenger is. In fact, this particular scene toward the end of the video can be interpreted in this way; some camera angles and gesturing by the girls do suggest that an additional passenger is present. Some have suggested that this unseen passenger is Morrissey, although this is purely conjecture. While his possible participation in this scene is compelling, the implications of such will not be explored in this present discussion. The last image of the vehicle in the video shows it skidding out of control, which may signify a sort of victory for Morrissey. Morrissey's ability to drive a vehicle is made impossible by the police officers, who in turn disable him from having girlfriends and perhaps sexual pride as well. The car can be read as a symbol of mobility and action, and Morrissey's inability to drive relegates him to inactivity and immobility. This is affirmed by Morrissey's lack of movement toward the end of the video, despite the raucous and driving music of the band. Morrissey again reflects difference and inactivity, being forced into feminine immobility by the male police officers.

Injury

In terms of gender constructions of celebrity, the video presents an interesting case: Morrissey as injured, and as an object of the gaze of the audience. Carol Vernallis discusses various aspects of music video in her article "The Kindest Cut: Functions and Meanings of Music Video Editing," and places particular emphasis on the role of the close-up. She suggests that the close-up serves to ground the music video in a single image, much like a hook or riff.[28] Furthermore, the close-up that features the pop star can serve as a high point in the video, a moment of unprecedented emotional weight. Throughout the video, Morrissey's face is seen in extreme close-up, which reveals to the viewer certain features he or she may not have noticed. The singer's face bears marks of a fight or accident; he has scratches and bruises across his cheek and the bridge of his nose. While his injuries might fit into the implied narrative of the video in some way, his injuries are unexplained.[29] The fact that the viewer is drawn to the close-up makes sense; the image in close-up is of the performer, the star of which the video is a showcase. But the nature of the subject of the close-up is interesting because the image is not necessarily an attractive one. While Morrissey is certainly not injured to an extent as to completely repulse a viewer, the injuries are noticeable and jarring. They seem to derail the notion of the close-up as providing a grounding effect for the video.

Morrissey as an injured figure is prevalent in many of his music videos and live performances, and the cause of the injury is unknown. Simpson suggests that these perceived injuries lend to the singer a "ruffian" air, as do his songs from the mid–1990s, like "Spring-Heeled Jim" and "We'll Let You Know," with their references to hoodlumery, and album titles like *Southpaw Grammer*, referring to boxing slang for a left-hander. Interestingly, Simpson suggests that by 1995 "Morrissey appeared to have lost both his ruffian and his *relative* peace of mind."[30] Yet, during this time, he continues to present himself as injured. The mystery of his injury but his performing despite it lends him an enigmatic air. If Morrissey's apparent injuries were sustained in a concert setting, or any other setting for that matter, they could be easily concealed by make-up and so forth. Rather, these injuries, whether actual or fabricated by make-up themselves, are especially prominent in various close-up shots of Morrissey's face. Does this presentation of Morrissey injured suggest weakness and thus make him less traditionally masculine? If so, then this provides a problem for the notion of Morrissey as more masculine.

Vernallis continues by describing how she engages with the performer in a music video:

> As I watch a video and follow the song, I casually study the performer's body, just as I do when I look at models in magazines. I admire the lines of the jaw, the look in the eye, the light. Suddenly the performer's head turns towards me, the eyes gaze into mine, the singing voice demands my attention, and I am struck. Music can transgress both physical space and the borders of the body, changing our sense of time and of these boundaries themselves. At this moment, the performer crosses the limits of the screen and addresses me as a person, and I can no longer view this face and body as an object. Just as quickly, the head turns, the rhythm changes, the soul has gone, and again I am simply watching a blank human form.[31]

She is suggesting that the figure in the close-up becomes the subject of much scrutiny. Her suggestion might seem obvious: the performer in the video becomes the object of the viewer's gaze, in a particularly striking manner. The viewer is able to see physical properties that might not have been overly apparent in the performer's face in other media. For instance, one might notice irregularities or particularities in facial features that might have been hidden in promotional or album artwork. While the close-up might provide a kind of grounding within the often-confusing and non-narrative string of images and cuts that make up music videos, such revelations regarding new or unnoticed physical features can serve to be just as jarring as some edits.

Vernallis considers the construction of the images in music video and its similarity to sonic properties, evoking Barthes' "Grain of the Voice." She states:

> All gestures in music video — the flick of a wrist, the flickering of light, or the fluttering of fabric — become like dance. We use sound to register the interiority of objects, whether hollow or dense. The way that the camera in music video hovers over the figures, slowly taking in their bodies, may look pornographic, but it might also be a way to register the sounds emanating from these bodily sources. If we think of a singer's voice as reflecting the rhythms of her body, and the instruments as extending the voice, then the camera can be thought of as creating a fantasy of what lies inside the body — the spring of the muscles, the heartbeat, the flow of blood.[32]

If one is to accept Vernallis' reading of the function of the roaming camera to create a sense of the vitality of the artist, the close-up and revelation of personal injury shows such vitality directly. The viewer is able to see with her own eyes the blood and muscle that lie inside the body. The vitality of the performer is heightened in this view, but also exposed in a potentially damaging way. The performer, in an injured state, is shown as vulnerable and perhaps in danger. The exposure of Morrissey to the camera exposes him also to further danger but also displays him as a kind of hero in terms of defiance and bravery. He puts himself on display, although injured, to make a stand for something, and to show that he is not afraid to show his weaknesses, in the form of injury.

Gender

In the 1980s, there emerged the "new man," as suggested by Sean Nixon. Analyzing an advertisement from the mid–1980s by the clothing company Levi's, Nixon discusses some of the characteristics of the "new man" image:

> First, the appropriation and glamorization of 1950s style was important. It set the terms for the signification of an assertive masculinity. Secondly, the surface of the models' bodies — and specifically developed muscles — were displayed. Thirdly, the assertive masculinity of both the "fifties" style and the models' physiques, were signified together with the coding of softness and sensuality.... Fourthly, the display of these bodies was presented to the viewer in highly distinctive ways. Cuts to arms, chest, face, bottom and thighs, together with a focus on the unbuttoning of the jeans and ... a cut of the water seeping over the model's jean-clad crotch, undermined more conventional significations of power and aggression associated with displayed masculine bodies. Fifthly, the male hero was represented as self-contained and on his own.[33]

The models are not only sensitive and sensual but also concerned with a well-groomed appearance and a sense of fashion. It is interesting that there would be a juxtaposition of masculine assertiveness with sensuality and softness. In the May 1991 edition of the British men's magazine *Arena*, Sean O'Hagan identifies the "new man" as sensitive, charming and considerate: "He hoped one day to own an Audi and an Armani. But he'd do the housework and not be afraid to shed a tear."[34]

While magazines like *GQ* and *Arena* discuss men's issues as well as fashion and personal presentation and grooming, a new magazine in Britain, *Loaded*, begins to cater to a slightly different kind of man. While maintaining a certain level of sensitivity, this "man" is more aggressive; the editor of *Loaded* explains it as follows: "Don't take us too seriously, we're blokes and we're useless.... We like football, but that doesn't mean we're hooligans.... We like looking at pictures of fancy ladies sometimes but that doesn't mean we want to rape them."[35]

Masculinities continue to form, and in 2002 Mark Simpson describes a new masculinity, which might have emerged from the "new lad." He calls this "well dressed, narcissistic and bun-obsessed" man a *metrosexual*.[36] In fact, Simpson first uses the word in a newspaper article printed in November 1994, where he describes a "metrosexual" as a "single young man with a high disposable income, living or working in the city (because that's where all the best shops are)." While maintaining the fashion consciousness of the "new man" and the love of football of the "new lad," the metrosexual is most associated with homosexuality, except that the metrosexual is generally not gay. Simpson bases this new category of masculinity on David Beckham, the popular British football player. Simpson explains that Beckham is comfortable in Indian sarongs, clothing conventionally created for women, and in wearing nail polish and his wife's underwear. He has also been open to posing naked on the cover of *Esquire* and sporting a different — and what Simpson calls "tricky" — haircut every week. Simpson continues: "In the interview with the Brit gay mag Attitude, this married father of two confirmed that he's straight, but as he admits, he's quite happy to be a gay icon; he likes to be admired, he says, and he doesn't care whether the admiring is done by women or men." Simpson's metrosexual is an able consumer living in a metropolis, which allows him to maintain a certain look: "He might be officially gay, straight or bisexual, but this is utterly immaterial because he has clearly taken himself as his own love object and pleasure as his sexual preference." Interestingly, Simpson seems to evoke the same gendered frameworks in discussing the rise of female metrosexuality: "Female metrosexuality is the complement of male metrosexuality, except that it's active where male metrosexuality is passive. No longer is a straight man's sense of self and manhood delivered by his relationship to women; instead it's challenged by it." He then takes aim at the "new lad" magazines exported to the United States from the U.K., suggesting that they perform a "hysterical metrosexuality of tits, beer, sports, cars, and fart-lighting," but actually deliver "glossy male models selling male vanity." For Simpson, this new way of presenting oneself is a successful, if not benign, masculinity, but one that he thinks will last into the future.[37]

It is within the development of these various models of masculinity that Morrissey, and this music video, can be situated. Is he — or *was* he — a sensitive "new man," or did he transform himself into a "lad"? The video presents an aggressive and masculine Morrissey, perhaps "lad-ish," who is refused admittance into the masculine world of mobility and vitality, through his inability to drive an automobile. The only moment the viewer sees him in the driver's seat is the moment in which he is asked to leave it. His agency to transport himself is removed, and his jealousy and animosity toward the "boy racer" are revealed, although the singer is relegated to the performance space and removed from the city streets. For Morrissey, his inactivity or injury does not affect his gender; he is overwhelmingly masculine due to both his bodily appearance and his aggressive demeanor. Perhaps his inability to be like the "boy racer" signifies that he can never achieve a "new lad" masculinity, or perhaps that British society, in the guise of police officers, will not allow him to. Thus he is able to employ a further different type of masculinity, or something of the sort that embraces lack. Also, Morrissey is relegated to performing with injury. With his display of injury as well as his restriction to performance away from the streets, Morrissey is of no danger to anyone, even if the words he sings suggest his intent to murder.

Another interesting element in the video is the handsomeness or attractiveness of the performer as compared to the antagonist figure of the "boy racer." Morrissey is displayed as physically larger than the "boy racer," and although he is not driving, he seems comfortable and particularly capable of performing. The singer is poised in a stance that suggests confidence and is unmoved by the further thrusts of the music toward the end of the video; his seriousness and strength is showcased in his stillness. While some might note that his stillness situates him in a category of difference in comparison to the musicians around him, it also serves to point out his strength and *immovability*.

The Spectator and Desire

As is discussed in previous chapters, much of the writing on celebrity and mediation in terms of gendered frameworks of desire addresses issues of the "feminization" of the celebrity as an eroticized object. On the other hand, there is the consideration of the audience and its "masculinization." Mulvey's ideas are problematized both by the presentation of a male celebrity and also, importantly, by the presence of a female spectator. Furthermore, the presentation of a mediated celebrity affects the audience, in terms of self-realization and its relationship with what it sees.

Christian Metz expands on the subjects of identification and the mirror in cinema. First, Metz tries to distinguish cinema from other media, such as written text and music, as "more perceptual." Furthermore, for those media that are similar, such as theater and opera for instance, "the perceptions they offer to the eye and the ear are inscribed in a true space … the same one as that occupied by the public during the performance."[38] Thus, the film is a grand signifier of environments and stories but is in fact a symbol of absence; Metz suggests that a film canister obviously does not really contain all that a film presents. As a recorded medium, film points to an absence of that which it presents. Metz explains,

> More than the other arts, or in a more unique way, the cinema involves us in the imaginary: it drums up all perception, but to switch it immediately over into its own absence, which is nonetheless the only signifier present.
> Thus film is like the mirror. But it differs from the primordial mirror in one essential point: although, as in the latter, everything may come to be projected, there is one thing and one thing only that is never reflected in it: the spectator's own body. In a certain emplacement, the mirror suddenly becomes clear glass.[39]

Thus, while in the primordial mirror the child sees him- or herself as an other and with others, as an object, the "mirror" of cinema can be like clear glass because the spectator already has a sense of subjectivity and is "thus able to constitute a world of objects without having first to recognize himself within it." Metz then asks the important question, "But *with what*, then, does the spectator identify during the projection of the film?"[40]

It should be noted that there is little distinction made between various media and the perceptions they offer in this present discussion. While Metz' descriptions regarding the perceptual engagement of various media are noteworthy, there is a certain sense of the "more perceptual" that occurs when an audience is engaged with material and media that focuses on that which it is enamored with, such as might be the case with a celebrity. As outlined earlier, it could be argued that an audience enters the "world" of the celebrity and will engage completely, with all its attention, with the "stream(s)" offered by the specific medium, whether audio music or the "more perceptual" of music video. It is with these considerations in mind that the discussion continues.

The screen only displays the Other; there is no perceiving of the self, as the self is already established. The spectator is what Metz calls "all-perceiving," knowing not only that she is apart from the film (not in it) but also that the film is imaginary, that she is not dreaming, and that she is ultimately the one who is taking in the information from the screen and forming it into the experience of cinema.

> In other words, the spectator *identifies with himself*, with himself as a pure act of perception (as wakefulness, alertness): as the condition of possibility of the perceived and hence as a kind of transcendental subject, which comes before every *there is*.[41]

What the spectator ultimately perceives is her presence but also the absence of what is on the screen: the cinematic signifier (the film and that which it contains) "installs a new figure of the lack, the physical absence of the object seen."[42] Metz clarifies the process of desire in terms of voyeurism:

> [Desire] in the end has no object, at any rate no real object; through real objects which are all substitutes (and all the more numerous and interchangeable for that), it pursues an imaginary object (a "lost object") which is its truest object, an object that has always been lost and is always desired as such.[43]

Thus the film can contribute to this desiring by pointing to absence; film is

> something in whose definition there is a great deal of "flight"; not precisely something that hides, rather something that *lets* itself be seen without *presenting* itself to be seen, which has gone out of the room before leaving only its trace visible there.[44]

The music video can work in a similar way. The images conveyed in the video give the viewer limited information, about both the singer and the events that are occurring within the video. The viewer might seek to follow the trace that remains after the video is presented. Such a trace is made more vital and striking because of the charged images of injury in close-up. Therefore, the video works to maintain and continue the draw of the celebrity; perhaps the spectator notices her own lack, in terms of the absence of the celebrity and her desire for it.

John Ellis explains this phenomenon in discussing the star as an "impossible image," much like the cinematic image, the picture that exists and then does not. He states,

> The star is tantalisingly close and similar, yet at the same time remote and dissimilar. Further, the star is a legitimate object for the desire of the viewer in so far as the star is like the viewer, and an impossible object for the desire of the viewer in so far as the star is extraordinary, unlike the viewer.[45]

Furthermore, this image is always absent though present:

> The star image in subsidiary forms of circulation [television, magazines, newspapers, etc.] is not a complete and settled identity. If it was, it would be a satisfactory phenomenon and would not produce the curiosity necessary to encourage cinema attendances. This curiosity seems to be produced in two ways: first by the enigma of star paradox (ordinary-extraordinary) and second by the resultant promise of cinema (or presence-absence).[46]

Thus, Ellis accounts for the presence through absence that is hinted at by Metz, suggesting that such is required for the celebrity to function. Cinema promises the trace of presence and the possibility of contact. This is how the celebrity works, both in cinema and in what Ellis calls "subsidiary forms of circulation."

Concluding Remarks

Morrissey is a charismatic and enigmatic performer who seems to capture the audience in the context of various media. In music video, the singer has established an interesting history of conveying images of contradictory stereotypes of gender, as well as incorporating "lack," impairment, or a sense of need into that image. Interestingly, Morrissey's persona presented in the video for "The Boy Racer," while situated within a certain evolutionary context in terms of conceptions of masculinity, is both traditionally masculine (and "attractive" as such) and also extremely jarring in terms of injury. These images can also be read as unsettling; Morrissey's stillness toward the end of the video, in contrast to the raucous output of the musicians in the band, points to an inactivity, an indifference.

Nevertheless, it could be argued that the images *do not* ultimately avert the viewer, and it is not only the brevity of the close-ups or the relative "tameness" of the injuries that is to be credited. Metz provides an argument as to why the video continues to work, even with contradictory information and potentially uncomfortable images. Perhaps, in a sense, the spectator wants that which the spectator does not — or cannot — have. Morrissey "goes away" once the video is over, unless the spectator has the opportunity to view the video at will, at which time Morrissey "returns." The narrative, though, is incomplete, much like the singer with his injury. This incomplete narrative, coupled with the concern of the spectator as to how such events have come to pass, propels the desire of the spectator for the object on the screen. Contradictory stereotypes of gender and the complexity of Morrissey's performance of masculinity simply add to the mystery of the performance, a mystery that might be solved if only the absent figure on the screen might be physically present with the spectator. The inconsistency of the persona on the screen might be somehow made consistent by his physical presence.

5

"At Last I Am Born"
Morrissey in Live Performance

Mona Venkateswaran, a chartered accountant who oversees the finances of the Canadian Broadcasting Corporation website, CBC.ca, discusses her experience in attending the Morrissey concert in Toronto in October 2004 and meeting the singer. She writes of adult men and women singing every lyric to Morrissey's songs, climbing onto the stage hoping to give him a hug, hand him flowers or give him a handwritten note. She writes, "He once said at a concert, 'Welcome to the Church of Morrissey.' It couldn't have been put more perfectly."[1] For many fans, the ultimate way to experience the music of Morrissey is in live performance. Those who are unable to attend a concert by the singer must resort to engaging with his live material through "bootleg" audience recordings, television and Internet broadcasts of concerts, and official releases of Morrissey concerts on videocassette or DVD. Morrissey's concerts are a fascinating spectacle, a display of affection and energy almost unrivaled by other popular musicians. Morrissey, where the venue's physical layout allows, has only cursory (and often local) security personnel between him and the audience. This configuration allows for many of the more athletic members of the audience to climb onto the stage for a moment with the singer. These moments usually consist of a quick hug or kiss, or just a handshake, after which an on-stage security person escorts the stage invader away from the singer. It is obvious that the security personnel are purposefully told to treat those that make it onto the stage in a lenient manner, resulting in a generally non-violent and relatively gentle sequence of events.

Morrissey's live concerts are uncharacteristically short, running no more than an hour and a half, including the traditional encore song, but they are full of fascinating moments, some of which involve vocal and physical gestures employed by the singer. For instance, Morrissey often growls or makes extraneous noises. Vocally, he often seems to force his vibrato, resulting in an unnatural flutter in his voice, perhaps in order to highlight certain lyrics or melodic moments. As is further explored later in this book, he often seems to use questionable tuning in his singing, although this might also be a result of technical difficulties in live performance. In addition to these vocal gestures, he often makes particular physical movements, such as whipping his microphone cord in time with the music. In many concerts in the last decade, he has made reference to Julia Riley, a fan with whom he converses during the concert, and whose website he uses as an "official" mouthpiece. Her story and affiliation with the singer are now legendary. She has appeared at most shows since at least 2000 and often gets preferential treatment from security personnel and can be snubbed by fans as a result. His relationship to "superfans" has become somewhat personal, as his response to the death of Melinda Hsu in 2010 made evident. At most shows, Morrissey removes his own shirt and throws it into the audience, providing a "relic" for his fans to revere. This has become an anticipated occurrence.

There are other interesting aspects of Morrissey's live performance. For instance, during his tour to support *You Are the Quarry* in 2004, Morrissey performed in front of giant lighted letters that spelled out his name. It could be argued that such a display might be a form of narcissism and may contribute to a sense of narcissistic masculinity surrounding him and perhaps also may offer Morrissey another instance to display an alternate mode of masculinity.

This chapter will serve to map out certain characteristics and peculiarities of Morrissey's live performance. These various peculiarities come together to color or enhance his enigmatic star image. Unlike when Morrissey is mediated through various media, Morrissey is *actually physically* available to his audience in concert, and vicariously in the case of live performance captured in video or audio recording.

Physicality and Morrissey's Public Performance

A constant characteristic of a Morrissey concert is its sense of physicality, in terms of the proximity of the singer to the audience and in his interaction with them. This physicality has been discussed in chapter 1 in terms of Morrissey's "simultaneous remoteness and availability," according to Rogan, and the division — or lack, thereof— between audience and star.[2] In chapter 4 aggression and the audience's desire for contact with the singer were discussed in terms of Morrissey's live concert performance and the change in musical style with the release of *Your Arsenal* in 1992. It was also discussed that physicality in terms of perceived injury is an important part of Morrissey's star image. Interestingly, Morrissey has appeared in concert with bandages on his face as recently as July 2006.

In August 1987, Morrissey stated that the thrill in live performance is "totally, totally gone.... I no longer feel that it's something I want to continue doing. I wouldn't like to go on a stage if I just felt 55 per cent of an interest, and that really is the case. So I don't think I should do it."[3] Of course, Morrissey has since continued to tour and perform live concerts. His first concert as a solo performer occurred in December 1988; he did not perform live during the year that followed. In an interview with Mat Snow in *Q* magazine a year after that first solo concert, Morrissey recalls the emotions of that night and his physical interaction with the fans.

> In the hall that night there was a great aura of love and gentleness, and all the people who came on stage treated me in a very gentle way. I wasn't kicked or punched or dragged, although they were very emotionally charged. I came away with no bruises.[4]

It is hard to imagine that such interactions would be gentle, especially with the emotion of the fans being so high. As noted earlier, though, Morrissey considers the physical interaction with his fans a "gentle ballet."

The interaction between Morrissey and his adoring audience as a "gentle ballet" is given particular vitality in the official concert video *Introducing Morrissey*, released in 1996, which features many instances of these "invasions." At the end of the live performance and before the credits, director James O'Brien constructs a collage of clips of Morrissey repeatedly being embraced by fans. These clips are stitched together and presented in slow motion, accompanied by an instrumental track of "Interlude," Morrissey's duet with singer Siouxsie Sioux. Middleton discusses the possible meaning of repetition by suggesting that

> popular common sense ... associates [repetition] with the phenomenon of being "sent," particularly in relation to the "hypnotic" rhythmic repetition and "prim-

itive" audience trance: a collective "loss of the subject" in a state, perhaps, of *jouissance*.[5]

It is difficult to ascertain how a "collective" experience might occur when members of the viewing audience are separated by time and space, able to watch the sequence whenever and wherever they might wish. Nevertheless, an audience that experiences the same content, whether or not at the same time or place, might constitute a collective, as per Benedict Anderson's "imagined communities" or "reading coalitions." Anderson calls a group of people who read the same language yet are not part of the same political nation, or do not reside in the same geographical space, a "reading coalition," constructing their own "imagined community" because they are reading the same kind of written text.[6] Because of the slow-motion presentation of the clips, and the accompaniment of soft and beautiful music, as opposed to "rhythmic" or "primitive," and the lack of the voices of the singers, it is unclear if there would be a collective loss of the subject. Although the sequence might in some ways be lulling, it is not particularly hypnotic in terms of rhythm. Actually, Middleton is speaking of the repetitive rhythms of popular music. However, he also makes the point that the "very force of repetition can, as it were, obliterate the significance of content."[7] In other words, the repetition of the content might make that content less significant, less meaningful. Why, then, would that content be included at the end of the video in such a manner that might ultimately desensitize the viewer?

There might be a sense that the audience might in fact experience a "loss of the subject," as Middleton suggests. The presentation of person after person engaging physically with Morrissey, and doing so *so slowly*, might suggest that a member of his viewing audience can also be in such a position, in a sense. In watching these repeated episodes of successful "stage invasions," a viewer might share in the experience vicariously. The audience then, as a "reading coalition" all "reading" the same video sequence, is allowed to touch Morrissey. The audience as a whole is able to knock him down.

Vocal and Physical Gestures

In live performance, Morrissey is the focus of attention on stage. He is often situated in the center and toward the front of the stage relative to the other band members. There is most often only a spotlight on him as he is singing, relegating other members of the band to the shadows. While he does introduce the other musicians, giving them the credit for their contributions to the live music of the evening, he does not interact with them in any particularly substantial way. He is the focus of attention during the concert; he is also the singer. Therefore, it would seem that what Morrissey presents in vocal performance is of utmost importance.

There are moments when Morrissey's vocal performance differs from what is presented in his recordings. For instance, Morrissey seems to force an unnatural vibrato or flutter to occur in his voice. It is possible that Morrissey produces this sound by employing a succession of glottal stops. The term "glottal stop" refers to the sound made when the vocal chords close and thus stop the flow of air, and then immediately release that air (a common example of the glottal stop in the English language is the sound between the syllables in the word "uh-oh"). The sound of the glottal stop is produced in the throat rather than in the mouth, and the sound is made possible by the exhalation of air from the lungs, rather than any articulation of that air by the mouth or the tongue. The overuse of this technique can be damaging to the voice, especially when used at the beginning of singing tones. Morrissey provides an example of this phenomenon during a performance of "Still Ill" on The Smiths' live concert recording, *Rank*. He utilizes this particular vocal gesture when he asks whether he is "still ill," predominantly on the sustained portions of the lyric, at the end of the question, and on the word "no." This vocal technique is also evident during a performance of "First of the Gang to Die," featured on Morrissey's 2005 release, *Live at Earls Court*. In a more noticeable instance, Morrissey changes his vibrato in the delivery of certain lyrics, especially when he refers to "Hector," the dead gang member. This vocal style is not evident in any of Morrissey's studio recordings and perhaps can then be linked to the energy of live performance.

The use of glottal stops in popular singing seems to be a somewhat rare occurrence. A glottal stop can be used at the start of a singing tone in aggressive styles like punk, allowing the singer to make a sudden attack on the sung pitch. This technique is considered dangerous, though, and potentially harmful to the voice. The glottal stop is used for ornamentation in other musics, though, like *Sean-nós*, a form of Irish song. Types of melodic ornamentation in *Sean-nós* songs include grace notes (short notes that serve as ornaments to the melody), rolls and wavers, and short glottal stops. Sean Williams suggests that in the context of the Irish song type, glottal stops, along with the other ornamental gestures, are used to "glorify the story told by the song."[8] Regarding the specific ornament of the glottal stop, Williams suggests that it brings attention to the particular line of text during which it occurs: "By stopping for a fraction of a second, the word immediately preceding the stop can be echoed in the listener's mind, and the words just following the stop can be heard more clearly because of the stop."[9] It is unclear, though, whether Morrissey was ever exposed to this kind of Irish singing. Interestingly, Nick Kelly, in a review of Morrissey's concert in Dublin in October 2002, notices a link between Morrissey's presentation and Irishness. He writes that Morrissey has recently lived in Dublin, and "he mimicked the local accent, lacing his loquacious banter with knowing references to the streets and suburbs of the fair city." He has taken this experience and translated it to the stage, "gleefully annunciating every last syllable and making subtle changes to the lyrics."[10] Nevertheless, Morrissey's use of the glottal stop is markedly different from its use in Irish song in that he repeats the stop during a held note, with the succession of stops replacing the normal and natural flutter of his vibrato. This "melodic ornamentation" may function in several ways. It might in fact emphasize the word or phrase that precedes it, such as might be the case in the song "Still Ill," placing importance on the words of the narrator, asking whether he or she is "still ill." Also, it might provide a sense of ambivalence, because of its substitution of a natural occurrence. The resulting sound of forced flutter is louder and more pronounced than Morrissey's natural vibrato and seems out of place, especially when the gesture does not occur in any studio recordings.

There is another vocal gesture that Morrissey employs liberally in live performance and that he refrains from using in his studio recordings. Morrissey often growls in performance, evoking either anger or extreme emotion. Neva Chonin describes Morrissey's live singing as "punctuated by arch guttural vocal effects."[11] Often he will growl a few of the words of a song, resulting in those lyrics being indecipherable. Thus, while presenting his songs in a physical proximity to his fans, he shrouds some of his lyrics by masking them in growls and grunts. In some of these cases, he squeals and screams, perhaps imitating the yells of the audience. Such actions and sounds are not consistent with his crooner image. The production of unnatural vibrato and growls and squeals suggest what musicologist Robert Walser calls an "overflowing" of the natural function of the voice. In his discussion of the use of distortion and power chords in Heavy Metal music, Walser suggests that these sounds can be explored in terms of power:

> Distortion functions as a sign of extreme power and intense expression by overflowing its channels and materializing the exceptional effort that produces it.... Distortion begins to be perceived in terms of power rather than failure, intentional transgression rather than accidental overload — as music rather than noise.[12]

Therefore, when Morrissey's voice does crack or distort in growls or squeals, or when he engages in the production of unnatural vibrato, he is perhaps simply "overflowing its channels." Certainly, Morrissey's vocal gestures can be read as "music rather than noise."

In a review of a concert at London's Royal Albert Hall in 2002, Sean O'Hagan writes that the anger that seems to permeate some of his vocal performance points to a greater discomfort: "Between songs he paws at his chest continuously, nervously strokes his quiff and repeatedly hitches up his pants.... Throughout, he seems oddly uncomfortable in his own body.[13] In addition to the growls, which might suggest anger, Morrissey whips his microphone cord, often in time to the music. This action is evocative of self-flagellation, a form of mortification, leading Mark Mordue to call Morrissey "a curious, strange creature ... arcing the microphone lead like a great whip to the music's pulses."[14] Historically, self-mortification is an action associated with asceticism, a way of subduing the body through self-discipline. Asceticism and corporal penance have historically been linked with Roman Catholicism and monastic Christianity. Interestingly, Morrissey seems to be increasingly drawing upon Catholicism, the religion of his childhood. In an interview with Douglas Coupland, Morrissey states, "'Those Catholics, they really nab you when you're young.' [Makes gesture of cowpoke searing calf with branding iron.] 'They sear you. They sear you, they do.'"[15] This stance is further reinforced with his wearing of a priest's outfit during the tour in support of *You Are the Quarry* in 2004.

The Ultimate Fan: Julia Riley

For many years, there has been a constant in the experience of Morrissey in live performance. Morrissey has made reference to a "Julia" from the stage, usually aiming his comments to the front of the audience. He almost always asks this "Julia," Julia Riley, how she is and usually makes reference to her multiple times during the concerts that she attends. Riley maintains a fan-made magazine dedicated to Morrissey called *True to You*, first published in 1994, according to her website. Based in Massachusetts, Riley has released 15 issues of the magazine as of July 2010 and has readers in over 35 countries. She has been a constant fixture in the discourse of Morrissey because of her presence at almost all of his concerts since at least 2000. She apparently garners special treatment by concert organizers and Morrissey's own security personnel.

Many fans question her ability to travel and attend the number of Morrissey concerts that she does, and many wonder how she could have a conversational (while somewhat strange) relationship with the singer, if only in the context of a live performance. Away from a concert setting, though, Morrissey does use her website as an official outlet for comments and announcements, as is demonstrated by his posting of answers to fan-submitted questions. Although the site is technically a "fan" site, and not an official site, the inclusion of its web address on the packaging of many of Morrissey's recent recordings, including 2009's *Years of Refusal*, as well as the singer's obvious support, lends the site an air of extreme credibility. It has become a sort of rival to the other major fan website, *Morrissey-Solo*, whose visitors often criticize Riley's site for its lack of updates. As for Riley herself, many fans posting on the *Morrissey-Solo* discussion boards consider her friendly, while some are jealous of her and suggest that it would be "an empty life" to continuously follow Morrissey on tour.[16] Of course, many might simply be envious of her unprecedented access to the singer and his acknowledgment of her existence.

There is a story that circulates in the fan community that she came into a fortune because of a mishap that has rendered her sickly. She apparently delivered to Morrissey a first edition of an Oscar Wilde book, a treasure that would cost a considerable amount of money. Some have suggested, perhaps in jest, that she is in fact Morrissey's wife; others have suggested that she is a charity project for Morrissey, an example of the downtrodden and sickly figure so often present in his songs. It is unclear how much of a relationship the two figures have, away from the live concert experience and the few messages posted on the *True to You* website. Nevertheless, her life has become part of Morrissey's discourse, and her interaction with the singer has become an item of jealousy and envy.

Another fan who has had the opportunity to interact with Morrissey is Melinda Hsu, whose master's thesis on the singer is mentioned earlier in this book. Hsu's death in early 2010 prompted Morrissey to release a statement through Riley's website, expressing his sympathies. He writes, "I felt as if I knew Mel because she was always there—wherever 'there' happened to be." In his statement, Morrissey expresses his thoughts regarding fans such as Hsu and Riley. He writes,

> Those who travel from concert to concert as Mel did possibly don't realize the contribution they make. They are as much a part of the night as I am, but I sometimes feel embarrassed because I think they are asking for more than there is, and, mustily, I can't give it. The goat-like vocals and tipsy monologues are all that I am.[17]

Morrissey's Shirt

The most-anticipated moment in a Morrissey concert, apart from seeing the singer himself, is when he throws a shirt into the crowd, something that he has continued to do for many years. Chonin describes the scene at a concert in San Francisco:

> The venue's floor was a crush of bodies and flailing, loving arms. When Morrissey (affectionately known as Moz) reached into the crowd to accept bouquets, hungry hands attempted to pull him in; when he pulled off his shirt and tossed it into the front rows, the audience shredded it like hyenas at a kill.[18]

Kelly describes part of the appeal that a piece of shirt might provide. The concert in Dublin ended "with Morrissey ritually discarding shirt and tossing it into the excitable crowd, for whom he still remains, at 42 [in 2002], a potent sex symbol."[19] A piece of Morrissey's shirt is considered a real rarity, something to fight for and to treasure. It is common to find discussions on message boards at the fan websites discussing the possible brand name of the shirt, as well as the brand of fragrance with which a fragment might be infused. A piece of Morrissey's shirt is a site of connection with the physical Morrissey. It is a "relic" for some, kept as an object of reverence, pointing to the "sainthood" of Morrissey. Morrissey's audience might agree with his own words in describing his concert as a service in the "Church of Morrissey." Chonin writes, "He froze, arms outstretched like a solemn scarecrow, between verses of 'Jack the Ripper' (only Morrissey would strike a Christ pose while singing from a serial killer's perspective)."[20] Simpson writes:

> [Morrissey] has achieved in life the transcendence that other performers have only achieved in death (or real, clinical, certifiable madness). This is the twisted miracle of Morrissey's life that his fans, his congregation of Beautiful Bastards, bear witness to. Morrissey is the only "saint" to be canonised before his death, and the only one to intercede on behalf of his supplicants not from heaven but from his bedroom.[21]

In addition to being a part of something that might be religiously revered, a piece of Morrissey's shirt is a part of a whole that is ultimately unattainable, that being the man himself. The shirt is something that is physically *on* his skin, something that becomes permeated with his sweat, and the closest part of his physicality that a member of his audience can possess. In fact, Simpson suggests that there is a conscious effort made by the singer to deny the giving of himself to all of the external forces that would like a piece of him. Simpson, while suggesting that Morrissey is "mad," writes:

> Morrissey's "looniness" is an extreme form of self-preservation, self-regard and self-love which compels him to say the one thing people don't want to ever hear from a pop star: "No."
> Over and over again.
> No to the loss of himself. No to the ravenous, slavering
> demands of everyone who wants a piece of him: fans, the music industry, associates, biographers, even and especially friends.[22]

Yet Morrissey gives of a physical tangible part of himself, the clothing that he wears, to those fans who reach for it, and often fight over it, in hopes of obtaining a fragment. This small gesture of generosity provides for the audience — or, more specifically, those few who are able to secure a piece of the shirt — a lasting remnant of the physical being, a swatch of the physical man that they can take home and treasure. This fragment is special because it is often or otherwise purposely withheld. As Simpson suggests, Morrissey denies access to himself on all sides *except* in concert, where his voice — and body — are available to all.

Narcissism and Morrissey's Name

An interesting aspect of Morrissey's 2004 tour in support of *You Are the Quarry* is the stage backdrop. Bruce Scott describes the scene at the concert in Toronto on 12 October 2004:

> Behind the musicians, on a raised platform, the word "MORRISSEY" was spelled out in 15-foot-high capital letters illuminated by Vegas-style light bulbs. It was strangely reminiscent of Elvis's comeback tour, or a Tom Jones album cover, but it worked perfectly with the tone of the evening.[23]

Sofi Papamarko suggests that "the fixture was cheeky and over-the-top, like the man himself."[24] The bright red letters are featured on the cover of Morrissey's live concert video, *Who Put the "M" in Manchester?*, a cover that also evokes the posturing of Elvis Presley, with Morrissey leaning to the left of the frame with his arm and hand pointing upward. Although the letters are the most visible elements on the stage, the letters actually function to single out Morrissey. They literally point to Morrissey as the only figure on the stage, focusing the gaze of the audience on that one person. The large display of that single name points to a kind of narcissism on the part of Morrissey. This extreme selfishness and egotism also invite the audience to look at Morrissey, to explore aspects of his physical self and to desire him. Such a stance reinforces the suggestion that Morrissey acts as a "metrosexual," as argued by Mark Simpson. As recently as July 2006, Morrissey has introduced the band and himself as "We are Morrissey," upon their emergence onto the stage. Although the large lit-up letters are gone (now that the *You Are the Quarry* tour is over), the focus still remains on the singer, so much so that the other members of the band are in a secondary position. Chonin describes the pleasure that Morrissey seems to derive from the adoration of the audience:

> Like Narcissus gazing into a pool of adoration, he blithely toyed with his fans' obsession: "Nice try," he quipped to one trying to clamber onstage; "Fly, boy, fly!" he instructed another. To one especially hopeful acolyte, he drawled, "You can crash at my place tonight."[25]

Why, then, the evocation of a time past, whether Elvis or Tom Jones, or the perceived superficiality and kitsch of Las Vegas performers? It seems that this performing context, with its reference to a historical time that is now out of fashion, might be a way in which Morrissey effaces himself, while knowingly accepting the praises of his audience. The lowering of himself will arguably garner a greater response from the audience to raise him up. Therefore, the appropriation of kitsch elements, like the large lettering outlined by blinking lights, not only acts as an indication of who should be the focus of the stage presentation but also works to, in a sense, deface Morrissey, soliciting a greater response from the audience. This can be read as selfish and self-serving.

Perhaps a Morrissey concert might not always be perceived as selfish. Robert Everett-Green writes that "his concert was a generous affair, in its flood of arresting song, and in Morrissey's tolerance of people clambering on stage to embrace him," though it seemed "indicative of the public isolation of rock stars like Morrissey, beloved by strangers who will always remain strangers."[26] Everett-Green, then, not only recognizes the possible generosity of Morrissey in concert but is also sympathetic toward the loneliness of a narcissistic celebrity.

Concluding Remarks

This chapter outlines particular characteristics of the live Morrissey concert experience. These characteristics serve to color or add to the otherwise enigmatic star image of the singer, evident in his presentation through other types of media. A particularly strong characteristic of a Morrissey concert is the physicality displayed during it. Various members of the audience might attempt to clamber onto the stage for a moment with the singer. Some might be successful in embracing or kissing Morrissey, an action that seems to be condoned and expected by Morrissey and his security personnel.

Morrissey's voice is also characteristic, with the singer using successive glottal stops, and growls and squeals. None of these vocal effects are used in studio recordings, thus making the live Morrissey vocal a different species than the recorded output. He seems to reinforce his sense of "sainthood" by his physical gesture of whipping his microphone cord. He also consistently mentions audience member Julia Riley, engaging in conversation with her from the stage. Her life has become part of the Morrissey discourse, and her background the subject of wide conjecture and rumor, all of which is impossible to verify.

A piece of Morrissey's shirt remains as one of the most treasured Morrissey "relics," as a site of physical connection with the singer. The fragment of the shirt has actually had physical contact with Morrissey's skin and sweat, thus bearing a bit of his physical self. Finally, the signage during Morrissey's 2004 tour points to the singer himself as the sole focus of the concert, lending him a sense of narcissism. While the style of the signage might seem nostalgic or kitschy, it serves to deface the singer so as to solicit a greater response from the audience.

6

"We'll Let You Know"
Inactivity and the Musical World of Morrissey

Morrissey is a complex example of the male pop vocal celebrity. In terms of his star image, Morrissey seems to problematize gendered frameworks of desire by maintaining a kind of "masculinist" power while becoming subject to the eroticizing "gaze" of the audience. One way that this is accomplished is through the constant production of discourse, that does not allow an audience to know all the details of his life and persona. This discourse is produced in many ways. For instance, Morrissey's persona carries with it controversies which constantly call into question the singer's own views, in terms of racism and nationality. Morrissey's gender and sexuality are also continuously in flux. This ambivalence can be achieved through a complex presentation of gender, which is particularly evident in his music videos. It is possible that such discourse production — or discourse *obscuration*—can be seen within his musical output as well. As McClary and others argue, there are musical codes and conventions that are considered gendered. It is fascinating how Morrissey engages with these gendered musical codes; it is important to consider how Morrissey's music is presented while taking into account how Morrissey's persona problematizes gendered frameworks of desire.

This chapter explores, through a musical analysis of the song "We'll Let You Know," how Morrissey elicits desire and delays its satisfaction. Before presenting the analysis, it is worthwhile to discuss two important musicological works that focus on Morrissey. Stan Hawkins and Nadine Hubbs provide interesting readings of Morrissey, his star image and his performance practice. Hubbs' analyses provide a basis and starting point for the discussion presented in this chapter, with her notion of Morrissey's "inactivity" in relation to the accompanying band and rock music as a whole. Hawkins' work is important in that he takes into account Morrissey's problematic gender presentation and touches upon themes similar to those of this book. Both articles deal with the music of Morrissey in a musicological context and are valuable for that very fact. Unfortunately, the music of Morrissey has largely been overlooked both in musicology and in the realm of popular music studies. This chapter works to contribute to a greater academic, and musicological, discourse on Morrissey, his persona and the music that he presents.

Hubbs: Morrissey as "Fourth Gender"

Nadine Hubbs begins her article by discussing Morrissey's public persona, stating that the overall aim of the article is to "examine some of the ways in which powerful regulatory practices of gender, sexuality, and desire are constructed by popular music, Morrissey's songs in particular, and music in general." She presents an elegant analysis of Morrissey's lyrics with the following:

> His narratives suggest a gay viewpoint in some instances, and a straight viewpoint in others, but every instance is fraught with ambiguity. This ambiguity ... manifests an intriguing and rather specific schema in the Smiths songs: that is, most often the identity of the male as object of desire is shrouded in mystery; the female object appears more clearly identified, but more ambivalently desired.[1]

Hubbs then points to Henke's *Rolling Stone* article and Morrissey's apparent proclamation as being "a prophet for the fourth gender." She provides some clarification of the term "fourth gender" by suggesting what it does not refer to, and by clarifying other categories of gender. Hubbs states:

> Thus he evidently passes on not only the first and second, but skirts the "third gender" as well, what the nineteenth-century sexologists' category of the gender invert—a female soul in a male body, or vice versa.[2]

Hubbs suggests that the "fourth gender" embodies a kind of gender ambiguity; the problem with using such a label to describe Morrissey is that the singer is not generally ambiguous in his gender performance. She states that Morrissey's appearance "has always been rather conventionally masculine, and is quite possibly the least subversive aspect of his work and persona." She continues, "His 'fourth gender' standpoint rests on a refusal of both heterosexual and homosexual classifications, and dissension from the binary genders that make these possible."[3]

Hubbs suggests that Morrissey is an "inactive figure." Attempting to analyze the music of The Smiths in a musicological framework, she suggests that Morrissey's melodies are different from the music that accompanies them, due to their apparent "inactivity" or restriction to a certain range of musical pitches: "[Morrissey's] melodic contour ... is extraordinarily flat.... It is very typical for his vocal melodies to present extended stretches of repeated pitch." She continues by suggesting that these melodies are doubly gendered as feminine, being both different and inactive. Hubbs explains:

> [The static melodic quality] functions, in relation to relevant melodic norms, as a mark of difference — specifically a difference of inactivity. Such difference arises, of course, by contrast with other singers' levels of rhythmic activity and melodic contours.
>
> But it is also created by contrast with the level of activity of the other members — the instrumentalists — of Morrissey's own (all-male) bands. This is true with the Smiths, and equally so with the bands that Morrissey has worked with in his solo career.[4]

Hubbs suggests that the activity of the band is in accordance with the normative standard of rock music, citing Frith and McRobbie's term "cock rock." By referring to Frith and McRobbie, Hubbs suggests that musical "inactivity" can be understood in gendered terms.[5] Morrissey's vocal delivery contrasts with the band's "activity"; Hubbs characterizes it as "'droning,' and literally monotonous — that is, static and nonteleological — whereas the singing is not at all speechlike."[6]

Hubbs continues by discussing song as a narrative form: "One usual function of melody, text, and other available means is to represent and characterize a narrating subject, embodied by the singer." She points out that there exist "boys' songs and girls' songs," and that it is easier for a woman to sing a man's song than for a man to sing a woman's song, since "she is understood to take on the purportedly neutral and universal masculine perspective of the song's first-person subject." Furthermore, Hubbs suggests that musical rhetoric, which makes up certain musical works, can be gendered (this is reminiscent of John Shepherd's thoughts on the gendered framework that surrounds the discipline of music). Hubbs states,

"Morrissey's songs ... transgress masculine convention through identifications with feminine subjectivity, and with other distinctly unmasterful ways of being." She then embarks on a textual analysis that illustrates ways in which Morrissey defies gendered expectations in his lyrics, and how these "unexpected addition[s] to the text and dramatic narrative [are] *mirrored* by [their] musical setting—painted, and hence amplified, by a melodic extension."[7]

Such unexpected moments come also in the ways the lyrics are presented. Discussing the printed lyrics of one of The Smiths' songs, "Girlfriend in a Coma," Hubbs states:

> This marriage of tragic seriousness with transparent artifice is characteristically Wildean and quintessentially camp, as is the peculiar usage of capitalization and quotation marks—just what does it mean to "murder" or "strangle" in quotes? Meaning is precisely indeterminate: Morrissey's caps and quotes cultivate enigma, like the italics used similarly by generations of campy writers.[8]

Hubbs' point is as follows: "Morrissey's work resists, subverts, and transvalues cultural terms of sexuality and gender on verbal, visual, and musical levels. I have argued that Morrissey's melodies signify difference, specifically a difference of inactivity."[9] Hubbs continues by culturally situating Morrissey as a celebrity who has neither confirmed nor denied a gay subject position, but who is comfortable with what she calls "queer insider language."[10] Perhaps Hubbs is referring to songs like "Picadilly Palare" or "All the Lazy Dykes," although Bret has read the latter as being "the most offensive song in the Morrissey catalogue."[11] Bret's complaint comes from the fact that although the homosexual community has followed other oppressed communities in disempowering offensive terms by adopting them, Morrissey has not acknowledged his membership in that community. About Morrissey's ambiguous presentation, Hubbs suggests that "ambiguity is not particularly confusing to queer subjects, to whom its utility and indeed necessity are intimately known." As for Morrissey's reception by heterosexual fans, Hubbs states,

> I also know of straight fans who harbor no notion that Morrissey or his work has anything to do with queerness. This perspective (not so rare as it may seem improbable) is readily afforded by mainstream ignorance of queer codes, and supported by the economy of compulsory heterosexuality.[12]

Hubbs suggests that Morrissey's "project of resistance" is aimed at both conventional masculinity and standard sexuality: "His approach involves not visual signs of cross-dressing and -comportment, but the more subliminal means of musical rhetoric, and allusively, sophisticated textual identifications with feminine subjects." About Morrissey's choice of celibacy, Hubbs adds, "This conventional form of celibacy is weakened by Morrissey's presence, and the distinct erotics of his work and persona."[13]

Finally, Hubbs suggests that the singer's resistance to conventional categories of gender and sexuality work to keep him relevant and "susceptible to the identification needs and desires of even widely divergent audiences." She ends her article with the following point:

> Clearly, any listening or criticism of Morrissey's oeuvre that ignores the relevant codes and secret languages neglects a crucial part of the picture. But to ghettoize this music under some reductive rubric of "gay rock" ... is also to miss the point rather completely.... Far more rewarding than either of these extremes is to claim all the potential resonances of the work, in its rich multiplicity and adroit resistance to univocal interpretation.[14]

It should be noted that even if one chooses to accept Hubbs' suggestion of the "inactivity" of Morrissey's melodic output in relation to the "active" accompaniment of the band, Morrissey is not actually "inactive" at all. He is, of course, singing. His vocal delivery is very active in terms of melodic inflection and phrasing, as well as in communicating the lyrics of the song. Hubbs uses the term "inactivity" in a relative sense; her article deals with other elements of Morrissey's performance, specifically the pitches and range of his melodic lines, without taking into account the specifics such as his pitch inflection. More "active" aspects of Morrissey's vocal performance are presented in further detail later in this chapter.

Hawkins: Morrissey as "Anti-Hero"

Stan Hawkins explores how The Smiths constructed a kind of "authenticity" and how this affected Morrissey's persona. Hawkins is "concerned with how musical expression creates empathic responses." In his study, he uses musical codes to discuss aspects of Morrissey's distinct performing style while also exploring both his lyrical distinctiveness and his "ironic expression and playfulness." Hawkins states,

> I seek to demonstrate that the multiple voices in Morrissey's performance are inseparable from their cultural historical roots ... his musical rhetoric becomes

a channel for addressing the local space in relation to the central while opposing the dominant positions that instill power and belief ideologically.[15]

Hawkins argues that Morrissey's lyrics work on two levels: as an ambivalent approach to himself, in terms of self-deprecation; and as a lament for Arcadia, or pre-modern England and the values that accompany it. Hawkins suggests that modernization and suburbia emerged in opposition to the notion of pre-modern England, creating for some a sense of "statelessness" between these two mentalities. It seems that The Smiths might have gone to great lengths to dwell within this "statelessness," merging the old sentiments of Arcadia with new musical tastes and a fascination with feminism and a woman's place in society. Hawkins further explains:

> In one respect, [Morrissey's] apparent confusion about his own sexuality has led him to a curiously non-committal position in which he has repeatedly stressed his asexuality and disinterest in sexual activity. On the one hand, such declarations might be read as distinctly English, reflecting a moralistic and satirical take on the Victorian approach to sex. On the other hand, they could be evaluated alongside many of the pop stars of the 1980s whose display of sexuality concertedly conflicted with heteronormative models of masculinity.[16]

Hawkins suggests that The Smiths reflect a certain authenticity due to both their mundane or ordinary name and their "back to basics" approach to music making, constructing their sound without what Hawkins calls "clichéd musical features ... that appealed enormously to their fans, primarily because it contrasted boldly with the pop and rock of the day [the 1980s]." Hawkins characterizes the music of The Smiths as avoiding "harmonic teleology," through chord progression and voice-leading. Rather, Hawkins states, "it is through [Morrissey's] unique manner of controlling rising and falling pitches in his melodic lines that our attention is drawn to the special quality of his delivery."[17] Hawkins also makes a point regarding Morrissey's voice and his vocal range, suggesting that he "strains to pitch notes in his falsetto register," and thus "evokes a sense of increased emotional intensity for the receiver through the sheer effort invested on the part of the artist."[18] Hawkins' reading of Morrissey's melodic output is interesting in light of Hubbs' earlier proclamations of its "inactivity." Many would argue, though, that Morrissey is a singer who in fact *does not* strain his voice, in comparison to other popular music vocalists; this is perhaps why some have considered Morrissey a "crooner." For example, Jon Pareles describes Morrissey's voice in concert as a "sustained croon."[19] Morrissey himself seems to associate himself with the crooners rather than with rock singers. He states,

> I've always stood by so-called crooners like Matt Monro [best known for performing the title song from the 007 movie *From Russia with Love*] and, to a lesser degree, people like Doris Day — people who could really belt out an emotional number. I've never stood by rock'n'roll singers.... It was always the older generation of stately crooners that attracted me.[20]

While it may be true that forceful singing on Morrissey's part might evoke "increased emotional intensity," there is more to the singer's presentation and allure than just the straining of his voice, which occurs almost exclusively in live performance. In the context of a concert, the straining of Morrissey's voice is probably due to the excitement of the live performance and his feeding off the emotions of the audience. Nevertheless, Hawkins' focus on the aural signs of Morrissey's physical investment in the music is perhaps simplistic.

Regarding Morrissey's performance of masculinity, Hawkins states:

> In ridiculing dominant forms of masculinity by claims to asexuality, Morrissey actually appropriates qualities of Otherness in order to highlight the awkwardness of his difference. Yet actually, such a strategy could be interpreted as a deliberate attempt to foil our grasping the orientation of his sexual identity.[21]

Hawkins suggests that Morrissey characterizes the "anti-hero," emphasizing his "attachment to women and gay men, albeit in a non-sexual manner." He explains, "The implications of this are that his identity is constantly renegotiated through the process of performance, appropriation, and representation." Hawkins refers to the work of Julian Stringer on The Smiths, where Stringer considers the band "genderless through ... typical English lack or concealment of sexual desire." Hawkins explains:

> Such a positioning is helpful for us in understanding the qualities of Morrissey's identity, an identity that promotes celibacy, put-on awkwardness, ordinariness and ambiguity. In this way, his construed genderlessness could be perceived as a construction intended to set up a special tension through the play on difference. The possibilities opened up on this level thus present us with a useful starting point for considering the nature of musical expression alongside identity.[22]

It is here that Hawkins makes his first analysis of Morrissey's musical expression in terms of the singer's identity:

> Frequently, in his songs, misery and despair are masked by euphoric musical gestures that blend countless references. It is as if Morrissey's ongoing crisis is in constant need of relief through the execution of jovial musical narratives —

a strategy that pinpoints the counternarrative quality of his musical expression.[23]

Morrissey couples violent or angry lyrics with "simple, polite, musical gestures" to continue the crisis. By presenting the listeners with ambiguous messages, both through the juxtaposition of lyrical content and musical convention, and by presenting himself as an "ill-treated subject," Hawkins suggests that the singer employs these "manipulative strategies" to receive the empathic response from his fans, upon which "his dependency ... truly relies."[24] Hawkins clarifies this further:

> My conception of empathy is that pop artists are aware of their dependency on audiences and accordingly measure their voices through the complex channels of communication. This is central to the way in which identification makes us *feel* for the artist. In this sense, Morrissey's musical traits become statements on their own and therefore represent the trademarks of his identity.[25]

While Hawkins' analyses are welcome in terms of the ways in which Morrissey, obviously an intelligent performer and probably the master of his star image (in as much as this might be possible), engages with his fans, the author's suggestions also rely upon the notion of manipulation and playing of games on the part of the singer. Hawkins suggests that Morrissey is able to "cajole him knowingly in a way that flatters the fan's social competence," referring to author David Bret, also a Morrissey fan. Hawkins' use of the term "cajole," suggesting manipulation, is questionable. It is unclear why Hawkins sprinkles his text with terms that can be read as pejorative.

One of Hawkins' points is that Morrissey employs irony in his performance, "as a *relational strategy*." He states, "By this I am referring to the way in which it pulls together diverse meanings in order to create something ambiguous."[26] Hawkins goes on to attempt an analysis of "ironic markers" within Morrissey's songs, the most prevalent being "fluctuations in voice register, emphases of specific words, stylistic referents, and instrumental gestures in the overall musical material."[27] The author provides a reading of the song "Billy Budd" from *Vauxhall and I*. He states:

> Now when Morrissey delivers these lines, the music is structured around simple harmonic patterns set against an up-tempo, cheerful, regular rock groove. With a superficiality underlined by the very stylistic features of these musical codes, the protagonist's enunciation is sarcastic while deadly serious, and certainly succeeds in its aim. The pleasure derived from this song, as with all his others, lies in how Morrissey highlights his choice of words through musical expression.[28]

Hawkins concludes:

> Morrissey's texts are representative of a type of performativity that opens up new spaces for considering identity in a culturally defined setting. For me, the nature of Morrissey's social space is one of crisis where the shifts and rearrangements of masculinity in the 1980s and 1990s exist in a permanent state of tension. The effect of his performance lies in the emotions that are evoked when we experience his music.[29]

Musical Analysis

The object of analysis for this chapter is the song "We'll Let You Know," from the album *Your Arsenal*, released in 1992. The song begins in the key of D major, but after a lengthy instrumental section, it moves into the key of E minor in a prominent second section. The song maintains a regular and somewhat slow harmonic rhythm; the harmony changes primarily with every passing measure, with very few exceptions. Hawkins suggests that the characteristic of a slow harmonic rhythm links Morrissey's music to that of the post-punk *milieu*. The instrumental accompaniment, played by the band, follows a primarily simple harmonic progression, which repeats itself with little or no change.

The song begins with a short instrumental introduction comprised of eight measures, outlining the harmonic progression that is predominant in the next sections: D major — D major over B-flat — D major — B minor — E minor — B minor — E minor — G major — A major. This is a tonal progression that — except for a somewhat interesting anomaly, which will be explored in greater detail below — coincides with rather simple tonal harmonic conventions.[30] Morrissey then begins singing a verse consisting of 12 measures, accompanied by what sounds to be multiple guitars. As the bass guitar enters on the second verse, Morrissey sings a similar melody over an identical accompaniment. On the third verse, a penny whistle or flute enters, while on the fourth verse, the drums enter softly in the background. The fifth verse introduces some processed vocal sounds behind the melody line. Following this initial five-verse section comes an "instrumental interlude," in which the harmonic material from the verses is played in an identical manner a full five times, essentially replicating the amount of time that was spent with Morrissey's vocal, but now without that voice. The next tonal section moves to the key of E minor and signals a shift of affect from a somewhat pastoral sound to one suggesting a more aggressive feeling, although the section continues the same meter. This section is 16 measures long, only slightly longer than a single verse from the first section; the song ends abruptly with some spoken words and various instrumental noises fading out at the end.

Morrissey chooses to begin the song with an eight-measure section, with the other verses running a full 12 measures. Interestingly, Morrissey sings five verses of lyrics, all within a musical context of fours: each verse is in 4/4 time, and there are 12 measures per verse, and the second major section is 16 measures long. To have five verses with vocals and then five "verses" without vocals is somewhat unexpected.

This analysis takes into account the general harmonic progression of the first section in D major, as well as the melodic line of the bass guitar, which features quite boldly in this section. While the guitars provide somewhat static harmonic accompaniment in the higher sonic range, the bass guitar provides a melodic line that is in movement, and works to supply tension to the section, in contrast to Morrissey's vocal line, which is primarily static melodically. It is with this melodic line in mind that this analysis continues.

The second chord in the progression of the verse is a D major chord, and the guitars play a full chord with an A tone in the highest pitch, as if to highlight the stability of a root-position chord. This strong chord is played over a B-flat tone in the bass, a tone that does not fit into the chord above it, or the key of the whole piece. Therefore, the combined chord can be considered musically unstable, delaying a sense of resolution until the following measure. It seems that the D major chord over the B-flat, played by the bass guitar, serves as an expansion of the tonic—D major—at the beginning of the verse, perhaps to *destabilize* this part of the verse, but at the very least to provide a strange sound with delay of resolution, a resolution that occurs only in the next measure. It might function as a kind of *neighboring* tone, an upper neighbor to the pitch of A that precedes it, and an imaginary A following, suggested by the move of the bass melody down to a D, the root of the chord in that measure. Since B-flat does not belong to the key of this section, it is considered *chromatic*: "A chromatic neighbor lends more tonal color to a passage, and it tends to draw more attention to the pitch that it is embellishing."[31] Interestingly, the pitches that lead up to the B-flat move quickly, step-wise, using eighth notes, which might cause one to read the B-flat not as a neighbor to a fleeting A before it and a nonexistent A after it, but rather as an anomaly. Also, this non-chord tone, and non-key tone, is placed in an accented position; the B-flat occurs on the first beat of the measure and is sustained for a full four beats until "resolving" down to the pitch of D in the next measure. The stress of this non-chord tone adds a certain amount of power to this measure.[32]

While the above note combination occurs in the second through fourth verses, the fifth verse features the bass guitar playing a different passage. Instead of moving stepwise from a pitch of F-sharp to B-flat, the bass line moves from the root D to G, occurring in the place of the previous B-flat, in the second measure of the verse. While a tone of G is also not a chord-tone, it does fit into the key of D major; unlike the occurrence of the B-flat tone in previous verses, which did not fit into the key of D major, the G tone is not chromatic. Therefore, the occurrence of this G tone is rendered less powerful than the B-flat in previous verses. The G tone might serve a neighboring function, but the same reservations apply as in earlier instances. The step-wise motion that leads to the G tone is very quick, in eighth notes, while the G tone occurs on an accented beat, sustains over the measure and resolves down to an implied F-sharp, nonexistent but suggested by the D, which is in fact the following note.

It is interesting to discuss what lyrics might be highlighted during these peculiar musical moments. Hubbs suggests that there could be a relationship between musical gestures and the lyrics, in what she might call a "mirroring" in the music of "unexpected addition[s] to the text."[33] The first verse of lyrics, which are expressed without the striking bass line, conveys a sense of sadness, that the narrators in the song have always been in such a state of despair. The bass guitar enters on the next verse, where the narrators exclaim that the listener (or the subject of the song) has wondered how they have made it up to this point in their despair. The interesting melodic event occurs while Morrissey sings the word "how" in this second verse, and the bass returns to the pitch of D as he begins the next line. The first sentence of the verse is injected with a certain instability with the appearance of the B-flat in the middle of it. The lyrics continue in the next verse, with the suggestion that the narrators might appear kind and happy (but they're not), and that it is the turnstile, assumedly at the entrance to a stadium, that makes them angry. In this verse, the B-flat tone appears while Morrissey sings the word "smiles" in the very first musical phrase of the verse. It is interesting that Morrissey juxtaposes "smiles" with the following lines suggesting hostility. In normal usage, one usually suggests that being "all smiles" is simply an act when one is actually upset or angry. Thus, to suggest that "we're all smiles" and then to follow with an explanation that is qualified as "honest" suggests that the blame being laid on the turnstiles is misplaced. Morrissey's delivery is ironic, suggesting that there is a deception occurring. It is with this verse that the listener might be able to formulate what the song is about, in terms of narrative. Bret explains:

> It is a sad state of affairs that the archetypal Briton in the eyes of many Europeans is the thug who attends football matches solely in order to make life a misery for genuine fans. The song, a lilting ballad embellished with the creaking of turnstiles and muted stadium screams, is a direct contrast to the raucous chanting one hears at these events — Morrissey is mocking the hooligans much as he ridicules the National Front for attending a disco.[34]

Bret is referring to the song "The National Front Disco," which appears directly after this one on the *Your Arsenal* recording. Adding to this, Simpson analyzes the song, and the others with similar sentiments that appear on the album, as follows:

> Morrissey is expressing a will-to-believe in the flawed nobility of those who express themselves spontaneously and directly, relying on their fists and fast friendships, instead of insipid, faithless, fickle words (or laws) in the way that "nice" (i.e. lying) people do.[35]

The hostility continues in the third verse, with the protagonist (antagonist?) of the song threatening to hurt those unable to defend themselves. Here, the B-flat falls again on the end of that first line, on the word "descend," giving a rather ominous atmosphere to this verse. It is with the following verse that there is a slight but significant change to the bass line. Here, Morrissey alludes to the meaningless of the song sung by them (him?): they have no meaning. Instead of a B-flat tone played by the bass guitar, while Morrissey sings the lyric "sing," which also happens to be the highest pitch of his melody line in the song as a whole, the bass guitar plays a G tone, which does not carry the same degree of instability as a B-flat, as G actually fits into the key of this section of the song. Therefore, one might read this verse as relatively stable, in comparison to the ones that have come before. The previous verses, with stressed words like "how," "smiles" (and its ironic usage) and "descend," might be read as rather negative ones, pointing to an overall fatalistic feeling or atmosphere during this part of the song. The less-intense fifth verse, with the more comfortable harmony coinciding with the word "sing," and the suggestion in the lyrics that these songs are meaningless, might deflect the power of the previous verses. Since Morrissey is portraying a character included in the "we" and also the one who is singing a song, this verse negates, so to speak, the other verses, asking the listener to disregard them as meaningless.

Following this are five verses during which Morrissey does not sing at all. The chord progression from the previous section continues to repeat itself with various guitar noises and highly processed sounds akin to voices on top of it. In a live version of the song on the video release *Introducing Morrissey*, this interlude is considerably shorter. During the filmed performance, the director of the video chooses to focus on the physical image of Morrissey, taking time to study his leg and torso and to highlight his still form. When listening to the audio version of the song, Morrissey is quite absent without the video component, but if one remembers the live video presentation of the song, Morrissey is then extremely "present." Thus, although the singer is "present," the listener must wait for the continuation of the song with the reentry of Morrissey's vocal line.

This instrumental section consists of the same harmonic material repeated multiple times. In one sense, the repetition works to delay any kind of musical or emotional resolution for the listener, or any progression in the song to a climactic point, if there should be one. On the other hand, the repetition of the section points to something that Hubbs calls a "melody of obsession":

> It sets its own narrow confines and paces back and forth within them, frequently retracing its own path—and thus acts as ideal musical counterpoint to Morrissey's narratives of compulsion, with their *idées fixes*, and their voyeuristic and sometimes agoraphobic preoccupations.[36]

While Hubbs applies her comments to another of Morrissey's songs in which the melody line itself is comprised of repetition and a narrow range of pitches, the same can be said not only of the melody line in question but also when considering that the harmonic accompaniment is repeated over and over again, without the focusing power of the singer's voice above it. Therefore, there is a possible reading of the section as symbolizing obsession, perhaps with the singer himself.

When Morrissey's voice does return, the music is altogether different, much darker and much more aggressive. These lyrics solidify the hostility of the previous verses. They are alarming, though, in their harshness. Morrissey suggests that some might consider them (the subjects of the song) cold or depressing. But, in the end, they are the last group of people that could really be called British. This is all seemingly dripping with harshness, something absent from the previous parts of the song.

Throughout the song, Morrissey sings a melody around the pitch of F-sharp, sometimes singing a G or outlining a descending B minor chord. This new section is immediately firmly established in E minor, with Morrissey singing a melody beginning on the pitch of E but also spending much time on F-sharp. He hovers around this pitch, resolving back down to the pitch of E; the singer does not so much move to the higher pitch — to G — but rather he leans into the pitch, perhaps only approaching it microtonally. This is true not only in this section but also throughout the whole song. These "leanings" or microtonal movements might be attributed to style or slight intonation or tuning problems rather than actual tonal variety. His vocal intonation throughout this song suggests a certain instability or vulnerability while also remaining primarily static melodically. If one considers the song as a whole, Morrissey sings the melody around a single tonal center of F-sharp. This points to a supreme inactivity in the sense that, although harmonically there has been a definite change of key, the melody remains based around a single note. If one considers a melodic reduction of the song, his melody line is predominantly dedicated to the single pitch of F-sharp, surrounding it with neighboring notes.

In addition, Morrissey often attacks the pitch with questionable tuning. Such an approach to a pitch can work in several ways. Hawkins suggests that "subtle variations in pitch inflection function to emphasize certain words in a way that accent the lyrical connotations." He continues to suggest that these performance techniques also emphasize his style as "natural" or untrained, and thus a singer with whom one might be able to identify.[37] There is a tension inherent in a voice that is not squarely on a pitch or note, in that the voice might completely lose the pitch center and veer off completely. On the other hand, if a voice hits the proper note without any pitch variation, and that voice, in a sense, "pushes" on the correct pitch — whether through dynamic change or some change in lyric delivery — then there also exists a tension, that the voice will break. Such "stress" on the pitch also occurs in the song, particularly at those points when Morrissey in fact hits the F-sharp properly and with the right inflection.

His vocal delivery in this song is characteristic; Morrissey delivers the lyrics in a relaxed manner, verging on speaking. This manner of delivery is evident in live performance, where, toward the end of this song, Morrissey could easily append the melody line with a spoken "and so on," as he does in the filmed *Introducing Morrissey* concert performance. Hawkins explains the possible meaning of this:

> Importantly, the offsetting of vocal pitches with the chords to which they belong emerges as one of the most prevalent features of Morrissey's performance style. Seldom are his melodies aligned vertically with the harmonies. The effect of this lies in the contrapuntal tension that draws us into the emphasis of specific words and sentiments. Thus, the nature of vocal linearity not only defines the musical idiom but also heightens the level of poignancy, especially in terms of resistance and expectation.[38]

Inactivity

In order to explore the possible meanings of Morrissey's melodies, it is worthwhile to consider how melodic stasis is discussed in a musicological context. Siegmund Levarie and Earnst Levy discuss stasis in their study of musical morphology, or the study of musical form. They state:

> Musical forms reveal much of ourselves. In this sense, one may refer to music as a language. There are people who restrict thought to verbal expression, but the musician is clearly aware of thinking in music. In the light of this broader definition of thinking, the grammars of music seem no more arbitrary than those of language. They are, in fact, less arbitrary inasmuch as, being purely formal, they give a large role to the objective component whereas linguistic grammars are determined by convention. Hence there are many languages.[39]

While one might choose to disagree that grammars of music "give a large role to the objective component," and suggest that they might also be determined by convention as linguistic grammars, Levarie and Levy do place due emphasis on the communicable power of musical form. The authors discuss musical form from the perspective of either static or dynamic, ontic or gignetic. Ontic refers to being outside of time or absolute, while gignetic evokes the sense of being in time, or relative. These terms can often be used in the context of musical analysis, when one discusses various elements of a musical piece: ontic elements of a piece might be its overall form (such as sonata form in classical music, or the verse and chorus structure in pop songs), while gignetic elements might be single pitches in the changing context of a melody or tune. The authors expand on the various relationships within a melody:

> The tones themselves, not unlike points in a graph, are guide marks of a continuous line. This line arises from the morphé produced by an energetic process. In addition to this function as the phenomenalized points in an energy curve, tones form relationships with each other according to harmonic principles. We are thus faced with three layers: tone relations at the surface, tone points behind them, and an energetic process at the source. While merging into one total quality in the actuality of melody, the separate phenomena possess properties specific to each which contribute to the character of the final product.[40]

Morrissey's melodic content in this case might be considered monotone, but perhaps still "harmonically energized" in terms of teleological progress, or the movement toward an expected resolution. In a conventional case of monotone melodic contour, Levarie and Levy suggest that "the music is signally subordinate to the text.... One hears monotone in situations in which the intelligibility of the words remains paramount," such as in religious services or prayers.[41] It is improbable that "We'll Let You Know" can be compared to a prayer; perhaps Morrissey considers the words to be very important, but it is hard to believe that a popular musician would consider the music subordinate.

Richard Middleton categorizes a static melody within a "note-frame" called *chant*: "Tunes in the *chant* category virtually never leave a single note."[42] For Middleton, all melody lines, including a *chant* type, "can be regarded as having deep structural gestures lying behind them." He continues, "These can be represented graphically, but are better acted, or 'felt,' as kinetic patterns."[43] Middleton attempts to make a connection between musical gesture and physical gesture to try to understand the possible meanings of melodic form; what, then, does a static gesture signify, or what kind of affect does melodic stasis bring?

The performance of the song evokes a sense of Morrissey as being ambivalent, not giving any more than he needs to his audience. Hawkins suggests, "Emphasis on detachment as an entity allied to self-reflexivity, provides us with evidence that Morrisssey seeks to address and moderate levels of excess in stardom status."[44] In a sense, the singer is playing with his audience, holding back affect and practicing restraint. He withholds resolution so as to refuse the listener a certain pleasure; it should be noted that the tension in the song, due to this lack of resolution, is also pleasurable in a sense, in that one is being held in this state by the figure whom one desires. The resolution remains unattainable, and this state is controlled by the desired figure. Hawkins explains,

> Morrissey's refusal to be tied down to the explicit terms of his emotions becomes a main factor for exploiting oppositionality through music. In more general terms, a form of detachment boosts the sense of irony to the point that its intent can become enshrined in blatant indifference and superiority. In other words, Morrissey's ambivalence through ironic intent demonstrates how the passively aggressive character operates.[45]

Another issue arises when one considers how such an "inactivity" on Morrissey's part might affect the singer's star image. As a celebrity and a mediated figure, it might be argued that Morrissey can become eroticized as spectacle, and thus "feminized." Hubbs might also point to his "inactivity" as a sign of femininity, while the masculinity of the accompanying band is further reinforced. But, obviously, Morrissey is not a particularly feminine figure, as Hubbs would acknowledge. For instance, in the *Introducing Morrissey* video, the singer is sweating and physically active, responding to fans and their affections in an active manner. He displays marks that might lead one to think he has been in a fight or brawl. As discussed earlier, Morrissey's perceived injuries might point to his vulnerability, but they might also be read as a sign of his strength or bravery, suggesting involvement in physical combat. Also, if one compares Morrissey's physical presentation in the film to that of the singer in The Smiths, he is much larger, which might also mark a "bulking up" of his body, an attaining of a certain musculature and a further characteristic of traditional masculinity.

Concluding Remarks

As both Hubbs and Hawkins have pointed out, Morrissey problematizes the gender binary within which he might be categorized, but he does so without being obvious; he does not transgress physical masculinity by appropriating physical feminine traits. Rather, Morrissey works with tools around him, namely his artistic expression as well as his celebrity discourse, to perplex the public's perception of his persona. This is true in the case of the song that is the object of analysis in this chapter. Not only is there a glimpse into the ironic in terms of lyrical content, as Hawkins would argue is so prevalent in Morrissey's music, but there is also a demonstration of a kind of "inactivity." This stasis in terms of melodic output could be a *gesture*, to use Middleton's language, of a cautious discouragement of excess. Morrissey gives little away; lyrically, he moves to and fro from hostility and negativity to nonchalance, offering the listener no easy answer as to what his own position might be. Musically, Morrissey lets the listener wait for a resolution that ultimately does not arrive; instead, he allows the listener to languish in a lengthy instrumental section before a blistering, hostile and abrupt ending, all the while basically remaining on a single pitch. On the other hand, the singer leaves himself somewhat vulnerable if one takes into account the visual presentation of the song in the *Introducing Morrissey* film; the camera focuses on Morrissey's physical presence. During this time, Morrissey is no longer defined by his voice or by his lyrics, but rather simply by his physical being. This is something that might translate into the recording as well: Morrissey is present in the mind of the listener, although absent in terms of his voice during the instrumental portion of the song.

This song shows how difficult it is to decode Morrissey's persona and to untangle all of its complexities. This is probably how Morrissey would like it, and such a state allows for his enigma to continue to develop. To solve Morrissey would be to negate him. Furthermore, his songs reveals to the audience a mysterious part of itself. George Haas sums it up as follows:

> The words form pictures, the music evokes emotion. Morrissey uses the music and the lyrics in unison, forming a single message/metamessage. When he evokes our shadow side, the parts of our experience we have repressed, we fall from the state of innocence and become wretched like orphans cast out of our families. His lyrics describe our lives from the inside.[46]

7

"The Harsh Truth of the Camera Eye"
Morrissey's Enigma Through Mediated Performance

Morrissey's presentation of his celebrity persona on television and radio is worthy of study in terms of how he maintains his enigmatic character in the context of inquiry. The way that the singer answers and deflects questions in an interview context, and in a mediated context like a television or radio interview, reveals much about how his mystery is generated and maintained. This chapter will explore the various elements in the construction of the enigma as outlined by Roland Barthes in his book *S/Z*, in which he undertakes a structuralist study of Honoré de Balzac's story *Sarrasine*. Barthes shows, through what he calls "dilatory morphemes," how the enigma in the story is set up and maintained. The various tools that he describes can be recognized when dealing with Morrissey and the discourse that surrounds him.

Furthermore, there is a sense that the members of the press desire to solve some of his mysteries, including his insularity, his song craft and how he conducts himself in his leisure time. This desire is especially evident in the television and radio interviews that are the subject of this chapter. The hosts from both *The Late Late Show with Craig Kilborn* and *Friday Night with Jonathan Ross* search for answers from the singer but come away with little new knowledge. The answers provided by Morrissey in the interviews give the viewer some insight into how his enigma is created and maintained. His use of what Barthes describes as "dilatory morphemes" allows him to postpone the revelation of truth and to maintain his mystery.

He continues to use such tools in a radio interview with Janice Long, in which he both answers her questions in a misleading manner and also shifts the questions to her, moving the focus away from himself and his own personal life and leisure time.

Barthes' S/Z

Roland Barthes describes various methods and tools for delaying the revelation of truth in discussing Balzac's *Sarrasine*. Barthes identifies a point in the narrative where a character provides an answer to one of the central questions of the story up to this point. Yet this answer is only partial: "The truth is submerged in a list whose parataxis sweeps it along, hides it, holds it back, and finally does not reveal it at all." The parataxis (referring to the placing of phrases in sequence without any indication as to their importance) to which Barthes is referring is as follows, from *Sarrasine*: "The beauty, the wit, the charms of these two children, came solely from their mother." Barthes calls this example of "ineffective solving" an "equivocation."[1] That term also suggests the use of ambiguity to conceal truth or to avoid commitment. Barthes characterizes the equivocation further by stating that it is a "mixture of truth and snare which frequently, while focusing on the enigma, helps to thicken it." For Barthes, the snare is "a kind of deliberate evasion of the truth."[2] He suggests that the snare, "the feint, the misleading answer, the lie," is the main type of delay.[3] Barthes calls the snare and the equivocation "dilatory morphemes," part of his "hermeneutic code." In addition to the snare and the equivocation there are the partial answer, the suspended answer, and jamming, all working to "*arrest* the enigma, to keep it open."[4] Barthes also adds the "false reply" to the hermeneutic code; the false reply differs from the snare because the former emerges from error rather than from a lie or the intention to mislead.[5] The partial answer "only exacerbates the expectation of the truth."[6] The suspended (or avoided) answer occurs when the narrative itself delays the solving of an enigma; Barthes, in the context of his analysis of *Sarrasine*, describes it as follows: "Had the discourse not moved the two speakers off to a secluded sofa, we would have quickly learned the answer to the enigma." Barthes adds that if the mystery had been solved (in this case, revealing the source of the Lanty fortune), "there would have been no story to tell."⁷ Jamming refers to an "acknowledgment of insolubility."⁸ Barthes suggests that jamming occurs when "the discourse declares the enigma it proposed to be unresolved." Barthes quotes from *Sarrasine* to illustrate an instance of jamming: "Was it affection or fear? Those in society were unable to discover any clue to help them solve this problem."⁹

Barthes also links desire to the process of discovering truth: "Truth predicates an incomplete subject, based on expectation and desire for its imminent closure."¹⁰ Thus, Barthes proposes the "hermeneutic sentence." He explains:

> The proposition of truth is a "well-made" sentence; it contains a subject (theme of the enigma), a statement of the question (formulation of the enigma), its question mark (proposal of the enigma), various subordinate and interpolated clauses and catalyses (delays in the answer), all of which precede the ultimate predicate (disclosure).¹¹

His suggestion is that any enigma could be inserted into this structure of "sentence." Similarly, Barthes contends that an enigma is like a *fugue*:

> Both contain a *subject*, subject to an *exposition*, a *development* (embodied in the retards, ambiguities, and diversions by which the discourse prolongs a mystery), a *stretto* (a tightened section where scraps of answers rapidly come and go), and a *conclusion*.¹²

Barthes also considers the narrative to be like the "gradual order of melody" in a *fugue*, polyphonic, with various "voices" occurring at the same time. Barthes goes as far as setting up a kind of musical table, with rows of music notes indicating "events" that occur throughout the narrative, divided temporally into columns. This is an interesting analogy considering the subject matter of this book, a musician and the multi-faceted discourse that surrounds him. Therefore, like music, "the classic text ... is actually tabular (and not linear), but its tabularity is vectorized, it follows a logico-temporal order."¹³

In a similar way, the discourse that surrounds the celebrity is tabular, with various "streams" or "voices" constructing the celebrity's persona. Discourse provides fragments of truth, which in turn allow for the delay of answers to enigmas by the emergence of various "dilatory morphemes," in order to keep the question at the forefront of the persona. Without such "incomplete truth" with regard to the persona, there is no desire for closure, and thus no desire for sustained attention.

Another way that Barthes identifies the construction of the enigma is in terms of power. The enigma fascinates and spellbinds; Barthes formulates these elements as seduction on the part of the enigma and pleasure for the audience, for lack of a more elegant term. Power over an audience is not something that can be documented in interviews, at least explicitly, but it can be implicit in the discourse. For Barthes, in the narrative that he uses as a case study, Sarrasine is, in a sense, both freed and captured when he hears the music, *in anticipation of* the entrance of La Zambinella, the object of his desire. Barthes states, "The first (sensual) pleasure is initiatory: it serves as a basis for memory, repetition, ritual: afterwards, everything is organized to recapture this *first time*." This statement suggests that there is a certain power at work that demands from Sarrasine to continue to be exposed to the enigma; the audience is seduced by the enigma, compelling the audience to repeat the experience. The pleasure of such an experience is evident in the returning of the audience to experience it again. Barthes suggests that the pleasure can come from simple proximity to the desired object: "Proximity to the stage, and thus to the desired object, serves as a (fortuitous) point of departure for a series of hallucinatory feelings which will lead Sarrasine to solitary pleasure."[14]

Some have had similar experiences with Morrissey. A fan named Loretta Pasilas describes her meeting with Morrissey at a signing in Los Angeles:

> I was so nervous when I actually walked up to the desk. I couldn't believe I was face to face with him. It was very brief. I said, "Hello, how are you?" and he smiled and said, "Hello, Loretta, how are you?" He said my name! I almost died. I replied, "Oh, a little cold from standing outside for so long." Then he made a funny face and grabbed my hand, and said, "Oh," as if sympathizing with me. I couldn't believe he was holding my hand, so I grabbed his with both of mine and held on! Then his security people made me let go and that was it. It happened so, so fast.[15]

Morrissey was aware of Loretta's name from a post-it note attached to the DVD she wanted him to sign. Loretta's experience of pleasure is similar to Sarrasine's experience with La Zambinella, because of his proximity to her: "The proximity of La Zambinella ... is of an hallucinatory order: it is an abolition of the Wall [of Reality], identification with the object; what is involved is an hallucinatory embrace." Loretta's embrace might be construed as perhaps more literal, as she had actual physical contact with the man. Sarrasine also states, "La Zambinella's features are no longer described according to the aesthetic, rhetorical code, but according to the anatomical code (veins, planes, hair)."[16] Similarly, Loretta states, "His hair still looks good, thinning a little bit, but not too much. He looks great."[17] Her lament at the end of her description of her meeting with the singer seems to mirror the lament of Sarrasine after the performance. The experience is over: "Overcome by an inexplicable sadness, he sat down on the steps of a church. There, leaning back against a pillar, he fell into a confused meditation, as in a dream. He had been smitten by passion."[18]

Barthes' characterization of the relationship between a desired object and the one who desires it is a physical one: there exists an initial desiring, an embrace, a climax and subsequent fatigue and sadness. The desiring is established by a seduction; the seductive power of the enigma, as well as the draw that the enigma has on the desiring one, evoking sadness and eliciting the desire for more contact, imbues the desired object with a certain power. Barthes links seduction with intense pleasure and thus an intense desire for repetition.

Approaching the issue from the perspective of the performer, Mark Simpson comments:

> Morrissey has no need of sex with people so long as he continues to have it with his audience. Each stage performance is so obviously a sexual release—one of the things which makes his concerts so memorable and so sublimely, indecently unprofessional. If the yelps and yowls and the desperate, ecstatic falsettos on [various] tracks ... hint powerfully at an orgasmic release, onstage they turn into a form of musical pole dancing—a protruding, curling fleshy tongue, a salacious smile, a sadistic whipping of his mike cable, a coquettish swing of those magnificently inhibited hips, a tempting spasm of his shiftless body, a golden sparkly shirt torn from his back and flung into an audience which, as one, pounces on it and renders it to the tiniest, dampest, most fragrant fragments, while the curious love-object himself lies on the stage writhing around in ecstasy-agony or on his back, legs akimbo airborne or draped over a monitor in an obliging gesture towards his audience.[19]

In Simpson's view, the relationship between the enigma and the audience is reciprocal. Even so, pleasure is fleeting for both parties; La Zambinella states, "For me, the world is a desert. I am an accursed creature, condemned to understand happiness, to feel it, to desire it, and, like many others, forced to see it flee from me continually." This sentiment might be applied to Morrissey as well, or certainly to the persona suggested by the discourse that surrounds him. By his own admission, he is a "creature belonging nowhere: he is excluded from difference, from antithesis: he transgresses, not the sexes, but classification."[20]

Helen Dansette, while conducting an interview with Mark Simpson, tries to explain the phenomenon of physical adoration exhibited by fans at a Morrissey concert:

> As anyone's noticed who's been to a Smiths or Morrissey gig, or seen footage of them, it's intriguing the way that "straight" men behave. It's as if they are secretly titillated/intrigued, so that Morrissey's "ambiguous"/"not straight" persona allows them to explore the "not straight" aspects of themselves in a "safe" way.[21]

The intrigue or titillation experienced by these fans, then, is part of the power that Morrissey possesses over them. Sarrasine experiences a similar, rather violent, sentiment.

> Sarrasine wanted to leap onto the stage and take possession of this woman: his strength, increased a hundredfold by a moral depression impossible to explain, since these phenomena occur in an area hidden from human observation, seemed to manifest itself with painful violence.[22]

In the case of Morrissey fans, though, they follow through with their desires and often do leap onto the stage. Simpson explains, "the 'straight' boys all try to mob him and kiss him, finding in him possibly the only way to express their straight non-straightness, if you will."[23] Thus, the enigma is seductive, and its mysteries are part of that seduction as well.

Craig Kilborn: "Come Armageddon ... Now?"

In September 2002, Morrissey appeared on *The Late Late Show with Craig Kilborn*, a popular late-night talk show in the United States and Canada. Airing after the New York-based *The Late Show with David Letterman*, Kilborn's Los Angeles talk show seemed to target a younger demographic, although it aired at 12:30 A.M. every weekday. About his show, one viewer comments:

> His set looked like an erudite bachelor's lair, with wood tones, a fully stocked bookcase, overstuffed and distressed warm leather chairs, a bar cart and a sound system where he could play the stylish music of Sergio Mendes, Antonio Carlos Jobim or sample the hits of a performer on the program. There was also a "windowseat," to which he brought several female guests to do some canoodling, most famously, Catherine Zeta-Jones.
>
> When he was not figuratively or literally kissing up to his guests, the host of the show was clearly trying to do something a little different from other late

night talkers. His affirmational concepts including his catchphrase, "Proud of you," were a constant, and he had a metrosexual air, even before that term became part of the vernacular. His attempt to bring back the Ascot was only one in a series of style choices, and he was typically well groomed, keeping a hand mirror as one of the props on his over-sized Bavarian Oak desk.[24]

This description helps to contextualize Kilborn's presentation style as younger and current, yet sophisticated and trendy. Keeping with this image, Kilborn invited Morrissey on his show in 2002, at a time when the singer was without a record deal. After a period of name-dropping and begging for Morrissey to contact him, even suggesting a new show segment called "Tuesdays with Morrissey," which would showcase the singer on a weekly basis, Kilborn featured Morrissey on the show in conversation and with the performance of two songs over two nights.

After Kilborn announces that "for months, we've been searching the globe for our next guest," Morrissey emerges onto the stage to a great amount of applause, not only in terms of noise provided by the somewhat small studio audience, but also in terms of the length of time that the applause takes. Kilborn repeatedly tries to quell the applause by questioning Morrissey as to how he has been and by saying "All right, here we go." Morrissey simply basks in the attention and suggests that Kilborn not "interrupt the cheering." Interestingly, Morrissey here refers to the cheering fans as "my family," suggesting to Kilborn that they are "lovely people," terms that solidify the thought that Morrissey's relationship with his fans is an intimate one. While being alone himself, at least in terms of his public persona, being without a significant family image, he derives a certain sense of belonging from the screaming and applauding fans in the audience. While many fans know of the existence of Morrissey's mother, as well as his sister, these actual familial relationships are not in the public eye. If Morrissey were married, or if he had a public romantic relationship, perhaps there would be some connection to another "family" figure, as might be the case with other celebrities.[25]

When Morrissey is asked about what is most attractive about his performance, whether it is his lyrics or his voice, Morrissey replies, "Neither, it's just the way I look." He then adds that it is both his lyrics and his voice, but that people like the way he sings, "really." Before answering the question, Morrissey deprecates himself by suggesting that fans like nothing about him, a gesture that, in another context, might end a conversation.

His comment also suggests that people only concern themselves with physical appearances, although he ends up denying this and then answering in a more sincere manner. While his initial answer fits in the context of a late-night talk show functioning as a joke, even garnering a response from Kilborn that "it's the jaw" that attracts people, it also keeps Morrissey from having to provide his honest opinion as to what he thinks is attractive.

When Kilborn mentions that Morrissey's lyrics are sad, the singer suggests that life is "disturbing." Kilborn suggests that his own life is charming and that he never gets depressed; Morrissey responds to this by looking to the audience and repeatedly stating, "No, we don't believe that." Morrissey brings the audience into the conversation with Kilborn as part of his "family" yet again, by agreeing with them, and joining with them in disputing Kilborn's comments. Again, the spotlight moves away from Morrissey and onto Kilborn's personal life, with the audience, along with Morrissey, casting into doubt Kilborn's charming life. Morrissey does admit that he is, as a person, very positive and very happy, but that the lyrics come from a sincere and realistic worldview.

When asked from where a particular lyric emerged, Morrissey enters into a diatribe against current practices within the music industry. Instead of commenting on the original context from within which the lyric was written, Morrissey applies the lyric to current issues to which he thinks it can be applied. This is not to say that his application is wrong or that the lyric cannot be reworked to apply to the current state of affairs when he sings it; rather, his answer deflects the truth. While we hear a possible meaning for the lyric, the meaning is a current one for a song that was originally released in 1988; it is quite conceivable that the song "Everyday Is Like Sunday," actually might *not* be a "general observation of life and the Arts," as Morrissey suggests. Morrissey's answer can be considered an example of what Barthes would call an equivocation in this context; while his answer is truthful to the extent that the lyric can be applied to current conditions, his answer provides little insight into the writing process or the emotion or personality from which the particular lines were written. His application of the lyric to the current state of the American music industry in particular allows Morrissey to avoid committing to answering the question as it was originally posed. Instead, the singer takes the opportunity to discuss the state of an industry that, at the time of the interview, had no room for him.

Morrissey makes a case for himself, suggesting that record companies in America only care for "young teenagers who won't ask for money," who "assume that they're idols because they're on the television." In a way, Morrissey elevates himself above these current stars, suggesting perhaps that his longevity—and popularity despite being without a recording contract—makes him a more worthy artist, a true "idol." In turn, the record companies' interest in younger and cheaper product, as Morrissey argues in this interview, is "really destroying music." Kilborn recognizes that Morrissey has made a lot of money over the years, but the singer counteracts this by suggesting that he has been around for a long time, and that he has a strong audience, who then burst into applause. Morrissey distances himself from the current roster of celebrities in the music business by touting the length of his career, suggesting that his monetary success took place over a period of time rather than very quickly, perhaps like a singer who might be featured on a television program like *American Idol*.

When Kilborn asks Morrissey if Los Angeles is "too sunny for Morrissey," the singer doesn't really answer, but rather changes the subject. He states, "No," but then goes on to suggest that it is interesting how physically close the television studio is to his home while Kilborn was searching for him. In a way, this could be read as a kind of suspended answer, to use Barthes' terminology. While Morrissey does not really answer the question, Kilborn quickly moves on, without hesitation, to a discussion of the singer's home and life in Los Angeles. The juxtaposition of Morrissey, often considered a morose and melancholy performer, and the sun of Los Angeles, associated with happiness, vacation and activity, is a dichotomy left for another time. Kilborn's interview moves the conversation along, so that the question need not be answered; if Kilborn would have pressed the issue, perhaps the viewer would have learned a bit about how Morrissey's emotional character functions in the context of sunny Los Angeles, and how melancholy might be generated within such a bright atmosphere. Instead, the narrative of the interview moves to a brief discussion of the history of Morrissey's house: it was built by Clark Gable for his wife. Another suspended answer is provided by Morrissey when he tells Kilborn that he does like the "old history of Hollywood," but continues to talk about the house and its past inhabitants without going into any detail.

One of the more striking mysteries that is brought to light in this interview concerns what Morrissey's "typical Saturday" might be like: Morrissey answers, "I just sit around. I just stay in bed all day and watch television." When asked what he watches, he says, "Nothing." These answers are examples of Barthes' snare, a deliberate evasion of the truth. From this evasion of the truth, he begins a second diatribe concerning his dislike of commercials, again citing the prevalence of corporate greed in America. Kilborn simply agrees and tries to put the focus back onto Morrissey by suggesting that the singer is "not greedy." It seems that the host has learned from the last few minutes and acknowledges that Morrissey has been around for a long time and has always put out "good songs" without being greedy. Instead of confirming Kilborn's assumption that Morrissey has been in the business since the mid–1980s, Morrissey answers, "Since the late '40s," seemingly playing with Kilborn, but also refusing to answer the question.

Because this is apparently the first interview for an American talk show in which Morrissey has ever engaged, Kilborn feels that they might have a special bond, as they are "just chatting." When Kilborn invites Morrissey to go out with him and have a beer, Morrissey simply exclaims, "I'm available." This statement seems to sum up much of his persona, as a lone figure, uncommitted and unwanted. When Kilborn attempts to quote another line from "Everyday Is Like Sunday" and makes a mistake ("Come Armageddon ... now?"), Morrissey again brings the audience into the conversation; as fans, they know the lyric perfectly. Morrissey looks at the audience while pointing at Kilborn and says, "Nearly." When Kilborn suggests that he does not listen to Morrissey's music much because of his current love for jazz, Morrissey suggests that jazz is "going nowhere." Kilborn ends the interview abruptly by asking the viewing audience to return after the break to hear Morrissey sing a new song that has been featured on Morrissey's successful tour.

Morrissey seems to mark himself as a special celebrity, an anomaly in the music industry worthy of a record deal on his terms rather than those of the current record companies. Mark Simpson suggests that "by 1998 he had managed to bring about a state of affairs where he was such a 'special' pop star that he was actually without a record deal of any kind." He continues,

> Despite his tendency to blame record companies/the press/the Marylebone Cricket Club for these things and the fact that he stubbornly remains "merely" the most famous cult performer in the world, one that everyone has heard of

even if most don't actually own any of his records, he knows he has no one to thank but himself.²⁶

In the interview with Kilborn, Morrissey acknowledges, almost happily, that he is in fact without a record deal, but that he is taking part in a successful world tour. Nevertheless, Morrissey presents himself as a loner.

> Whatever it might do for your mental health, not to mention your bank balance and marriage prospects, this is a great strategy for holding on to one's artistic edge. Nosing into middle age, surrounded by the evidence of his past successes and acclaim, and of course the continuing love from his fans, Morrissey is still a voice sobbing in the wilderness, still complaining bitterly of the things he complained to himself as a child: that he is unloved, underrated, overlooked, neglected.²⁷

Interestingly, Morrissey suggests in this interview that although he spends his days alone watching television, he is happy. He refers to the screaming fans in the audience as his "family." There exists this constant dichotomy in his presentation.

> For all his bravura posturing as the loneliest monk, he can't quite make up his mind whether he is rejected or rejecting, which is in itself the basic and irresolvable problem of self-consciousness. He keeps people at a distance because he feels too good for the world and the people in it, and because he feels he isn't nearly good enough for the world or the people in it.²⁸

Simpson seems to capture much of what the singer conveys through the interview, Morrissey as "unloved, underrated, overlooked, neglected," willing to be the subject of Kilborn's jokes and wrongly quoted lyrical references.

Even so, his fans in the studio audience are with him and for him, audibly agreeing with Morrissey that "we all feel that way most of the time," referring to the song "Suedehead," in which the narrator describes his physical discomfort with the state of his world. They support him on the tour during which he has no record deal, and they scream at the announcement that the new song is called "First of the Gang to Die," a song many of them have heard countless times on unofficial concert recordings or at live concerts themselves. But as for Morrissey's personal life, with questions referring to the emotional or personal context from which a particular lyric emerged and the juxtaposition of a disturbed singer and sunny and "carefree" California, the viewer learns little. As such, the question of Morrissey's enigma remains, its answers delayed for the next morsel of persona in the discourse of celebrity narrative.

Jonathan Ross: "It Just Says 'M.'"

David Bret suggests that it was a "grave mistake" for Morrissey to appear on *Friday Night with Jonathan Ross*, a television program recorded live and aired on 14 May 2004 on BBC One. Bret describes the scene as follows:

> Half-expecting Ross to interview him on the stage and no doubt keen to get it over with, he stalled before being invited to the sofa, where he fidgeted constantly, tugged at his hair, often seemed short of breath on account of his frayed nerves, and persistently glanced off-camera as if in search of the nearest escape route.[29]

Bret concludes the description of the interview as "quite possibly the longest 25 minutes of [Morrissey's] career."[30] He even calls the appearance on Ross' show a "fiasco," which, according to Bret, adversely affected the next few months of promotional appearances for the singer.

Morrissey's interview with Ross might have not been as bad as Bret suggests. While Bret makes an argument that there was a homosexual subtext to one of the preceding interviews, that there was a bit of a pairing of a male guest, apparently "crazy" about Dean Butterworth, Morrissey's "straight" drummer, by Ross, this subtext is not apparent in the interview with the singer. Bret does not make it clear why this would be uncomfortable for Morrissey, in any case. While it might be construed that Morrissey was uncomfortable during the interview, his wit is still very evident, and he does not appear to be upset. His constant fidgeting and "shyness" could be read as simply an expected pattern of behavior for the singer, given his mystery and reclusiveness; as announced by Ross in Morrissey's introduction, this was apparently his first British television interview in 17 years. What is strikingly evident in this interview is Morrissey's humor.

For instance, Ross asks the singer if he could call him "Steven," the singer's given name. Morrissey immediately says no. In a manner similar to Kilborn's, Ross is attempting to become friends with the singer, even if only for appearances, and for the short time of the interview. Morrissey suggests that even though that was his name when he was a little boy, he "wasn't a very happy little boy," and that he changed his name to distance himself from the past, a move that he himself believes was "quite clever."

When asked what might appear on Morrissey's driver's license, Morrissey jokes that it says "Mozzer," one of the many variations on his name used by fans and the press, as well as by Ross later in the interview. On an even more humorous note, Morrissey adds, "No, it just says 'M.'" Again, Ross asks for friendship, which Morrissey declines, because of Ross' Oscar Wilde haircut. When Ross asks Morrissey, "Don't you think this tousled boy's look works for me?" Morrissey answers emphatically and with a change of vocal tone, "No, I don't," garnering applause from the audience. It should be noted that the audience present for this interview, though polite and certainly quick to make noise, is not as raucous as the obviously more fan-centric crowd present at the Kilborn taping. There are no screams or vocal responses from this audience.

Ross then moves on to promote the upcoming album, *You Are the Quarry*, suggesting that it is the singer's best solo album, to which Morrissey responds, "I think it's my best *ever* album." This is the second instance in this interview where Morrissey attempts to distance himself from his past, earlier by refusing the use of his childhood name, and presently by discounting not only his earlier solo work but also the critically acclaimed work of The Smiths. He obscures his past accomplishments by suggesting that the new album is his "fifty-second" solo release instead of his tenth, as erroneously suggested by Ross. Ross suggests that the album is so good that he almost cried. Morrissey, unfazed, asks why he did not, to which Ross responds, "Because it wasn't quite that good."

The interview continues with an exploration of Morrissey's relationships with those around him. Ross asks him if people try to get close to him, "because you seem like someone who isn't easy to get close to," and that this would be an enticement for them to try to get close to the singer. Morrissey does not agree with this and answers, "No, I've not noticed that, to be honest." He does not recognize the desire that he elicits in his fans or, in the context of the question, in those around him; he does not acknowledge this publicly.

Morrissey is presented here as a difficult and solitary figure, only able to befriend a few loyal people who have been around for a long time; to "suffer fools" is a "waste of time" for Morrissey. Morrissey suggests that those who have wanted to become closer to him have backed away when they "found out what I'm really like." Jonathan Ross asks the important question, "What are you really like, then?" Morrissey's answer is an example of Barthes' jamming. He states, "I haven't a clue. I've got no idea." The answer cannot be revealed because not even Morrissey knows what he himself is like, apparently. There can be no resolution to the enigma through this line of inquiry.

Like in the Kilborn interview, Ross asks Morrissey what he does with his time, to which Morrissey again refers to very mundane things: listen to music, eat and listen to the radio. Notice that unlike the Kilborn interview, he doesn't mention television at all, or staying in bed for that matter, a fact that indicates the dubious nature of his answers.

Ross, like Kilborn, also recognizes Morrissey's good physique and musculature, and asks him if he works out. Again, like the Kilborn interview, Morrissey responds that he never works out, but that he refrains from eating meat, which contributes to his health. Like his diatribe against commercialism in the Kilborn interview, Morrissey takes the opportunity here to discuss his views on vegetarianism; this is an issue that has been at the forefront of Morrissey's public image since at least the release of the album *Meat Is Murder* in 1985.

The conversation moves to the subject of Morrissey's audience at this point. Ross acknowledges the diversity of the singer's fan base and wonders if the fans appreciate him now more than in the past. Morrissey agrees that this might be the case, but it is because he is "quite real," as opposed to simply being respected because of his longevity in the music business. Evoking some of the same sentiments as in the Kilborn interview, Morrissey expresses his disappointment with the current music scene, where "it's completely impossible to be natural in pop music."

Either trying to continue the joking or to make Morrissey uncomfortable, Ross shows the singer a clip from the British game show *Stars in Their Eyes*, in which a normal person (or, in this case, comedian Harry Hill) becomes a celebrity for the night (Hill becomes Morrissey). During the clip, in which Hill sings "This Charming Man," complete with Morrissey glasses, hearing aid and a fistful of flowers, the camera switches back to Morrissey with his fingers in his ears, trying to block out the sound. Ross notices that Morrissey did not like the performance by Hill. Morrissey states that he has not looked like that in 20 years, and that the old image of him from his days with The Smiths, assumedly a more recognizable image for older viewers, is not one with which Morrissey would like to be associated. It seems that although Morrissey at certain points wishes to embrace his past, like his early adoption of vegetarianism, he more often wishes to distance himself from it. The reinvention or evolution of his persona means the destruction of past images of himself, which suggests a certain instability of his celebrity persona. One can construct a persona of Morrissey, but it is increasingly fragmented, and when one constructs an image of some detail, it is discounted by the singer himself.

Ross moves the conversation to the topic of Morrissey's songwriting techniques. Morrissey suggests that songwriting is never a mechanical process and that he constantly feels the need to write an "account of life." After Ross poses a somewhat lengthy and detailed question, including options regarding how a Morrissey song might be put together, Morrissey states that "it all just falls into place," a statement that tells the viewer nothing about his writing process, neither discounting nor approving Ross' suggestions. Morrissey quickly states that Ross is also quite talented, moving the attention away from himself.

At this point of the interview, Ross asks if Morrissey is writing an autobiography, something that Morrissey told Janice Long he was doing on a radio interview in October 2002. (Morrissey claims that he has been approached by "several people" that were interested in publishing his autobiography, but he doubts its publication, due to so many "injunctions," on BBC Radio Two on 2 October 2002.) Morrissey confirms this but suggests that he has "a few chapters left." Simpson, though, seems to doubt this rumor. He explains, "I can't help thinking that such a book from him is a little ... superfluous. After all, he's already written and published his biography over the last twenty years or so, and it's note perfect."[31] Simpson, of course, is referring to Morrissey's music, apparently the most accurate window into the authentic Morrissey.

Ross again refers to Morrissey's difficult personality, suggesting that every album Morrissey releases seems to settle old scores, and that an autobiography would function in the same way. Morrissey simply replies, "Life is a serious subject." Ross suggests that he should relax, and "come out with me and play tennis." Similar to Kilborn, Ross wants to spend leisure time with the singer, and similar to that earlier interview where Morrissey confirms his availability, Morrissey considers the invitation, asking at what time they might want to meet.

In reference to Morrissey's media exposure around the release of *You Are the Quarry* in 2004, Simpson suggests that the singer was a sort of "media whore," but that he saved himself with his "difficult personality": "His performance on the Jonathan Ross show reminded us why he could never become a regular on TV couches. He's just too prickly."³² In addition, Simpson is relieved that Ross does not mention sexuality in the interview, considering his penchant for playing with "gender identity, camping about with his Oscar Wilde hairdo and telling everyone to be a 'metrosexual.'" Simpson explains, "I suspect that if Jonno had used the 'M' word [metrosexual] Moz would have spontaneously combusted. I doubt Moz would allow himself to be categorised as anything other than a *Mozzasexual*."³³ When asked if Morrissey is in fact a metrosexual, Simpson replies, "No, he's more transsexual. He's Rita Tushingham trapped in the body of a rather handsome, retired midfielder circa 1961."³⁴

Janice Long: "The Rumour Is More Important Than the Truth."

In December 2004, toward the end of the promotional period for *You Are the Quarry*, Morrissey and his band recorded a session for Janice Long's radio show at the BBC's Maida Vale studios. In this session, they performed four songs including two new tracks and a remake of Patti Smith's "Redondo Beach," and Morrissey took a few moments for an interview in which Long recognizes the successes that 2004 brought to the singer. It is obvious throughout this interview that Morrissey and Long have a fine rapport, and this interview is an effective example of Morrissey's ability to shift the focus of the interview from himself to another person. This shift is perhaps facilitated by the very comfortable relationship that he and Long seem to enjoy, which is in itself a rare occurrence if the singer's character is as difficult or repelling as he might have one believe. Thus, Long seems almost willing at certain times in the interview to engage with Morrissey in a more conversational manner than might befit other interviewers.

The exchange begins with Janice Long referring to Morrissey by his full name, as "Steven Patrick Morrissey," something that Morrissey discourages Ross from doing. Morrissey does not protest and goes on to suggest that Long has been "perfect," as opposed to Morrissey's past year, which has been enjoyable "for the most part," but "there's always room for improvement." As to rumors of Morrissey's retirement, he replies, "The rumour is more important than the truth," a statement that perhaps sheds more light on Morrissey's strategies than any other. His intention is not to quell rumors but rather to perpetuate them. Instead of either admitting or denying the rumor, he commits to no answer, at one point suggesting that the new songs he is performing might simply be for this session only rather than for another album.

Because of the timing of this interview, taking place at the end of the promotional period for his album, Morrissey is able to take a critical look at his performance during the past year. Long exclaims that she has seen Morrissey on television appearing in contexts she would never have expected. In answering Long, Morrissey speaks in a careful manner. Here, and throughout this interview, Morrissey is very hesitant to refer to himself. He rarely uses the personal pronoun in answering these questions but rather uses a more generic "you." For instance, instead of saying, "I think somehow I feel I have a duty to be less invisible," he states, "*You* feel *you* have a duty to be less invisible." While this might simply be a style of speaking when one discusses expected behaviors, it is noteworthy that Morrissey rarely refers to himself anywhere in this interview. By justifying his appearance on various "odd" television shows because "you have a duty to be less invisible, especially if people are buying the songs you've placed out there," does not necessarily suggest that he has in fact made himself any less invisible, or that he has not hidden himself, in a sense, from the audience that views him.

Long asks if Morrissey would ever appear on the British reality game show *I'm a Celebrity*, which features minor celebrities in a jungle-like environment to be voted off of the show by viewers, Morrissey replies, "I've never been approached in any way for anything." Morrissey would not place himself in the same context as minor celebrities, nor would he consider himself worthy of such a spectacle, it would seem. His addition of "for anything" at the end of that statement, and Long's subsequent accusations of Morrissey's dishonesty, have a somewhat sexual undertone to them. Morrissey has never been approached *in any way*, and Long does not believe it.

When asked if Morrissey would ever consider acting, the singer states, "I don't think you should do it," giving advice to Long rather than answering her question. For one who refrains from watching television, Morrissey is quite knowledgeable, not only about *I'm a Celebrity* but also about *Holby City*, a British medical drama. Morrissey asks Long for suggestions as to what kind of acting might be appropriate for him, although Long can supply no answers.

When Long asks Morrissey what kind of music he is listening to, he provides a snare, a lie, suggesting that he only listens to his own band. Long accuses him of lying and confronts him, saying that she knows he likes certain bands. Instead of acknowledging the truth, he asks Long which bands she thinks he likes. Morrissey again shifts from the one being interviewed to become the interviewer. This is a kind of suspended or avoided answer for Morrissey; the question does not need to be answered by him because Long instead can provide the answer, although not necessarily the one he himself might give. This stance is reinforced when Long asks Morrissey how he will be spending Christmas; Morrissey refuses to answer, telling Long to mind her own business. He asks Long where she is going for Christmas instead.

This portion of the interview is a triumph for Morrissey; he takes control of the interview by shifting the questioning toward Long. It seems that Long recognizes the jamming employed by Morrissey; she answers his question in detail, and in a conversational style. This portion of the interview indicates the kind of relationship that Long has with Morrissey, as she is willing to answer his questions that deal with *her* leisure time and *her* relationships.

The interview ends with Morrissey entering into yet another diatribe, this time about politics and the election of the latest President of the United States. The interview ends quickly with amiable departing words by both parties and the performance of a new song.

Concluding Remarks

It is interesting that there are similarities in the two television interviews, even though they were taped and televised two years apart. Both Craig Kilborn and Jonathan Ross attempt to befriend Morrissey, even if the friendship is meant to be only a cursory one. And, in both cases, that friendship is not explicitly accepted, with Morrissey simply stating his availability to Kilborn and asking what time he might come by for a tennis match with Ross. Morrissey has reservations, though; he disapproves of Kilborn's love for jazz, and he cannot be friends with a meat-eating Ross, except for over the phone. If either of these hosts got to know him, though, they might not like him; Morrissey himself does not know what he is like, so he is unable to identify what part of him causes offense.

Both hosts acknowledge Morrissey's physical presentation. They both mention that although he is in his mid–40, he appears exceptionally fit; he denies working out at all, but suggests that his diet has made him healthy. In these presentations, even his physical appearance becomes an enigma. Like the source of the Lanty fortune in Balzac's *Sarrasine*, the hosts and their viewers have no idea what contributes to Morrissey's fortunate physical condition; he provides a partial answer — that he refrains from eating flesh — and thus delays the truth.

In the interview with Janice Long, Morrissey seems more at ease, a state that is perhaps facilitated by the easy approach of Long, who, unlike Kilborn and Ross, is obviously a friend as well as a fan. This is so much the case that she is comfortable in disclosing familial information to the singer, and she seems to afford the privilege to have conversations with the singer away from the media, as suggested by her mention of their last meeting in Birmingham. As a friend, if Long could be considered such, she places herself in a position where Morrissey might be comfortable to enter into a conversation with her in the context of an interview. In other words, Morrissey — and, in turn, the listeners — gain information about Janice Long's personal life and leisure time while gaining no new knowledge about those aspects of Morrissey's life. When Long tries to get to the truth, Morrissey moves the dialogue to focus on Long. The shifting of the conversation away from Morrissey strengthens the mystery that surrounds him; it is probable that even if Morrissey is interested in personal details regarding Janice Long's Christmas vacation, the listening audience is more interested in personal details regarding Morrissey.

Morrissey's presentation of his celebrity persona through these interviews shows how he generates and maintains his enigmatic nature in the context of inquiry. Morrissey's use of "dilatory morphemes" allows him to control, in a sense, the discourse that surrounds him, and allows him to postpone the revelation of truth, to maintain his mystery and, in turn, the desire to know him and details of his personal life. These interviews present Morrissey in the context of speaking with another person, where most fans would only dream of being. Instead of answering questions directly, Morrissey lies or shifts the focus. He rarely provides concrete answers to the questions, using his time to embark on diatribes, even if they are worthy ones. His enigma remains intact even in this highly revealing context in which, unlike print, every physical attribute is observable in real time and, in the case of a television interview, in close-up rather than in the edited and processed arena of music video. Morrissey presented through interviews maintains his enigmatic character; no harsh truth is revealed through the camera eye.

Conclusion

It is important to contemplate the process of how a celebrity maintains a sense of enigma, because it reveals the starting point and development of desire. This work attempts to outline some ways by which a celebrity can continually generate the discourse that surrounds his or her star image. Due to the inherent characteristics of celebrity discourse, it is impossible for a fan or audience to know all that there is to know about a certain celebrity. In fact, the very nature of a celebrity persona suggests that a fan could never know the true person that exists behind that persona. Thus, there is always a sense of the unknown when dealing with celebrities; they are not ever completely revealed to the fan. Their true identity is further obscured by the media, which serves to reveal information in pieces over time.

The discourse surrounding Morrissey has been developed through various means, including through album reviews, some of which appear in the second chapter. Morrissey's biographical details provide a backdrop upon which his discourse unfolds. It is clear that his star image and the discourse that surrounds him is constructed from the reviews and controversies presented in the first and second chapters, and that his celebrity discourse continues to be produced. With every new interview or review, or any new detail of Morrissey's personal life, this discourse becomes richer, in terms of how new elements interact with those already present in the discourse and the depth that new facts give to a persona. It is interesting how Morrissey both relies upon and dismisses elements that are part of his past. While he seems to have a respect for the past, in some cases he is quick to let go of it.

As an example of an enigmatic celebrity, active in terms of the creation of new discourse, Morrissey can be read as a celebrity who gains a kind of "masculinist" power while being under the eroticizing gaze of an audience. Morrissey is subject to that gaze, but he retains a "masculinity" because of his continual ambiguity. The conflicts and mysteries that are presented in the case of Morrissey serve to maintain his enigma. Furthermore, Morrissey plays with gender performance and conventional gender roles. As is evident in chapter 4, Morrissey in a music video is certainly the focus of an audience's gaze, but his appropriation of certain visual elements makes him a difficult figure to label as "passive."

Morrissey has often appropriated elements that could be considered to indicate "lack" and injury in his music videos. Morrissey is presented as injured and, in a sense, incomplete. Furthermore, he displays a sense of both presence and absence, present on the screen, yet physically absent from the viewer, and ultimately unknown. His "lack" lends a complexity to his star image, and one with which the viewer engages when watching one of his videos.

Morrissey in live performance presents unique and peculiar elements of his otherwise-enigmatic star image, including physicality and a sense of narcissism. It is in live performance that one is introduced to Julia Riley, a fan who is present at almost all of his concerts, and someone whom the singer knows on a first-name basis. His throwing of a shirt into the crowd allows an audience member lucky enough to receive a piece to take home a part of Morrissey's physical self, or at least something that has actually touched his skin and soaked in his sweat. The large letters that spelled out Morrissey's name on stage during the 2004 tour led to no confusion as to who was the center of the concert experience and pointed to a powerful narcissism on the part of the singer. The concert experience is an interesting and rich example of a site within which the audience engages with a physically present Morrissey.

The audience also engages with the music of Morrissey, and this musical output contributes in an important way to the discourse of the singer. It is usually through the avenue of music, and specifically Morrissey's voice, that one is introduced to him. Therefore, there should be much weight placed on the music as a site of contact with Morrissey. As is clear in chapter 6, there are certain elements of inactivity that Morrissey presents in his music. The analysis of "We'll Let You Know" illustrates both the larger picture of inactivity in terms of melodic contour and also the nuances of harmonic dissonance and their effects on the communication of meaning.

The final chapter presents Morrissey featured in the arena of inquiry, mediated through television and radio. His enigma continues to be built and preserved through tools that could be documented using Barthes' "hermeneutic code." By postponing the solution to his enigma, these tools allow him to remain a mystery. Morrissey's ability to shift the focus from himself to his interviewer is clear in these interviews, and while this tactic demonstrates the effectiveness of the tools that Barthes identifies, it also indicates Morrissey's cleverness in the environment of a spoken interview. Furthermore, the interview with Janice Long is a rare example of Morrissey in a comfortable atmosphere, apparently with someone with whom he speaks away from the context of the media. Conversely, Long is comfortable with Morrissey, which allows the singer to more effectively shift the focus away from himself.

Ringleader of the Tormentors

Morrissey continues to confound his fans and his critics; he has stated recently that he has moved to Rome, because of the "crush" of fans in Los Angeles, a city that he also found particularly frightening. Morrissey explains: "I just find everybody so free and stylish in Rome. Nothing really matters, tomorrow doesn't matter and people will bump into you in the street and not even say anything, whereas in Los Angeles it's a horrible infringement."[1] His move to Rome from Los Angeles adds an interesting dynamic to the nationalistic element of Morrissey's star image. As the Italian magazine *XL*, commenting on the long-running popularity of The Smiths, states, "The Smiths are long gone, yet their icon is still intact. And it's getting a *tricolore* tinge [*tricolore* referring to the three colors of the Italian flag]. After London, Manchester and Los Angeles, Moz ... has chosen Rome."[2] While he seems to have called Rome his home, he has not yet lived there: "I don't live anywhere. I sold my Los Angeles home and all my things are in a cellar. I'm looking for a home, but in Rome, they all seem to hold on to their properties."[3] In an interview with Paul Morley, Morrissey states that he lives nowhere, yet he calls himself an "Italianophile." Morley attempts to get to the truth regarding Morrissey's reasoning for coming to Rome by suggesting that the singer fell in love with someone from the city:

[MORLEY:] You've moved to Rome to be with someone.
[MORRISSEY:] Something.
[MORLEY:] Because of someone.
[MORRISSEY:] Something.
[MORLEY:] Someone?
[MORRISSEY:] Something.[4]

Morrissey will not reveal to Morley what this "something" is, but he makes a point to refute any idea that he is in love with someone from Rome. Coinciding with this embrace of Italian-ness as a part of his persona is a collection of songs that Morley suggests reflect "a sonic discovery, an emotional discovery, a reawakening, a new focus."[5] The album is entitled *Ringleader of the Tormentors*, released in 2006.

The Italian influence is clear on the first single from the album, "You Have Killed Me," released in March 2006. In the song, Morrissey appropriates Italian cultural figures here by referring to Pier Paolo Pasolini, controversial film director and poet, and his first film *Accattone*, which takes as its subject matter the violent life of a pimp in the slums of Rome. He also refers to Anna Magnani, the lead actress in Pasolini's film *Mamma Roma*. About the films of Pasolini, Morrissey suggests that they are authentic, that they convey a sense of unmediated reality. For Morrissey, Pasolini was "an extreme genius. But he also looked great and he didn't seem to be impressed by other people. He didn't have to be anybody else, he was being himself in his own world and even though he was obsessed with the lowlife, that was all he wanted."[6] In addition to Pasolini, Morrissey refers to Luchino Visconti, whose film, *Rocco e i suoi fratelli*, Morrissey thinks is a masterpiece.[7]

Like Pasolini, Morrissey also strives to be himself, without the pressure of having to be someone else. He states:

> Whatever people invest within you, that's what you are and there's nothing I can do about that. People can say what they like. I can't really control how people view a situation so why obsess about it? And why set out to correct everybody on the planet with the view they have about you?[8]

His comments are sparked by the interest generated by lyrics in one of his recent songs, "Dear God Please Help Me." Tom Doyle writes, "Here, Morrissey is wry and explicit ... openly homoerotic ... though keen to offer more information than is perhaps necessary."[9] Criticized for his sudden gender-specificity in this song, Morrissey replies that he understands how his lack of gender specificity can be read as a way of avoiding truth: "But I don't think I'd be any less of a conundrum to people if I actually wrote or sang in a deafeningly specific way.... I am simply inexcusably me."[10] When Morrissey is asked about the song's detailed lyrics in *Mojo* magazine, Morrissey responds,

> Well, I didn't really think there was ever something I couldn't write about, but unless it was a strip of me then I didn't really want to venture into anything. The song has to be true, otherwise it's pointless. And it is, it's very true.[11]

Morrissey seems to suggest that the homosexual connotation of the lyric is true. By suggesting that the song is a "strip of me," he is "admitting" to a homosexual experience in the present tense. Doing so seems to be out of character for Morrissey.

In the *XL* interview, Gianni Santoro confronts him about the song: "Fans are already talking about it as the 'coming out' song. It has been marked that way." Morrissey answers, "Oh my God. Coming out? From where? Towards where? I am myself. Period."[12] When the *NME* suggests that the song is about one's battle between homosexuality and religion, Morrissey replies, "I don't think homosexuality is mentioned in the song." When confronted again with the specific gender reference, Morrissey answers, "We all have sexuality and why is mine so unique? So I very childishly feel inclined to say nothing at all and often wonder if I did say to people that I am very close to somebody who is female, what would the reaction be?"[13] If one can read Morrissey's comments in *Mojo* as an admittance of homosexuality, his comments in the *NME* can be read as an affirmation of his heterosexuality. It seems that even with a song that explicitly describes a physical encounter that can be read as homosexual, Morrissey's own sexual preference remains a mystery. Morrissey's answer to the *NME* is an equivocation, to use Barthes' term, an ambiguity to conceal the truth and, ultimately, to avoid commitment. It is left to the interviewer to decide how to interpret Morrissey's answer. Furthermore, Morrissey performed The Smiths' song, "Girlfriend in a Coma," during the opening concert of his tour in Tulsa, Oklahoma, on 13 March 2006. If "Dear God Please Help Me" could be considered as containing homosexual lyrics, "Girlfriend in a Coma" is arguably one of Morrissey's most heterosexual songs, and it is also gender-specific.

Italy has influenced Morrissey is other ways. The video for "You Have Killed Me" also bears a *tricolore* tinge in that it features Morrissey performing the song on a televised song contest or talk show stage from the 1970s, introduced in Italian, with bassist Gary Day sporting a tricolored guitar strap. The video evokes a past time not originating in England, but rather the context of the European song contests, like the annual Sanremo festival where The Smiths themselves performed in 1987. Keeping with this theme, Morrissey has stated that he loves the music of Gigliola Cinquetti and Rita Pavone. Cinquetti won the Sanremo festival in 1964 at the age of 16 and went on to win the Eurofestival that same year. Pavone, a singer and actress, was a success through the 1960s, enjoying multiple hits and successful movie and television appearances. On Italian music, Morrissey states,

> At six years old I bought *Heart* by Rita Pavone. I still have it. And then there was ... Gigliola Cinquetti, do you know the song *Sì*? She represented Italy at the Eurofestival [in 1974]. And she came in second place. My new video is a reference to the festival.[14]

As Bracewell and Zuberi suggest, Morrissey has evoked England's past; however, here Morrissey is evoking a past that is outside of his cultural context, although he does qualify himself by suggesting that he was exposed to Italian music as a child. In a sense, by evoking a past time, and one as perhaps *uncomfortable* to modern viewers as an early 1970s song contest, Morrissey relegates himself also to an older time. While in some cases such a move might imbue a kind of authenticity, with Morrissey it serves to ridicule rather than authenticate. Why would Morrissey present himself as showcased on a 1970s song contest, with visual style being decidedly unstylish? While such an approach might be *de rigeur* in 2006, with the popularity of 1970s references in popular culture, and while it might indicate a certain respect that Morrissey has for that era of Italian music, it also indicates another moment of Morrissey's lack. He is only able to be showcased in such a manner, relegated to an old and old-fashioned venue, away from his own cultural context, receiving polite applause from an unknowing — and, in actuality, a false — audience. Scenes of the audience are actually from stock footage from the time period.

It should be noted that Morrissey's humor is also evident here. For instance, throughout his performance in the video, Morrissey smirks and smiles, seemingly pleased with his performance. Furthermore, guitarist Alain Whyte is featured playing the drums while guitarist Boz Boorer is shown being rather serious and almost angry as he is playing this somewhat upbeat song. These elements, then, lend an air of irony to the video; Boorer is very serious even though his colleague is uncharacteristically playing the drums, a move that anyone who is familiar with Morrissey and his band would find humorous.

Morrissey evokes not only a certain sense of Italian-ness from a particular time but also a sense of other parts of Europe. In the final song on the album, "At Last I Am Born," Morrissey describes the evolution of the narrator of the song from a difficult child to Claude Brasseur. Brasseur is a French actor who appeared in almost 90 films, including those by Jean-Luc Godard, but is practically an unknown figure in North America. Godard's 1964 film *Bande à part* (or "Band of Outsiders") features Brasseur as "Arthur," one of a pair of petty criminals who attempt to rob an older woman of her money. It is unclear if Morrissey is evoking the actor for the role that he plays as a criminal or whether the actor's allure comes from the cultural context in which he worked.

Morrissey continues to move in and out of the public consciousness, beyond the realm of his fan base. On 27 March 2006, Morrissey made a statement available through his semi-official website, *True to You*. In the statement, Morrissey announces that he will not tour in Canada to promote his latest album, and he asks his fans to boycott all Canadian goods, in protest of the annual seal hunt. The seal hunt is a much-publicized hunting of the harp seal population in eastern Canada in late March, during which around 325,000 animals are killed. Their pelts and meat are then exported abroad. Morrissey not only condemns the slaughter of the seals but also equates the Canadian government with the Nazi regime. He writes:

> The Canadian Prime Minister ... states that the slaughter is necessary because it provides jobs for local communities, but this is an ignorant reason for allowing such barbaric and cruel slaughter of beings that are denied life simply because somebody somewhere might want to wear their skin. Construction of German gas chambers also provided work for someone — this is not a moral or sound reason for allowing suffering.... Canada has placed itself alongside China as the cruelest and most self-serving nation.[15]

Morrissey's comments were met with much anger by Canadian fans and were featured in a report on CBC news, Canada's national public broadcaster.[16] He reiterated his stance against Canada in a statement made on 31 March 2008, where he writes, "This Canadian government is happy to drag the global image of its own country down, and make it a place that people such as I couldn't bear to visit."[17] Most recently, regarding the animal welfare laws in China, Morrissey has stated, "You can't help but feel that the Chinese are a subspecies."[18] His actions demonstrate the power that he has to enter public consciousness. While some might suggest that his stance and controversial comments are simply means for greater publicity, Morrissey is obviously still able to command attention.

Violence

The singing voice has, in the past, been theorized as a site of pleasure for the listener. Roland Barthes and others explore the way that physicality in the voice translates into a kind of pleasure, perhaps a physical identification of the singer by the listener. The singing voice, though, in popular music in particular, can also be a site of violence. There are instances of violence *in* the voice, as might be argued in the case with Canadian songstress Leslie Feist, whose past vocal injury now permeates her performance and star image. Also, there are instances of violence *through* the voice, such as in the case of Morrissey.

Morrissey's song "It's Not Your Birthday Anymore," from his 2009 album *Years of Refusal*, is inundated with violence. The lyrics speak of some ambivalent event, perhaps sexual in nature, suggesting some sort of violence between two people, without specificity of gender. His voice, though, also exhibits evidence of violence, in terms of its timbre and intensity. As discussed earlier, Koestenbaum suggests that such intensity "interrupts and reverses our ground." As stated earlier, Wood suggests that such a voice points to a "thrilling readiness to go beyond so-called natural limits, an erotics of risk and defiance." Morrissey's song "It's Not Your Birthday Anymore" is a striking example of the manifestation of violence in the singing voice. It can be argued that the voice is a compelling site of pleasure because of its potential for violence, *in* and *through* the voice.

Leslie Feist, as a case study for violence in the voice, embodies the idea of popular music as something loud. During her time with the punk band Placebo in the 1990s, Feist began to bleed from her throat, due to the high volume and frequency of forced singing during a tour. The vocal injury that resulted from the "overflowing of her channels," to use Walser's terms, forced her to enter into a full year of therapy.

This injury forced Feist to sing softly but also allowed Feist to begin singing in a way that she describes as "jhai," a concept that might shed light on Morrissey's own vocal delivery. From publicity during the promotion of *Let It Die*, her album from 2004, "jhai" is described as "a detached manner of singing especially suited to very emotional material. The emotion is underplayed, never quite lets go and leaves room for the listener to crawl inside." Also, "Like line drawings as opposed to detailed paintings, these songs leave you space to fill in the emotional blanks."[19] This style of singing manifests itself with the singer no longer worrying about singing well or with precision. "Jhai" also carries with it a suggestion of relaxed singing, without much worry or stress. For Feist, "jhai" is also an opposite presentation of her teenaged self.

In the case of Feist, violence is experienced *in* the singing voice, a moment of violence that affects not only her star image but also her very artistic expression. In the case of Morrissey, violence is experienced *through* the singing voice. Of interest is the inherent violence in Morrissey's song "It's Not Your Birthday Anymore." The song begins with the description of someone saying no, with the narrator dismissing the negative response. The chorus features the narrator expressing that the time for niceties is over, now that the birthday has passed, suggesting that the overly kind things said the day before were not truly meant.

Later in the song, Morrissey sings that all the gifts given for the birthday cannot compare to what the narrator considers some sort of affection shown to the subject, at that moment, on the floor. Furthermore, there is no need to be kind to the subject, as the narrator no longer feels the need to see the subject happy or included now that the birthday has passed. So, then, what kind of affection, exactly, is the narrator offering, after the birthday is over, on the floor?

If "jhai" is manifest in Feist's voice due to the violence in the voice, is a kind of "jhai" manifest as well *through* the singing voice? Can Morrissey's singing voice in "It's Not Your Birthday Anymore" be considered "jhai," with the (terrible) emotion underplayed, never quite letting the listener go, leaving space for the listener to fill in the emotional blanks? Barthes writes of the violence inherent in language, due to the fact that "no utterance is able directly to express the truth and has no other mode at its disposal than the force of the word."[20] He continues: "We know that violence is always there (in language) and it is precisely this that can lead

Conclusion 189

us to decide to bracket out its signs."[21] Morrissey, then, "brackets out violence's signs."

Such a reading, though, is problematized when Morrissey sings in an explicitly emotional way, perhaps exhibiting a more explicit violence in the singing voice, a kind of "overflowing" of Morrissey's own "channels." Morrissey, generally, does not sing loudly. Consider the song "Used to Be a Sweet Boy," from his 1994 album *Vauxhall and I*. Morrissey's gentle vocal delivery is strikingly different from some of his singing in "It's Not Your Birthday Anymore."

Elizabeth Wood writes of the voice "overflowing sonic boundaries," of going beyond "natural limits" (again, evoking Walser's conception of distortion). Of interest is her suggestion that such an "overflowing of the channels" constitutes what Wood calls an "erotics of risk and defiance," terms that suggest a potential of injury and violence. Morrissey moves from singing about violence (that is, violence *through* the voice) to embodying this violence (violence *in* the voice). He moves from singing about violence to *singing violence*, from singing about committing an act of violence to committing violence — *in* the singing voice. This is not unlike Feist's injury, except without the (physical) blood.

Furthermore, as Wood suggests, this violence, overflowing, while also "bracketing out," is a kind of site for desire, "a desire for desire itself." If Koestenbaum suggests that there is an act of desire demonstrated in the consuming sound (that is, in listening to — in being in the same place as — the sound), can something be said, then, of the "consuming" sound, both for the listener and the victim in the song?

Violence and desire, both of these residing at the site of consumption, are experienced by the listener consuming the music, by the narrator of the song "consuming" a victim, by the listener being "consumed" by the sound, and finally by the victims — both the character in Morrissey's song, post-birthday, and Leslie Feist, the injured songstress. In the case of the listener, consuming and consumed, the violence leads to something else — a kind of knowing, what Barthes suggests is the source of language, that meaning that is unable to be expressed, causing all language to be brutal, violent.

What do we do with this violence, then? In Feist's case, violence *in* the voice, violence results in rebuilding. In Morrissey's case, the results are less easy to determine. If Morrissey moves from singing about violence (that is, violence *through* the voice) to singing violence (that is, violence *in* the voice), perhaps there is the possibility of rebuilding there as well. And perhaps that is where desire resides also, in the potential for something new, something Other, that which is not yet but might be. These are encouraging words for those of us who are consumed and those who are constantly being consumed, violently, by Morrissey's singing voice.

Avenues for Further Study

With this new material, it is clear that Morrissey continues to be an enigma to his audience. The construction of his star image is a process that can be studied in greater detail; there are many other aspects of his persona that should be explored. The depth of his persona would yield much in terms of how his enigma is constructed and maintained. In addition, Morrissey would be a worthy object of study simply in terms of his lyrical output as poetry. The singer has been associated with a group of 20th-century poets, often cited as his influences. For instance, Bracewell links Morrissey to W. H. Auden and Philip Larken. In the April 2006 issue of *Mojo*, Morrissey is included as an equal in a group of poets including Auden, Larkin, T. S. Eliot, John Betjeman and Stevie Smith.[22] Gavin Hopps' book, *Morrissey: The Pageant of His Bleeding Heart*, is a worthy step in this direction.

There continues to be a difficulty in approaching the voice and its allure. There is a definite lack of appropriate vocabulary with which to approach the study of the voice, due perhaps to its abstract nature, and because rock music that features the voice is generally, and certainly in the case of Morrissey, specifically written for — and by — that particular voice. Often in a discussion of an instrumental piece and its interpretation by a player of a particular instrument, the focus is on the piece itself, rather than on the tone of the instrument that performs it. In music like that of Morrissey, the voice is an intrinsic part of the piece being performed. The tone of the voice is part of not only the performance but also the composition. To quantify how the voice functions in the reception of the piece demonstrates the difficulty one encounters when trying to meaningfully discuss the voice. While Barthes provides a useful framework with which to approach the voice, with his concept of a voice's "grain," it is a notion that is somewhat difficult and abstract. Further work on a theoretical framework with which to approach the study of the voice in popular music should be attempted. Stan Hawkins has embarked into some of this territory, writing specifically about Morrissey in his book, *The British Pop Dandy: Masculinity, Popular Music and Culture.*

The model of the incomplete celebrity, which poses problems for the current gendered frameworks of desire, can be applied to other celebrities and to perhaps the very notion of the celebrity. A celebrity by definition can be thought of as incomplete, presenting a star image that generates an ongoing impulse for completion. The continual production of discourse in time also allows the celebrity to be "active" and allows the celebrity a "masculinist" power against the feminizing gaze of the audience. This can be the case not only with Morrissey but also with other male celebrities. Morrissey is an excellent case and would continue to be so, because his enigmatic character is a very important and obvious part of his star image.

As for Morrissey's opinion regarding a book like this one, it is unlikely that he would approve. Bracewell's comments at the beginning of this work suggest the singer's disfavor; it would be "nothing less than an abnegation of all that he has achieved" for him to give his approval.[23] In the recent interview with *Mojo*, Morrissey reveals his own project, to conceal the truth. In doing so, he also describes the basic workings of desire, which this book has attempted to identify. However, Morrissey summarizes it in a single final phrase:

[*Mojo*:] Have you found love?
[MORRISSEY:] Yes I have, yes I have. I mean, it's completely false of course.
[*Mojo*:] What? All love is false or the love you found was false?
[MORRISSEY:] The latter. But everything's fine. Have you found love? How do you know it's love?
[*Mojo*:] Because I feel incomplete without them.
[MORRISSEY:] Well, that's always the exchange. You have something I don't have and I have something you don't have. Which is OK.[24]

Chapter Notes

Introduction

1. Michael Bracewell, *When Surface Was Depth: Death by Cappuccino and Other Reflections on Music and Culture in the 1990's* (Cambridge, MA: Da Capo Press, 2002), 116.
2. This lyric is from Morrissey's song "The Public Image," which was released as a b-side for the single "I Have Forgiven Jesus," released in December 2004. The track was released on an expanded compact disc edition of *You Are the Quarry* in late 2004 (EMI Attack/Sanctuary 06076-86011-2, 2004)
3. These lyrics are from Morrissey's song "I Am Two People," which was released as a b-side for the single "Let Me Kiss You," released in October 2004. The track was also released on the expanded compact disc edition of *You Are the Quarry* in late 2004.
4. Morrissey shared this information on Kilborn's late-night talk show in 2002.
5. David Tseng, "Morrissey's Letter to The Times on British Army Guards Wearing Real Fur Hats," *Morrissey-Solo* (2 August 2010), available from www.morrissey-solo.com/article.pl?sid=10/08/02/1620212, accessed 2 August 2010.
6. Julian Stringer, "The Smiths: Repressed (But Remarkably Dressed)," *Popular Music* 11:1 (1992): 16–17.
7. This lyric is from The Smiths' song "I Want the One I Can't Have," from the album *Meat Is Murder* (Rough Trade/Sire CD 25269, 1985).
8. Paul Morley, "The Last Temptation of Morrissey," *Uncut* (May 2006), 68.
9. Roland Barthes, *S/Z*, trans. Richard Miller (New York: Hill and Wang, 1970), 19.
10. Mark Simpson, *Saint Morrissey* (London: SAF Publishing, 2004), 151–62.
11. David Bret, *Morrissey: Scandal & Passion* (London: Robson Books, 2004), 224–38.

Chapter 1

1. Johnny Rogan, *Morrissey & Marr: The Severed Alliance* (London: Omnibus Press, 1993), 32–33, 50–53. Rogan's book presents the most comprehensive account of Morrissey's young life, although David Bret's two books on Morrissey present somewhat more concise and readable accounts.
2. David Bret, *Morrissey: Landscapes of the Mind* (London: Robson Books, 1994), 10.
3. Paul Morley, "Wilde Child," *Blitz* (April 1988), available from http://motorcycleaupairboy.com/interviews/1988/blitz.htm, accessed 8 September 2009.
4. James Henke, "Oscar! Oscar! Great Britain Goes Wilde for the 'Fourth-Gender' Smiths," *Rolling Stone* 423 (7 June 1984), 45.
5. John Robertson, *Morrissey in His Own Words* (London: Omnibus Press, 1988), 10.
6. Colin Snowsell, "'My Only Mistake Is I'm Hoping': Monty, Morrissey, and the Importance of Being Mediatized" (Master's thesis, University of Calgary, 2002), 90.
7. Dave McCullough, "Handsome Devils," *Sounds* (4 June 1983), available from http://foreverill.com/interviews/1983/sounds1.htm, accessed 7 July 2010.

8. Simpson, *Saint Morrissey*, 100.
9. Ibid., 102.
10. Ibid., 106.
11. Ibid., 105–6.
12. Ibid., 123.
13. Ibid., 210.
14. Ibid., 115.
15. Bret, *Scandal & Passion*, 100.
16. David Fricke, "Keeping Up with The Smiths," *Rolling Stone* 484 (9 October 1986), 33.
17. Rogan, *Morrissey & Marr*, 18.
18. Chris Whatsisname, "Morrissey," *Les Inrockuptibles* (July 1987), quoted in David Bret, *Morrissey: Scandal & Passion* (London: Robson Books, 2004), 11.
19. Bret, *Scandal & Passion*, 19.
20. Ibid., 267.
21. Simpson, *Saint Morrissey*, 148.
22. Rogan, *Morrissey & Marr*, 2.
23. Andrew Harrison, "Home Thoughts from Abroad," *Word* 4 (June 2003), 71.
24. Dele Fadele, "Caucasian Rut," *New Music Express* (22 August 1992), available from http://motorcycleaupairboy.com/interviews/1992/caucasian.htm, accessed 8 February 2010.
25. Simon Frith, "Britbeat: Loose Tubes," *The Village Voice* 37 (1 September 1992), 86.
26. Armond White, "Anglocentric," *The Village Voice* 37 (1 September 1992), 70.
27. Andrew Perry, "Fame, Fame, Fatal Fame," *Mojo* 89 (April 2001), 72.
28. Jaan Uhelszki, "L.A. Confidential," *Mojo* 89 (April 2001), 84.
29. Coleman, "Your Arsenal," 69.
30. Adrian Deevoy, "Ooh I Say!" *Q* 72 (September 1992), 62.
31. For a more detailed discussion of Beethoven's use of Organicism, refer to Joseph Kerman and Alan Tyson (with Scott G. Burnham), "Beethoven, Ludwig van, §15. Middle-Period Works," *Grove Music Online*, ed. L. Macy, available from www.grovemusic.com, accessed 10 April 2006.
32. Ernest Renan, "What Is a Nation?" in *Nation and Narration*, trans. Martin Thom, ed. Homi Bhabha (London, New York: Routledge, 1990), 19–20.
33. Richard Taruskin, "Introduction [Studies in Nationalism and Music]," *Repercussions* 5:1–2 (Spring–Fall 1996): 6.
34. Ibid., 13. Taruskin is referring to Robert Morgan, *Twentieth-Century Music* (New York: Norton, 1991), 119.
35. Taruskin, "Introduction," 20.
36. John Covach, "Popular Music, Unpopular Musicology," in *Rethinking Music*, eds. Nicholas Cook and Mark Everist (New York: Oxford University Press, 1999), 453.
37. Keith Negus, *Popular Music in Theory: An Introduction* (Hanover: Wesleyan University Press, 1996), 165.
38. Middleton, *Studying Popular Music*, 13–15.
39. Negus, *Popular Music in Theory*, 177. Negus refers to Michael Tracey, "The Poisoned Chalice? International Television and the Idea of Dominance," *Daedalus* 114:4 (1985), 17–56.
40. Michael Bracewell, "Introduction," in Linder Sterling, *Morrissey Shot* (New York: Hyperion, 1992), 3.
41. Nadine Hubbs, "Music of the 'Fourth Gender': Morrissey and the Sexual Politics of Melodic Contour," in *Bodies of Writing, Bodies in Performance*, eds. T. Foster, C. Siegel, and E. Berry (New York: New York University Press, 1996), 270.
42. Michael Bracewell, *England Is Mine: Pop Life in Albion from Wilde to Goldie* (London: HarperCollins, 1997), 222–23.
43. Ibid., 226–27.
44. Nabeel Zuberi, *Sounds English: Transnational Popular Music* (Urbana: University of Illinois Press, 2001), 18–19.

45. Ibid., 62. Zuberi takes this quote from an interview in Tony Parsons, *Dispatches from the Front Line of Popular Culture* (London: Virgin, 1994), 95.
46. These lyrics are from the song "Glamorous Glue," released on the album *Your Arsenal* (Sire CD 26994, 1992).
47. Bret, *Scandal & Passion*, 257.
48. Jim Nelson, "Morrissey Returns!" *GQ* 74:4 (April 2004), 231.

Chapter 2

1. Red Saunders, "Super Starts," *Rolling Stone* 408 (10 November 1983), 35.
2. Bret, *Scandal & Passion*, 40.
3. Bret, *Landscapes of the Mind*, 35.
4. Kurt Loder, "Records: The Smiths," *Rolling Stone* 424 (21 June 1984), 56.
5. Kurt Loder, "1984 Record Guide," *Rolling Stone* 437–438 (20 December 1984), 113.
6. Don Watson, *New Musical Express* (25 February 1984), available from http://foreverill.com/disc/smithslp.htm, accessed 3 February 2010.
7. Ibid.
8. Danny Kelly, *New Musical Express* (8 August 1987), available from http://foreverill.com/disc/smithslp.htm, accessed 3 February 2010.
9. Rogan, *Morrissey & Marr*, 205.
10. Bill Black, "It's a Fair Cap," *Sounds!* (17 November 1984), available from http://smiths.arcaneoldwardrobe.com/disc/hatful.htm, accessed 12 September 2009.
11. Ibid.
12. The Smiths, *Hatful of Hollow* (Sire/Reprise CDW 45205, 1984).
13. The Smiths, *The Smiths* (Rough Trade/Sire CD 25065, 1984).
14. Tim Holmes, "Records: Meat Is Murder," *Rolling Stone* 448 (23 May 1985), 59.
15. Paul Du Noyer, *New Musical Express* (16 February 1985), available from http://foreverill.com/disc/meatmurd.htm, accessed 3 February 2010.
16. Mark Coleman, "Records: The Queen Is Dead," *Rolling Stone* 482 (11 September 1986), 94.
17. Jim Farber, "Records: Louder Than Bombs," *Rolling Stone* 500 (21 May 1987), 98.
18. David Browne. "Records: Strangeways, Here We Come," *Rolling Stone* 514 (3 December 1987), 84.
19. Ibid., 84–85. The song "Paint a Vulgar Picture" discusses the notion of reissuing recordings, perhaps with new packaging or song sequences. These reissues, the lyrics suggest, are ultimately of little worth.
20. Len Brown, *New Musical Express* (12 September 1987), available from http://foreverill.com/disc/strange.htm, accessed 3 February 2010.
21. Jim Farber, "Records: Rank," *Rolling Stone* 539 (17 November 1988), 153.
22. Len Brown, "Born to Be Wilde," *New Musical Express* (13 February 1988), available from http://motorcycleaupairboy.com/interviews/1988/chest.htm, accessed 22 May 2010.
23. Rogan, *Morrissey & Marr*, 286.
24. Mark Coleman, "Records: Viva Hate," *Rolling Stone* 526 (19 May 1988), 165.
25. David Fricke, "The Year in Records," *Rolling Stone* 541–42 (15–29 December 1988), 186.
26. Jim Farber, "Avant to Be Alone," *Rolling Stone* 585 (23 August 1990), 138.
27. Stuart Maconie, "Interesting Drag," *New Musical Express* (20 October 1990), available from http://motorcycleaupairboy.com/mozdiscl/bonadrag.htm, accessed 11 April 2010.
28. Rachel Felder, "Recordings — Kill Uncle by Morrissey," *Rolling Stone* 611 (22 August 1991), 68.
29. Mark Coleman, "Recordings — Your Arsenal by Morrissey," *Rolling Stone* 642 (29 October 1992), 69.
30. Simpson, *Saint Morrissey*, 144.

31. Steven Volk, "Recordings — Vauxhall and I by Morrissey," *Rolling Stone* 679 (7 April 1994), 74.
32. Adrien Deevoy, "Morrissey," *GQ* [British Edition] (October 2005), 275.
33. Paul Evans, "Recordings — World of Morrissey by Morrissey," *Rolling Stone* 705 (6 April 1995), 61.
34. Al Weisel, "Recordings — Southpaw Grammar by Morrissey," *Rolling Stone* 718 (5 October 1995), 68.
35. David Quantick, "Albums: School of Hard Knocks," *Melody Maker* 72 (26 August 1995), 37, available from http://motorcycleaupairboy.com/mozdisc2/southpaw.htm, accessed 21 June 2010. The website incorrectly cites the 26 August issue of the *New Musical Express* as the source for Quantick's review.
36. Matt Hendrickson, "Maladjusted," *Rolling Stone* 767 (21 August 1997), 112.
37. "Spins: *Maladjusted*," *Spin* 13 (September 1997), 160, available from http://motorcycleaupairboy.com/mozdisc2/mal.htm, accessed 21 June 2010.
38. Jude Rogers, "On Music: Morrissey's Misstep," *The Guardian* (13 March 2009), available from www.guardian.co.uk/music/2009/mar/13/morrissey-southpaw-grammar-maladjusted, accessed 29 July 2010.
39. Michael White, "Record Reviews: Morrissey — You Are the Quarry," *FFWD* (20 May 2004), available from www.ffwdweekly.com/Issues/2004/0520/cd1.htm, accessed 21 May 2010.
40. James Hunter, "You Are the Quarry," *RollingStone.com* (13 May 2004), available from www.rollingstone.com/reviews/ album? id=5280076&pageid=rs.Home&pageregion =triple1&rnd=1086016598076&has-player=true, accessed 31 May 2010.
41. Michael Idov, "Record Reviews: Morrissey — Live at Earls Court," *Pitchfork.com* (1 April 2005), available from www.pitchforkmedia.com/article/record_review/20043/Morrissey_Live_at_Earls_Court, accessed 26 July 2010.
42. Alex Needham, "NME Reviews: Morrissey — Ringleader of the Tormentors," *NME.com* (31 March 2006), available from www.nme.com/reviews/morrissey/7896, accessed 24 August 2010.
43. Ross Raihala, "Morrissey, Ringleader of the Tormentors," *Spin.com* (4 April 2006), available from www.spin.com/reviews/morrissey-ringleader-tormentors-attacksanctuary, accessed 24 August 2010.
44. Mark Beaumont, "NME Reviews: Morrissey — Greatest Hits," *NME.com* (7 February 2008), available from www.nme.com/reviews/morrissey/9460, accessed 28 July 2010.
45. Stephen Thomas Erlewine, "Greatest Hits [Deluxe Edition]," *allmusic.com*, available from www.allmusic.com/cg/amg.dll?p=amg&sql=10:d9fexzwjldfe, accessed 28 July 2010.
46. Ben Ratliff, "Critics' Choice: New CDs — Morrissey, 'Years of Refusal,'" *The New York Times* (16 February 2009), available from www.nytimes.com/2009/02/16/arts/music/16choi.html, accessed 28 July 2010.
47. Anthony Thornton, "NME Reviews: Morrissey — Years of Refusal," *NME.com* (18 February 2009), available from www.nme.com/reviews/10089, accessed 28 July 2010.
48. Joe Gross, "Morrissey, 'Years of Refusal' (Lost Highway)," *Spin.com* (28 January 2009), available from www.spin.com/reviews/morrissey-years-refusal-lost-highway, accessed 28 July 2010.
49. Evie Nagy, "Morrissey, 'Swords,'" *Billboard.com* (6 November 2009), available from www.billboard.com/#/new-releases/morrissey-swords-1004040720.story, accessed 28 July 2010.
50. Nadine McBay, "Morrissey Swords Review," *BBC Music* (26 October 2009), available from www.bbc.co.uk/music/reviews/hwd3, accessed 28 July 2010.
51. White, "Record Reviews: Morrissey — You Are the Quarry," available from www.ffwdweekly.com/Issues/2004/0520/cd1.htm, accessed 21 May 2004; "Spins: *Maladjusted*," *Spin* 13 (September 1997), 160, available from http://motorcycleaupairboy.com/mozdisc2/mal.htm, accessed 21 June 2010.

Chapter 3

1. Simon Frith and Angela McRobbie, "Rock and Sexuality," in *On Record: Rock, Pop and the Written Word*, eds. S. Frith and A. Goodwin (London: Routledge, 1990), 371.
2. Ibid., 373–74.
3. Ibid., 375.
4. Allison McCracken, "'God's Gift to Us Girls': Crooning, Gender, and the Re-creation of American Popular Song, 1928–1933," *American Music* 17:4 (Winter 1999): 365–66.
5. Ibid., 378.
6. Ibid., 389.
7. Sara Cohen, "Men Making a Scene: Rock Music and the Production of Gender," in *Sexing the Groove: Popular Music and Gender*, ed. Sheila Whiteley (London: Routledge, 1997), 30–31.
8. Ibid., 31, 33.
9. Barbara Bradby, "Sampling Sexuality: Gender, Technology and the Body in Dance Music," *Popular Music* 12:2 (May 1993): 156.
10. Ibid., 157.
11. McCracken, "God's Gift to Us Girls," 371.
12. Diane Railton, "The Gendered Carnival of Pop," *Popular Music* 20:3 (October 2001): 322–23.
13. Frith and McRobbie, "Rock and Sexuality," 376.
14. Railton, "The Gendered Carnival of Pop," 321.
15. Cohen, "Men Making a Scene," 21.
16. Mavis Bayton, "Women and the Electric Guitar," in *Sexing the Groove: Popular Music and Gender*, ed. Sheila Whiteley (London: Routledge, 1997), 37.
17. Susan McClary, "Narrative Agendas in 'Absolute' Music: Identity and Difference in Brahms's Third Symphony," in *Musicology and Difference: Gender and Sexuality in Music Scholarship*, ed. Ruth A. Solie (Berkeley: University of California Press, 1993), 329.
18. Ibid., 330.
19. Ibid., 331–32.
20. Susan McClary, *Feminine Endings: Music, Gender, and Sexuality* (Minneapolis: University of Minnesota Press, 1991), 10–12.
21. Ibid.
22. Ibid., 25.
23. Lori Burns, "'Joanie' Get Angry": k. d. lang's Feminist Revision," in *Understanding Rock: Essays in Musical Analysis*, eds. J. Covach and G. M. Boone (New York: Oxford University Press, 1997), 99.
24. Ibid., 110.
25. John Shepherd, "Difference and Power in Music," in *Musicology and Difference: Gender and Sexuality in Music Scholarship*, ed. Ruth A. Solie (Berkeley: University of California Press, 1993), 49.
26. Ibid., 50.
27. Ibid., 51.
28. Ibid., 52.
29. Ibid., 59.
30. Susanne G. Cusick, "On a Lesbian Relationship with Music: A Serious Effort Not to Think Straight," in *Queering the Pitch: The New Gay and Lesbian Musicology*, eds. P. Brett, E. Wood and G. C. Thomas (New York: Routledge, 1994), 78–79.
31. Elizabeth Wood, "Sapphonics," in *Queering the Pitch: The New Gay and Lesbian Musicology*, eds. P. Brett, E. Wood and G. C. Thomas (New York: Routledge, 1994), 27.
32. Ibid., 32.
33. Ibid., 32–33.
34. Ratliff, "Critics' Choice," n.p.
35. Barthes, *S/Z*, 21.

36. Jacques Lacan, "The Agency of the Letter in the Unconscious or Reason Since Freud," in *Ecrits: A Selection*, trans. A. Sheridan (New York: W.W. Norton, 1977), 167.
37. Roland Barthes, "The Grain of the Voice," in *Image—Music—Text*, trans. S. Heath (New York: Hill and Wang, 1977), 181.
38. Ibid., 185.
39. Ibid., 10.
40. Ibid., 188.
41. Roland Barthes, "The Adjective Is the 'Statement' of Desire," in *The Grain of the Voice: Interviews 1962–1980*, trans. Linda Coverdale (New York: Hill and Wang, 1985), 173.
42. Ibid.
43. Ibid.
44. Roland Barthes, "Listening," in *The Responsibility of Forms: Critical Essays on Music, Art, and Representation*, trans. Richard Howard (Berkeley: University of California Press, 1985), 254–55.
45. Barthes, "The Grain of the Voice," 179–81.
46. Barthes, "Listening," 259.
47. Roland Barthes, "The Phantoms of the Opera," in *The Grain of the Voice: Interviews 1962–1980*, trans. Linda Coverdale (New York: Hill and Wang, 1985), 183–84.
48. Richard Middleton, *Studying Popular Music* (Milton Keynes: Open University Press, 1990), 262.
49. John Potter, "The Singer, Not the Song: Women Singers as Composer-Poets," *Popular Music* 13:2 (May 1994): 194.
50. Middleton, *Studying Popular Music*, 288.
51. Wayne Koestenbaum, *The Queen's Throat: Opera, Homosexuality, and the Mystery of Desire* (New York: Poseidon Press, 1993), 16.
52. Ibid., 17.
53. Ibid.
54. Barthes, *S/Z*, 17.
55. John Ellis, "Stars as a Cinematic Phenomenon," in *Visible Fictions: Cinema, Television, Video* (London: Routledge, 1982), 91.
56. Richard Dyer, *Stars* (London: British Film Institute, 1979), 69–70.
57. Richard deCordova, "The Emergence of the Star System in America," *Wide Angle* 6:4 (1985): 11.
58. Barry King, "Articulating Stardom," *Screen* 26:5 (September–October 1985): 40.
59. Dyer, *Stars*, 70–71.
60. deCordova, "The Emergence of the Star System," 10.
61. Dyer, *Stars*, 72.
62. Ibid., 73.
63. Ibid., 24.
64. P. David Marshall, *Celebrity and Power: Fame in Contemporary Culture* (Minneapolis: University of Minnesota Press, 1997), 19.
65. Ibid., 49.
66. Ibid., 51.
67. Ibid., ix–xi.
68. Laura Mulvey, "Visual Pleasure and Narrative Cinema," *Screen* 16:3 (Autumn 1975): 6.
69. Ibid., 8.
70. Ibid., 11.
71. Ibid., 12.
72. Richard Dyer, "Don't Look Now: The Instabilities of the Male Pin-Up," *Screen* 23:3–4 (September–October 1982): 66.
73. Ibid.
74. Stephan Schindler, "What Makes a Man a Man: The Construction of Masculinity in F. W. Murnau's *The Last Laugh*," *Screen* 37:1 (Spring 1996): 33.
75. Ibid., 36.

76. Scott Benjamin King, "Sonny's Virtues: The Gender Negotiations of *Miami Vice*," *Screen* 31:3 (Autumn 1990): 283.
77. Ibid., 288.
78. Ibid., 293.
79. Pam Cook, "Masculinity in Crisis? [Tragedy and Identification in *Raging Bull*]," *Screen* 23:3–4 (September–October 1982): 43.
80. Ibid., 46.
81. Jeffrey A. Brown, "'Putting on the Ritz': Masculinity and the Young Gary Cooper," *Screen* 36:3 (Autumn 1995): 213.
82. Rachel Adams, "'Fat Man Walking': Masculinity and Racial Geographies in James Mangold's *Copland*," *Camera Obscura* 42 (September 1999): 6.
83. Ibid., 8–9.
84. Ibid., 21. Adams refers the reader to Andrew Ross, "The Great White Dude," in *Constructing Masculinity*, ed. Maurice Berger, Brian Wallis, and Simon Watson (New York, Routledge, 1995), 172.
85. Rey Chow, "Male Narcissism and National Culture: Subjectivity in Chen Kaige's *King of the Children*," *Camera Obscura* 25–26 (January/May 1991): 36.
86. Ibid.
87. Ginette Vincendeau, "Gérard Depardieu: The Axiom of Contemporary French Cinema," *Screen* 34:4 (Winter 1993): 356. Vincendeau quotes from an interview with Depardieu that appears in *Cahiers du cinéma*, May 1981, 111.
88. Ibid., 357.
89. Sean Nixon, *Hard Looks: Masculinities, Spectatorship and Contemporary Consumption* (New York: St. Martin's Press, 1996), 18.
90. Ibid., 13–14.
91. Ibid., 14.
92. Pat Reid, *Outlines: Morrissey* (Bath: Absolute Press, 2004), 86.

Chapter 4

1. Reid, *Outlines: Morrissey*, 96.
2. Taina Viitamäki, "I'm Not the Man You Think I Am. Morrissey's Fourth Gender," *Musiikin suunta* 3 (1997): 29–40.
3. Judith Butler, *Bodies that Matter: On the Discursive Limits of "Sex"* (New York: Routledge, 1993), x.
4. Ibid., 2.
5. Ibid., 12.
6. Judith Butler, *Undoing Gender* (New York: Routledge, 2004), 1.
7. Ibid., 2.
8. Butler, *Bodies that Matter*, 8.
9. Butler, *Undoing Gender*, 64–65.
10. Donna Haraway, "A Manifesto for Cyborgs: Science, Technology and Socialist Feminism in the 1980s," *Socialist Review* 80 (1985): 65.
11. Ibid., 72.
12. Ibid., 93.
13. Ibid., 96.
14. See Simpson, *Saint Morrissey*, 114–28. See *The Journal of Sex Research* 41:3 (August 2004): 279–87, and *New Scientist* 184:2469 (16–22 October 2004). Also see www.cnn.com/2004/TECH/science/10/14/asexual.study/index.html. Finally, websites that picked up the story are as follows: "See, maybe Morrissey was telling the truth," http://emjaro.blogspot.com/2004/10/see-maybe-morrissey-was-telling-truth.html, and www.morrissey-solo.com/articles/04/10/15/0853212.shtml.
15. Reid, *Outlines: Morrissey*, 12–13.
16. Ibid., 13.

17. Robertson, *Morrissey in His Own Words*, 8.
18. Ibid., 10.
19. Hubbs, "Music of the 'Fourth Gender,'" 277. Hubbs quotes an interview with Morrissey by Fred Hauptfuhrer, "Roll Over, Bob Dylan, and Tell Madonna the News: The Smiths' Morrissey Is Pop's Latest Messiah," *People Weekly* (24 June 1985), 106.
20. Simon Reynolds and Joy Press, *The Sex Revolts: Gender, Rebellion, and Rock 'n' Roll* (Cambridge: Harvard University Press, 1995), 214.
21. Deevoy, "Ooh I Say!" 66.
22. Reynolds and Press, *The Sex Revolts*, 215.
23. Ibid., 225–27.
24. Jaan Uhelszki, "The Mojo Interview: L.A. Confidential," *Mojo* 89 (April 2001): 84.
25. This information is from an informal conversation with Steve Redhead on 31 October 2000. He suggests that Morrissey takes on a kind of hypermasculinity with his 1994 album, *Vauxhall and I*, and suggests that an association with West Ham is another element contributing to this.
26. Linder Sterling, *Morrissey Shot* (New York: Hyperion, 1992), 76, 78.
27. The complete lyrics are available in the liner notes of Morrissey, *My Early Burglary Years*, Reprise, CDW 46874, 1998. n.p.
28. Carol Vernallis, "The Kindest Cut: Functions and Meanings in Music Video Editing," *Screen* 42:1 (Spring 2001): 42.
29. Andrew Goodwin, in his book, *Dancing in the Distraction Factory: Music Television and Popular Culture* (Minneapolis: University of Minnesota Press, 1992), explains how conventional narrative of the "classic realist text" is not needed for coherence in music video. He writes, "It is possible to see an enormous degree of stability and coherence in these texts, since they remain rooted rather than thrown into textual chaos by pop's musical characteristics" (p. 84).
30. Simpson, *Saint Morrissey*, 155.
31. Vernallis, "The Kindest Cut," 43.
32. Ibid., 39–40.
33. Sean Nixon, *Hard Looks*, 119.
34. "Our Decade: New Lad Rules the World," available from http://news.bbc.co.uk/1/hi/special_report/1999/02/99/e-cyclopedia/289778.stm, accessed 12 May 2010.
35. Ibid.
36. Mark Simpson, "Meet the Metrosexual," available from www.salon.com/ent/feature/2002/07/22/metrosexual/print.html, accessed 5 January 2010.
37. Mark Simpson, "Here Come the Mirror Men," *The Independent* (15 November 1994), available from www.marksimpson.com/pages/journalism/mirror_men.html, accessed 24 July 2010.
38. Christian Metz, "Identification, Mirror," in *Film Theory and Criticism: Introductory Readings*, eds. Leo Braudy and Marshall Cohen (New York, Oxford: Oxford University Press, 1999), 800–801.
39. Ibid., 802.
40. Ibid., 802–3.
41. Ibid.
42. Ibid., 810.
43. Ibid., 808.
44. Ibid., 811.
45. Ellis, "Stars as a Cinematic Phenomenon," 97–98.
46. Ibid., 108.

Chapter 5

1. Mona Venkateswaran, "Accountants Can Be Fanatics Too," *CBC News Viewpoint* (22 October 2004), available from www.cbc.ca/news/viewpoint/vp_venkateswaran/20041022.html, accessed 25 October 2009.

2. Rogan, *Morrissey & Marr*, 18.
3. Paul Du Noyer, "Oh, Such *Drama!*" *Q* 11 (August 1987): 60.
4. Mat Snow, "The Soft Touch," *Q* 39 (December 1989): 83.
5. Middleton, *Studying Popular Music*, 284–86.
6. Benedict Anderson, *Imagined Communities: Reflections on the Origin and Spread of Nationalism* (London, New York: Verso, 1991), 79.
7. Ibid., 291.
8. Sean Williams, "Melodic Ornamentation in the Connemara *Sean-nós* Singing of Joe Heaney," *New Hibernia Review* 8:1 (Spring 2004): 136.
9. Ibid., 140.
10. Nick Kelly, "Morrissey / Oct. 3, 2002 / Dublin (Ambassador Theatre)," *Billboard.com* (7 October 2002), available from www.billboard.com/bb/article_display.jspvnu_content_id= 1735207, accessed 26 November 2009.
11. Neva Chonin, "Morrissey Turns on the Charm," *San Francisco Chronicle* (16 September 2002), D1, available from www.sfgate.com/cgi-bin/article.cgi?file=/chronicle/archive/ 2002/09/16/DD21639.DTL, accessed 29 November 2009.
12. Robert Walser, *Running with the Devil: Power, Gender, and Madness in Heavy Metal Music* (Hanover: Wesleyan University Press, 1993), 42.
13. Sean O'Hagan, "Incredible Sulk," *The Observer* (22 September 2002), available from http://observer.guardian.co.uk/review/story/0,,7965459,00.html, accessed 26 November 2009.
14. Mark Mordue, "Morrissey, Enmore Theatre, Sydney," *12 Gauge Review*, available from http://12gauge.com/music_2003_mordue_morrissey.html, accessed 3 April 2010.
15. Douglas Coupland, "Papal Attraction," *The Observer* (19 March 2006), available from http://observer.guardian.co.uk/features/story/0,,1735254,00.html, accessed 24 July 2010.
16. This comment was posted on the *Morrissey-Solo* forums by user "jeane" on 20 July 2006, available from http://forums.morrissey-solo.com/showthread.php?t=61362, accessed 22 June 2010.
17. Morrissey, "Statement from Morrissey," *True to You* (30 April 2010), available from http://true-to-you.net/morrissey_news_100430_01, accessed 8 May 2010. A particularly touching passage from Morrissey: "Even after all she had done, even after all the money she had spent and the millions of miles she had hiked she still could not keep away from the squeeze and bend of yet another version of 'First of the gang to die'—never imagining, I'm sure, that it is she who would be the first."
18. Chonin, "Morrissey Turns on the Charm," D1.
19. Kelly, "Morrissey Dublin (Ambassador Theatre)," n.p.
20. Chonin, "Morrissey Turns on the Charm," D1.
21. Simpson, *Saint Morrissey*, 215.
22. Ibid., 197.
23. Bruce Scott, "Morrissey Pleases Toronto Crowd," *JAM! Music* (13 October 2004), available from www.canoe.ca/JamConcertsL2Q/morrissey_101304-can.html, accessed 19 October 2009.
24. Sofi Papamarko, "LIVE: Morrissey Drives Fans into a Frenzy," *ChartAttack.com* (13 October 2004), available from www.chartattack.com/damn/2004/10/1313.cfm, accessed 19 October 2009.
25. Chonin, "Morrissey Turns on the Charm," D1.
26. Robert Everett-Green, "This Charming Man Can Still Seduce," *The Globe and Mail* (14 October 2004), R4, available from www.theglobeandmail.com/servlet/ArticleNews/ TPStory/ LAC/20041014/MORISSEY14/ TPEntertainment/?query=morrissey, accessed 19 October 2009.

Chapter 6

1. Hubbs, "Music of the 'Fourth Gender,'" 268–69.
2. Ibid., 269.

3. Ibid., 270.
4. Ibid., 272.
5. Ibid., 282.
6. Ibid., 273.
7. Ibid., 275–79.
8. Ibid., 281.
9. Ibid., 282.
10. Ibid., 285.
11. Bret, *Scandal & Passion*, 282.
12. Hubbs, "Music of the 'Fourth Gender,'" 285.
13. Ibid., 286.
14. Ibid., 287–88.
15. Hawkins, "Anti-Rebel, Lonesome Boy: Morrissey in Crisis?" *Settling the Pop Score: Pop Texts and Identity Politics* (Aldershot: Ashgate, 2002), 66–67.
16. Ibid., 69. Hawkins cites Johnny Rogan's "very personal account of Morrissey's sexuality" (*Morrissey & Marr: The Severed Alliance*) as well as David T. Evans' book, *Sexual Citizenship: The Material Construction of Sexualities* (London: Routledge, 1993). Hawkins refers the reader also to William Simon, *Postmodern Sexualities* (London: Routledge, 1996).
17. Ibid., 70–71.
18. Ibid., 87.
19. Jon Pareles, "An Articulate Misfit with Rockabilly Sideburns," *The New York Times* (22 September 1992), C17.
20. Marc Spitz, "These Things Take Time," *Spin* 20:5 (May 2004): 64. Spitz informs the reader of Monro. For a comprehensive list of the recognition of Morrissey's "crooning" style in popular press, see Hubbs, "Music of the 'Fourth Gender,'" p. 291n33.
21. Hawkins, "Anti-Rebel, Lonesome Boy," 73.
22. Ibid., 74.
23. Ibid.
24. Ibid., 83.
25. Ibid., 88.
26. Ibid., 91.
27. Ibid., 92–93.
28. Ibid., 93.
29. Ibid., 97.
30. In Roman numerals, often used for harmonic analysis, the progression is as follows: I — I/Bb — vi — ii — vi — ii — IV — V. The B-flat played by the bass guitar is the anomaly because it has no place in the key of D major.
31. Stefan Kostka and Dorothy Payne, *Tonal Harmony with an Introduction to Twentieth-Century Music* (New York: McGraw-Hill, 1995), 179.
32. Another possibility, although somewhat dubious, is that the B-flat functions as an *augmented fifth* (the raising of the fifth note of the scale, or scale degree, by a semitone), which has a specific function in a chord. In four-part writing, upon which much of tonal harmony is based, the fifth scale-degree, the top note in a root triad, is raised to an augmented fifth and then raised by another semitone to become the third of another major chord. The raised fifth scale-degree acts as a passing tone between two chords, often I and IV or V and I. This progression does not occur in the Morrissey example. It is possible that, as is the case with an augmented fifth, this particular tone works to "create a tension that makes the tonic sound like V or IV" (Edward Aldwell and Carl Schachter, *Harmony and Voice Leading* [Fort Worth: Harcourt Brace Jovanovich College, 1989], 510). Furthermore, one can read the B-flat as a replacement for the A tone, simply to intensify the effect of the dissonance. This was a common occurrence, involving different specifics, around the beginning of the Baroque period, as a *contraction* (p. 56).
33. Hubbs, "Music of the 'Fourth Gender,'" 279.
34. Bret, *Scandal & Passion*, 175.

35. Simpson, *Saint Morrissey*, 145.
36. Hubbs, "Music of the 'Fourth Gender,'" 280.
37. Hawkins, "Anti-Rebel, Lonesome Boy," 86.
38. Ibid., 81.
39. Siegmund Levarie and Earnst Levy, *Musical Morphology: A Discourse and a Dictionary* (Kent, OH: Kent State University Press, 1983), 5.
40. Ibid., 184.
41. Ibid., 299.
42. Middleton, *Studying Popular Music*, 203.
43. Ibid., 205.
44. Hawkins, "Anti-Rebel, Lonesome Boy," 91.
45. Ibid., 95. Hawkins refers the reader to Linda Hutcheon, *Irony's Edge: The Theory and Politics of Irony* (London: Routledge, 1994).
46. Jo Slee, *Peepholism: Into the Art of Morrissey* (London: Sidgwick & Jackson, 1994), 157.

Chapter 7

1. Roland Barthes, *S/Z*, 38. Much of the expository material on Barthes' *S/Z* also appears in my essay on the enigmatic female in Joss Whedon's television series entitled "The Companion as a Doll: The Female Enigma in Whedon's *Firefly* and *Dollhouse*," pp. 239–247 in *Sexual Rhetoric in the Works of Joss Whedon: New Essays*, edited by Erin B. Waggoner (Jefferson, NC: McFarland, 2010).
2. Ibid., 75.
3. Ibid., 32.
4. Ibid., 75–76.
5. Ibid., 42.
6. Ibid., 75.
7. Ibid., 31.
8. Ibid., 76.
9. Ibid., 46–47.
10. Ibid., 76.
11. Ibid., 84.
12. Ibid., 29.
13. Ibid., 30. For Barthes, the "classic text" is one that can be read but not written, as opposed to "what can be written (rewritten) today"; he calls the "classic text" a "readerly text," while the other is called a "writerly text" (p. 4).
14. Ibid., 108.
15. Reid, *Outlines: Morrissey*, 44.
16. Barthes, *S/Z*, 118.
17. Reid, *Outlines: Morrissey*, 118.
18. Barthes, *S/Z*, 119.
19. Simpson, *Saint Morrissey*, 123–24.
20. Barthes, *S/Z*, 161–62.
21. Helen Dansette, "Mark Simpson: The Skinhead Oscar Wilde," available from http://prettypettythieves.com/followers/marksimpson.htm, accessed 25 January 2010.
22. Barthes, *S/Z*, 116.
23. Dansette, "Mark Simpson: The Skinhead Oscar Wilde," n.p.
24. This quote is from a user comment posted on the Internet Movie Database in early 2006. Available from www.imdb.com/title/tt0192906/usercomments, accessed 6 February 2006.
25. Morrissey himself has mentioned his actual family as recently as 30 November 2005 in a statement against the former Smiths drummer Mike Joyce posted on the website *True to You* (available from http://true-to-you.net/morrissey_news_051130_01, accessed 6 February 2010).
26. Simpson, *Saint Morrissey*, 202–3.

27. Ibid., 203.
28. Ibid., 124.
29. Bret, *Scandal & Passion*, 276–77.
30. Ibid., 278.
31. Dansette, "Mark Simpson: The Skinhead Oscar Wilde," n.p.
32. Ibid.
33. Ibid.
34. Andrew Williams, "60 Second Interview: Mark Simpson," *Metro* (15 September 2005), available from www.metro.co.uk/fame/interviews/article.html?in_article_id=504&in_page_id=11, accessed 6 July 2010.

Conclusion

1. Andrew Male, "Happy Now?" *Mojo* 149 (April 2006): 46.
2. Gianni Santoro, "Morrissey," *XL* (March 2006): 91. "Gli Smiths sono lontani, l'icona intatta. E si tinge di tricolore. Dopo Londra, Manchester e Los Angeles, Moz ... ha scelto Roma."
3. Ibid., 93. "Non abito da nessuna parte, Ho venduto la villa di Los Angeles e ho tutte le cose in una cantina. Cerco casa, ma a Roma tutti si tengono strette le proprietà."
4. Morley, "The Last Temptation of Morrissey," 63.
5. Ibid.
6. Male, "Happy Now?" 48.
7. Santoro, "Morrissey," 93.
8. Male, "Happy Now?" 50.
9. Tom Doyle, "Italian Stallion," *Q* 237 (April 2006): 108.
10. Male, "Happy Now?" 50.
11. Ibid., 47.
12. Santoro, "Morrissey," 95. "I fan ne parlano già come della canzone del coming out. É marchiata ormai.... [Morrissey:] Oddio. Coming out, venire allo scoperto? Da dove? Verso dove? Io sono me stesso. Punto."
13. "Exclusive Interview: Morrissey," *NME* (4 March 2006), 21.
14. Santoro, "Morrissey," 95. "A sei anni ho comprato *Heart* ['cuore'] di Rita Pavone. Ancora ce l'ho. E poi c'era ... Gigliola Cinquetti, conosci il brano *Sì*? Rappresentò l'Italia all'Eurofestival. E arrivò seconda. Il mio nuovo video cita il festival."
15. Morrissey, "Statement from Morrissey," *True to You* (27 March 2006), available from http://true-to-you.net/morrissey_news_060327_02, accessed 29 June 2010.
16. See "Rock Singer Snubs Canada to Protest Seal Hunt," available from www.cbc.ca/canada/newfoundland-labrador/story/2006/03/28/nf-morrissey-seals-20060328.html, accessed 29 June 2010.
17. Morrissey, "Statement from Morrissey," *True to You* (31 March 2008), available from http://true-to-you.net/morrissey_news_080331_01, accessed 8 May 2010.
18. Simon Armitage, "Morrissey Interview: Big Mouth Strikes Again," *The Guardian Weekend* (4 September 2010), 16, available from www.guardian.co.uk/music/2010/sep/03/morrissey-simon-armitage-interview, accessed 3 September 2010.
19. Author Unknown, "Feist Biography," *High Road Touring*, available from www.highroadtouring.com/hrtbin/apage?artist_id=180&page=biography, accessed 26 March 2010.
20. Roland Barthes, "Writers, Intellectuals, Teachers," in *Image Music Text*, trans. Stephen Heath (London: Fontana Press, 1977), 208.
21. Ibid., 214.
22. Male, "Happy Now?" 49.
23. Bracewell, *When Surface Was Depth*, 116.
24. Male, "Happy Now?" 48.

Bibliography

Adams, Rachel. "'Fat Man Walking': Masculinity and Racial Geographies in James Mangold's *Copland*." *Camera Obscura* 42 (September 1999): 5–28.
Aldwell, Edward, and Carl Schachter. *Harmony and Voice Leading*. Fort Worth: Harcourt Brace Jovanovich College, 1989.
Anderson, Benedict. *Imagined Communities: Reflections on the Origin and Spread of Nationalism*. London and New York: Verso, 1991.
Armitage, Simon. "Morrissey Interview: Big Mouth Strikes Again." *The Guardian Weekend* (4 September 2010), 16. Available from www.guardian.co.uk/music/2010/sep/03/morrissey-simon-armitage-interview. Accessed 3 September 2010.
Barthes, Roland. "The Grain of the Voice." Pp. 179–189 in *Image, Music, Text*, translated by Stephen Heath. New York: Hill and Wang, 1977.
———. *The Grain of the Voice: Interviews 1962–1980*. Translated by Linda Coverdale. New York: Hill and Wang, 1985.
———. *The Responsibility of Forms: Critical Essays on Music, Art, and Representation*. Translated by Richard Howard. Berkeley: University of California Press, 1985.
———. *S/Z*. Translated by Richard Miller. New York: Hill and Wang, 1974.
———. "Writers, Intellectuals, Teachers." Pp. 190–215 in *Image Music Text*, translated by Stephen Heath. London: Fontana Press, 1977.
Bayton, Mavis. "Women and the Electric Guitar." Pp. 37–49 in *Sexing the Groove: Popular Music and Gender*, edited by Sheila Whiteley. London: Routledge, 1997.
Beaumont, Mark. "NME Reviews: Morrissey—Greatest Hits." *NME.com* (7 February 2008). Available from www.nme.com/reviews/morrissey/9460. Accessed 28 July 2010.
Black, Bill. "It's a Fair Cap." *Sounds!* (17 November 1984). Available from http://smiths.arcaneoldwardrobe.com/disc/hatful.htm. Accessed 12 September 2009.
Bracewell, Michael. *England Is Mine: Pop Life in Albion from Wilde to Goldie*. London: HarperCollins, 1997.
———. *When Surface Was Depth: Death by Cappuccino and Other Reflections on Music and Culture in the 1990's*. Cambridge, MA: Da Capo Press, 2002.
Bradby, Barbara. "Sampling Sexuality: Gender, Technology and the Body in Dance Music." *Popular Music* 12:2 (May 1993): 155–76.
Bret, David. *Morrissey: Landscapes of the Mind*. London: Robson Books, 1994.
———. *Morrissey: Scandal and Passion*. London: Robson Books, 2004.
Brown, Jeffrey A. "'Putting on the Ritz': Masculinity and the Young Gary Cooper." *Screen* 36:3 (Autumn 1995): 193–213.
Brown, Len. "Born to Be Wilde." *New Musical Express* (13 February 1988). Available from http://motorcycleaupairboy.com/interviews/1988/chest.htm. Accessed 22 May 2010.

———. *New Musical Express* (12 September 1987). Available from http://foreverill.com/disc/strange.htm. Accessed 3 February 2010.

Browne, David. "Records: Strangeways, Here We Come." *Rolling Stone* 514 (3 December 1987), 84.

Burns, Lori. "'Joanie' Get Angry: k. d. lang's Feminist Revision." Pp. 93–112 in *Understanding Rock: Essays in Musical Analysis*, edited by J. Covach and G. M. Boone. New York: Oxford University Press, 1997.

Butler, Judith. *Bodies that Matter: On the Discursive Limits of "Sex."* New York: Routledge, 1993.

———. *Undoing Gender*. New York: Routledge, 2004.

Chonin, Neva. "Morrissey Turns on the Charm." *San Francisco Chronicle* (16 September 2002). Available from www.sfgate.com/cgi-bin/article.cgi?file=/chronicle/archive/2002/09/16/DD21639.DTL. Accessed 29 November 2009.

Chow, Rey. "Male Narcissism and National Culture: Subjectivity in Chen Kaige's *King of the Children*." *Camera Obscura* 25–26 (January/May 1991): 9–39.

Cohen, Sara. "Men Making a Scene: Rock Music and the Production of Gender." Pp. 17–36 in *Sexing the Groove: Popular Music and Gender*, edited by Sheila Whiteley. London: Routledge, 1997.

Coleman, Mark. "Recordings—Your Arsenal by Morrissey." *Rolling Stone* 642 (29 October 1992), 69.

———. "Records: The Queen Is Dead." *Rolling Stone* 482 (11 September 1986), 94.

———. "Records: Viva Hate." *Rolling Stone* 526 (19 May 1988), 165.

Cook, Pam. "Masculinity in Crisis? [Tragedy and Identification in *Raging Bull*]." *Screen* 23:3–4 (September–October 1982): 39–46.

Coupland, Douglas. "Papal Attraction." *The Observer* (19 March 2006). Available from http://observer.guardian.co.uk/features/story/0,,1735254,00.html. Accessed 24 July 2010.

Covach, John. "Popular Music, Unpopular Musicology." Pp. 452–70 in *Rethinking Music*, edited by Nicholas Cook and Mark Everist. New York: Oxford University Press, 1999.

Cusick, Susanne G. "On a Lesbian Relationship with Music: A Serious Effort Not to Thing Straight." Pp. 67–83 in *Queering the Pitch: The New Gay and Lesbian Musicology*, edited by P. Brett, E. Wood and G. C. Thomas. New York: Routledge, 1994.

Dansette, Helen. "Mark Simpson: The Skinhead Oscar Wilde." Available from http://prettypettythieves.com/followers/marksimpson.htm. Accessed 25 January 2010.

deCordova, Richard. "The Emergence of the Star System in America." *Wide Angle* 6:4 (Spring 1985): 4–13.

Deevoy, Adrien. "Morrissey." *GQ* [British Edition] (October 2005): 272–79.

———. "Ooh I Say!" *Q* 72 (September 1992): 61–66.

Doyle, Tom. "Italian Stallion." *Q* 237 (April 2006): 108–9.

Du Noyer, Paul. *New Musical Express* (16 February 1985). Available from http://foreverill.com/disc/meatmurd.htm. Accessed 3 February 2010.

———. "Oh, Such *Drama*!" *Q* 11 (August 1987): 56–60.

Dyer, Richard. "Don't Look Now: The Instabilities of the Male Pin-Up." *Screen* 23:3–4 (September–October 1982): 61–73.

———. *Stars*. London: British Film Institute, 1979.

Ellis, John. "Stars as a Cinematic Phenomenon." In *Visible Fictions: Cinema, Television, Video*. London: Routledge, 1982.

Erlewine, Stephen Thomas. "Greatest Hits [Deluxe Edition]." *Allmusic.com*. Available

from www.allmusic.com/cg/amg.dll?p=amgandsql=10:d9fexzwjldfe. Accessed 28 July 2010.
"Exclusive Interview: Morrissey." *NME* (4 March 2006), 21.
Evans, David T. *Sexual Citizenship: The Material Construction of Sexualities*. London: Routledge, 1993.
Evans, Paul. "Recordings—World of Morrissey by Morrissey." *Rolling Stone* 705 (6 April 1995), 61.
Everett-Green, Robert. "This Charming Man Can Still Seduce." *The Globe and Mail* (14 October 2004), R4. Available from www.theglobeandmail.com/servlet/ArticleNews/TPStory/LAC/20041014/MORISSEY14/TPEntertainment/?query=morrissey. Accessed 19 October 2009.
Fadele, Dele. "Caucasian Rut." *New Music Express* (22 August 1992). Available from http://motorcycleaupairboy.com/interviews/1992/caucasian.htm. Accessed 8 February 2010.
Farber, Jim. "Avant to Be Alone." *Rolling Stone* 585 (23 August 1990), 138.
_____. "Records: Louder Than Bombs." *Rolling Stone* 500 (21 May 1987), 98.
_____. "Records: Rank." *Rolling Stone* 539 (17 November 1988), 153.
"Feist Biography." *High Road Touring*. Available from www.highroadtouring.com/hrtb-in/apage?artist_id=180andpage=biography. Accessed 26 March 2010.
Felder, Rachel. "Recordings — Kill Uncle by Morrissey." *Rolling Stone* 611 (22 August 1991), 68.
Fricke, David. "Keeping Up with The Smiths." *Rolling Stone* 484 (9 October 1986), 33.
_____. "The Year in Records." *Rolling Stone* 541–542 (15–29 December 1988), 186.
Frith, Simon. "Britbeat: Loose Tubes." *The Village Voice* 37 (1 September 1992), 86.
_____ and Angela McRobbie. "Rock and Sexuality." Pp. 371–98 in *On Record: Rock, Pop and the Written Word*, edited by S. Frith and A. Goodwin. New York: Routledge, 1990.
Goddard, Simon. *Mozipedia: The Encyclopedia of Morrissey and The Smiths*. New York: Plume, 2010.
Goodwin, Andrew. *Dancing in the Distraction Factory: Music Television and Popular Culture*. Minneapolis: University of Minnesota Press, 1992.
Greco, Nicholas. "The Companion as a Doll: The Female Enigma in Whedon's *Firefly* and *Dollhouse*." Pp. 239–47 in *Sexual Rhetoric in the Works of Joss Whedon: New Essays*, edited by Erin B. Waggoner. Jefferson, NC: McFarland, 2010.
Gross, Joe. "Morrissey, 'Years of Refusal' (Lost Highway)." *Spin.com* (28 January 2009). Available from www.spin.com/reviews/morrissey-years-refusal-lost-highway. Accessed 28 July 2010.
Haraway, Donna. "A Manifesto for Cyborgs: Science, Technology and Socialist Feminism in the 1980s." *Socialist Review* 80 (1985): 65–107.
Harrison, Andrew. "Home Thoughts from Abroad." *Word* 4 (June 2003): 62–72.
Hauptfuhrer, Fred. "Roll Over, Bob Dylan, and Tell Madonna the News: The Smiths' Morrissey Is Pop's Latest Messiah." *People Weekly* (24 June 1985), 106.
Hawkins, Stan. "Anti-rebel, Lonesome Boy: Morrissey in Crisis?" Pp. 66–103 in *Settling the Pop Score: Pop Texts and Identity Politics*. Aldershot: Ashgate, 2002.
_____. *The British Pop Dandy: Masculinity, Popular Music and Culture*. Surrey: Ashgate, 2009.
Hendrickson, Matt. "Maladjusted." *Rolling Stone* 767 (21 August 1997), 112.
Henke, James. "Oscar! Oscar! Great Britain Goes Wilde for the 'Fourth-Gender' Smiths." *Rolling Stone* 423 (7 June 1984), 45.
Holmes, Tim. "Records: Meat Is Murder." *Rolling Stone* 448 (23 May 1985), 59.

Hopps, Gavin. *Morrissey: The Pageant of His Bleeding Heart.* New York: Continuum, 2009.

Hsu, Melinda. "Celibate Cries: Queer Readings of Morrissey's Sexual Persona." Master's Thesis, California State University, Fresno, 1996.

Hubbs, Nadine. "Music of the 'Fourth Gender': Morrissey and the Sexual Politics of Melodic Contour." Pp. 266–96 in *Bodies of Writing, Bodies in Performance,* edited by T. Foster, C. Siegel and E. Berry. New York: New York University Press, 1996.

Hunter, James. "You Are the Quarry." *RollingStone.com* (13 May 2004). Available from www.rollingstone.com/reviews/ album?id=5280076andpageid=rs.Homeandpageregion=triplelandrnd=1086016598076andhas-player=true. Accessed 31 May 2010.

Hutcheon, Linda. *Irony's Edge: The Theory and Politics of Irony.* London: Routledge, 1994.

Idov, Michael. "Record Reviews: Morrissey — Live at Earls Court." *Pitchfork.com* (1 April 2005). Available from www.pitchforkmedia.com/article/record_review/20043/Morrissey_Live_at_Earls_Court. Accessed 26 July 2010.

Kelly, Danny. *New Musical Express* (8 August 1987). Available from http://foreverill.com/disc/smithslp.htm. Accessed 3 February 2010.

Kelly, Nick. "Morrissey / Oct. 3, 2002 / Dublin (Ambassador Theatre)." *Billboard.com* (7 October 2002). Available from www.billboard.com/bb/article_display.jspvnu_content_id=1735207. Accessed 26 November 2009.

Kerman, Joseph, and Alan Tyson (with Scott G. Burnham). "Beethoven, Ludwig van; §15. Middle-Period Works." *Grove Music Online,* edited by L. Macy. Available from www.grovemusic.com. Accessed 10 April 2006.

King, Barry. "Articulating Stardom." *Screen* 26:5 (September–October 1985): 27–50.

King, Scott Benjamin. "Sonny's Virtues: The Gender Negotiations of *Miami Vice*." *Screen* 31:3 (Autumn 1990): 281–95.

Koestenbaum, Wayne. *The Queen's Throat: Opera, Homosexuality, and the Mystery of Desire.* New York: Poseidon Press, 1993.

Kostka, Stefan, and Dorothy Payne. *Tonal Harmony with an Introduction to Twentieth-Century Music.* New York: McGraw-Hill, 1995.

Lacan, Jacques. "The Agency of the Letter in the Unconscious or Reason since Freud." Pp. 146–178 in *Ecrits: A Selection,* translated by A. Sheridan. New York: W.W. Norton, 1977.

Levarie, Siegmund, and Earnst Levy. *Musical Morphology: A Discourse and a Dictionary.* Kent, OH: Kent State University Press, 1983.

Loder, Kurt. "1984 Record Guide." *Rolling Stone* 437–438 (20 December 1984), 113.

———. "Records: The Smiths." *Rolling Stone* 424 (21 June 1984), 56.

Maconie, Stuart. "Interesting Drag." *New Musical Express* (20 October 1990). Available from http://motorcycleaupairboy.com/mozdiscl/bonadrag.htm. Accessed 11 April 2010.

Male, Andrew. "Happy Now?" *Mojo* 149 (April 2006): 44–50, 89.

Marshall, P. David. *Celebrity and Power: Fame in Contemporary Culture.* Minneapolis: University of Minnesota Press, 1997.

McBay, Nadine. "Morrissey Swords Review." *BBC Music* (26 October 2009). Available from www.bbc.co.uk/music/reviews/hwd3. Accessed 28 July 2010.

McClary, Susan. *Feminine Endings: Music, Gender, and Sexuality.* Minneapolis: University of Minnesota Press, 1991.

———. "Narrative Agendas in 'Absolute' Music: Identity and Difference in Brahms's Third Symphony." Pp. 326–44 in *Musicology and Difference: Gender and Sexuality in Music Scholarship,* edited by Ruth A. Solie. Berkeley: University of California Press, 1993.

McCracken, Allison. "'God's Gift to Us Women': Crooning, Gender, and the Re-Creation of American Song, 1928–1933." *American Music* 17:4 (Winter 1999): 365–95.

McCullough, Dave. "Handsome Devils." *Sounds* (4 June 1983). Available from http://foreverill.com/interviews/1983/sounds1.htm. Accessed 7 July 2010.

Metz, Christian. "Identification, Mirror." Pp. 800–817 in *Film Theory and Criticism: Introductory Readings*, edited by Leo Braudy and Marshall Cohen. New York and Oxford: Oxford University Press, 1999.

Middleton, Richard. *Studying Popular Music*. Milton Keynes: Open University Press, 1990.

Mordue, Mark. "Morrissey; Enmore Theatre, Sydney." *12 Gauge Review*. Available from http://12gauge.com/music_2003_mordue_morrissey.html. Accessed 3 April 2010.

Morgan, Robert. *Twentieth-Century Music*. New York: Norton, 1991.

Morley, Paul. "The Last Temptation of Morrissey." *Uncut* (May 2006): 56–68.

———. "Wilde Child." *Blitz* (April 1988). Available from http://motorcycleaupairboy.com/interviews/1988/blitz.htm. Accessed 8 September 2009.

Morrissey. "Statement from Morrissey." *True to You* (27 March 2006). Available from http://true-to-you.net/morrissey_news_060327_02. Accessed 29 June 2010.

———. "Statement from Morrissey." *True to You* (31 March 2008). Available from http://true-to-you.net/morrissey_news_080331_01. Accessed 8 May 2010.

———. "Statement from Morrissey." *True to You* (30 April 2010). Available from http://true-to-you.net/morrissey_news_100430_01. Accessed 8 May 2010.

Mulvey, Laura. "Visual Pleasure and Narrative Cinema." *Screen* 16:3 (Autumn 1975): 6–18.

Nagy, Evie. "Morrissey, 'Swords.'" *Billboard.com* (6 November 2009). Available from www.billboard.com/#/new-releases/morrissey-swords-1004040720.story. Accessed 28 July 2010.

Needham, Alex. "NME Reviews: Morrissey — Ringleader of the Tormentors." *NME.com* (31 March 2006). Available from www.nme.com/reviews/morrissey/7896. Accessed 24 August 2010.

Negus, Keith. *Popular Music in Theory: An Introduction*. Hanover: Wesleyan University Press, 1996.

Nelson, Jim. "Morrissey Returns!" *GQ* 74:4 (April 2004): 198–205, 230–31.

Nixon, Sean. *Hard Looks: Masculinities, Spectatorship and Contemporary Consumption*. New York: St. Martin's Press, 1996.

O'Hagan, Sean. "Incredible Sulk." *The Observer* (22 September 2002). Available from http://observer.guardian.co.uk/review/story/0,,7965459,00.html. Accessed 26 November 2009.

"Our Decade: New Lad Rules the World." Available from http://news.bbc.co.uk/1/hi/special_report/1999/02/99/e-cyclopedia/289778.stm. Accessed 12 May 2010.

Papamarko, Sofi. "LIVE: Morrissey Drives Fans into a Frenzy." *ChartAttack.com* (13 October 2004). Available from www.chartattack.com/damn/2004/10/1313.cfm. Accessed 19 October 2009.

Perry, Andrew. "Fame, Fame, Fatal Fame." *Mojo* 89 (April 2001): 72.

Potter, John. "The Singer, Not the Song: Women Singers as Composer-Poets." *Popular Music* 13:2 (May 1994): 191–99.

Pareles, Jon. "An Articulate Misfit with Rockabilly Sideburns." *The New York Times* (22 September 1992), C17.

Quantick, David. "Albums: School of Hard Knocks." *Melody Maker* 72 (26 August 1995), 37. Available from http://motorcycleaupairboy.com/mozdisc2/southpaw.htm. Accessed 21 June 2010.

Raihala, Ross. "Morrissey, Ringleader of the Tormentors." *Spin.com* (4 April 2006). Available from www.spin.com/reviews/morrissey-ringleader-tormentors-attacksanctuary. Accessed 24 August 2010.

Railton, Diane. "The Gendered Carnival of Pop." *Popular Music* 20:3 (October 2001): 321–31.

Ratliff, Ben. "Critics' Choice: New CDs — Morrissey, 'Years of Refusal.'" *New York Times* (16 February 2009). Available from www.nytimes.com/2009/02/16/arts/music/16choi.html. Accessed 28 July 2010.

Reid, Pat. *Outlines: Morrissey*. Bath, UK: Absolute Press, 2004.

Renan, Ernest. "What Is a Nation?" Pp. 8–22 in *Nation and Narration*, translated by Martin Thom, edited by Homi Bhabha. London; New York: Routledge, 1990.

Reynolds, Simon. "Miserabilism: Morrissey." Pp. 15–29 in *Blissed Out: The Raptures of Rock*. London: Serpent's Tail, 1990.

——— and Joy Press. "Born to Run: Wanderlust, Wilderness and the Cult of Speed." Pp. 43–65 in *The Sex Revolts: Gender, Rebellion, and Rock'n'Roll*. Cambridge: Harvard University Press, 1995.

Robertson, John. *Morrissey: In His Own Words*. London: Omnibus Press, 1988.

"Rock Singer Snubs Canada to Protest Seal Hunt." Available from www.cbc.ca/canada/newfoundland-labrador/story/2006/03/28/nf-morrissey-seals-20060328.html. Accessed 29 June 2010.

Rogan, Johnny. *Morrissey and Marr: The Severed Alliance*. London: Omnibus Press, 1993.

Rogers, Jude. "On Music: Morrissey's Misstep." *The Guardian* (13 March 2009). Available from www.guardian.co.uk/music/2009/mar/13/morrissey-southpaw-grammar-maladjusted. Accessed 29 July 2010.

Ross, Andrew. "The Great White Dude." In *Constructing Masculinity*, edited by Maurice Berger, Brian Wallis, and Simon Watson. New York, Routledge, 1995.

Santoro, Gianni. "Morrissey." *XL* (March 2006): 90–95.

Saunders, Red. " Super Starts." *Rolling Stone* 408 (10 November 1983), 35.

Schindler, Stephan. "What Makes a Man a Man: The Construction of Masculinity in F. W. Murnau's *The Last Laugh*." *Screen* 37:1 (Spring 1996): 30–40.

Scott, Bruce. "Morrissey Pleases Toronto Crowd." *JAM! Music* (13 October 2004). Available from www.canoe.ca/JamConcertsL2Q/morrissey_101304-can.html. Accessed 19 October 2009.

Shepherd, John. "Difference and Power in Music." Pp. 46–65 in *Musicology and Difference: Gender and Sexuality in Music Scholarship*, edited by Ruth A. Solie. Berkeley: University of California Press, 1993.

Simon, William. *Postmodern Sexualities*. London: Routledge, 1996.

Simpson, Mark. "Here Come the Mirror Men." *The Independent* (15 November 1994). Available from www.marksimpson.com/pages/journalism/mirror_men.html. Accessed 24 July 2010.

———. "Meet the Metrosexual." Available from www.salon.com/ent/feature/2002/07/22/metrosexual/print.html. Accessed 5 January 2010.

———. *Saint Morrissey*. London: SAF Publishing, 2004.

Slee, Jo. *Peepholism: Into the Art of Morrissey*. London: Sedgwick and Jackson, 1994.

Snow, Mat. "The Soft Touch." *Q* 39 (December 1989): 78–84.

Snowsell, Colin. "'My Only Mistake Is I'm Hoping': Monty, Morrissey, and the Importance of Being Mediatized." Master's thesis, University of Calgary, 2002.

"Spins: *Maladjusted*." *Spin* 13 (September 1997): 160. Available from http://motorcycleaupairboy.com/mozdisc2/mal.htm. Accessed 21 June 2010.

Spitz, Marc. "These Things Take Time." *Spin* 20:5 (May 2004): 56–65.

Sterling, Linder. *Morrissey Shot*. New York: Hyperion, 1992.

Stringer, Julian. "The Smiths: Repressed (But Remarkably Dressed)." *Popular Music* 11:1 (1992): 15–26.

Taruskin, Richard. "Introduction [Studies in Nationalism and Music]." *Repercussions* 5:1–2 (Spring–Fall 1996): 5–20.
Thornton, Anthony. "NME Reviews: Morrissey—Years of Refusal." *NME.com* (18 February 2009). Available from www.nme.com/reviews/10089. Accessed 28 July 2010.
Tracey, Michael. "The Poisoned Chalice? International Television and the Idea of Dominance." *Daedalus* 114:4 (1985): 17–56.
Tseng, David. "Morrissey's Letter to The Times on British Army Guards Wearing Real Fur Hats." *Morrissey-Solo* (2 August 2010). Available from www.morrissey-solo.com/article.pl?sid=10/08/02/1620212. Accessed 2 August 2010.
Uhelszki, Jaan. "The Mojo Interview: L.A. Confidential." *Mojo* 89 (April 2001): 84.
Venkateswaran, Mona. "Accountants Can Be Fanatics Too." *CBC News Viewpoint* (22 October 2004). Available from www.cbc.ca/news/viewpoint/vp_venkateswaran/20041022.html. Accessed 25 October 2009.
Vernallis, Carol. "The Kindest Cut: Functions and Meanings of Music Video Editing." *Screen* 42:1 (Spring 2001): 21–48.
Viitamäki, Taina. "I'm Not the Man You Think I Am. Morrissey's Fourth Gender." *Musiikin suunta* 3 (1997): 29–40. Available from http://shoplifters.morrisseysolo.com/union/taina/morriss.htm. Accessed 8 May 2010.
Vincendeau, Ginette. "Gérard Depardieu: The Axiom of Contemporary French Cinema." *Screen* 34:4 (Winter 1993): 343–61.
Volk, Steven. "Recordings—Vauxhall and I by Morrissey." *Rolling Stone* 679 (7 April 1994), 74.
Walser, Robert. *Running with the Devil: Power, Gender, and Madness in Heavy Metal Music*. Hanover: Wesleyan University Press, 1993.
Watson, Don. *New Musical Express* (25 February 1984). Available from http://foreverill.com/disc/smithslp.htm. Accessed 3 February 2010.
Weisel, Al. "Recordings—Southpaw Grammar by Morrissey." *Rolling Stone* 718 (5 October 1995), 68.
Whatsisname, Chris. "Morrissey." *Les Inrockuptibles* (July 1987). Quoted in David Bret, *Morrissey: Scandal and Passion* (London: Robson Books, 2004).
White, Armond. "Anglocentric." *The Village Voice* 37 (1 September 1992), 70.
White, Michael. "Record Reviews: Morrissey—You Are the Quarry." *FFWD* (20 May 2004). Available from www.ffwdweekly.com/Issues/2004/0520/cd1.htm. Accessed 21 May 2010.
Williams, Andrew. "60 Second Interview: Mark Simpson." *Metro* (15 September 2005). Available from www.metro.co.uk/fame/interviews/article.html?in_article_id=504 andin_page_id=11. Accessed 6 July 2010.
Williams, Sean. "Melodic Ornamentation in the Connemara *Sean-nós* Singing of Joe Heaney." *New Hibernia Review* 8:1 (Spring 2004): 122–45.
Wood, Elizabeth. "Sapphonics." Pp. 27–66 in *Queering the Pitch: The New Gay and Lesbian Musicology*, edited by P. Brett, E. Wood and G. C. Thomas. New York: Routledge, 1994.
Zuberi, Nabeel. *Sounds English: Transnational Popular Music*. Urbana: University of Illinois Press, 2001.

Index

Accattone 183; *see also* "You Have Killed Me"
Adams, Rachel 103–104
"All the Lazy Dykes" 67–70, 145
"All You Need Is Me" 74
"Alma Matters" 65
"Alsatian Cousin" 50
"Ambitious Outsiders" 65
"America Is Not the World" 67–68
American Idol 168; *see also* Kilborn, Craig
American universalism 29–30
"Ammunition" 65
Anderson, Benedict 133
Anderson, Brett 112; *see also* asexuality
androgyny 20, 31
"Angel, Angel Down We Go Together" 51
animals, ethical treatment of 3, 41, 187; *see also* cyborg; "Meat Is Murder"; vegetarianism
anti-hero 7, 146, 148; *see also* Hawkins, Stan
Arcadia 147
Arsenal football club 30
asexuality 111, 112–113, 147, 148; *see also* anti-hero
"Asian Rut" 55
"Ask" 45, 50; *see also* "Everyday Is Like Sunday"
"Asleep" 46
"At Last I Am Born" 72, 186; *see also* God
Auden, W.H. 30, 190; *see also* Bracewell, Michael

Balzac, Honoré de 160, 178; *see also* Sarrasine
Band à part 186
"Barbarism Begins at Home" 41
Barthes, Roland 1, 9, 16, 88, 89–92, 94–95, 107, 122, 160, 167, 169, 172, 182, 184, 187–189, 190–191; *see also* grain of the voice; hermeneutic code; *S/Z*
Bartók, Béla 27
Battersea 27
Bayton, Mavis 82

Beaumont, Mark 73
Beckham, David 124; *see also* metrosexual
Beethoven (Ludwig van) 28
Beethoven Was Deaf 62
"Bengali In Platforms" 51; *see also* racism
Bennet, Keith *see* Moors murders
Berry, Chuck 29
"Best Friend on the Payroll" 64
The Best of Morrissey 116
Betjeman, John 190
"Bigmouth Strikes Again" 43, 44, 49
"Billy Budd" 60–61, 149
Black, Bill 39
"Black Cloud" 74
Bona Drag 53–55, 56, 60, 72, 114
Boorer, Martin "Boz" 59, 185–186
Bowie, David 117
"The Boy Racer" 7, 13, 30, 109, 115–116, 119–121, 125, 128
"The Boy with the Thorn in His Side" 43
Bracewell, Michael 3–4, 30–31, 185, 190, 191; *see also* Britishness
Bradby, Barbara 80–81, 107
Brady, Ian *see* Moors murders
Brasseur, Claude 186
"Break Up the Family" 52
Bret, David 14, 24, 34, 149, 153, 171
Britishness 1, 3, 18, 27, 30–32, 155; *see also* nationalism
Brown, Jeffrey A. 102–103
Brown, Len 49
Browne, David 49
Burns, Lori 84
Butler, Judith 13, 109–111
Butterworth, Dean 171

Catholicism 17, 31, 55, 68, 136; *see also* religion
celibacy 22, 46, 56, 146
"Cemetry Gates" 42
"Certain People I Know" 58
Chonin, Neva 135, 138, 140
Chow, Rey 104

213

Christianity 49, 54–55, 68, 136; *see also* Catholicism; God; Jesus
Cinquetti, Gigliola 185
cock rock 78–79, 144
Cockleshell Heroes 64
Cocteau (Jean) 36
Cohen, Sara 79–80, 82, 106–107
Coleman, Mark 26, 44, 53, 59
"Come Back to Camden" 68
Cook, Pam 7, 102
Cooper, Gary 102–103
Copland 103–104
Copland, Aaron 27–28
Coupland, Douglas 48, 136
Covach, John 29
crooning 42, 49, 61, 71, 79, 81, 147
Crosby, Bing 79
Cusick, Susanne 86, 107
cyborg 111–112

"Dagenham Dave" 63–64, 115
Dansette, Helen 165
Day, Doris 148
Day, Gary 59, 185
Dean, James 20, 24
"Dear God Please Help Me" 7, 16, 73, 183–184
death 35, 38, 41, 42, 43, 46, 48, 54, 62, 71, 73, 74, 76; *see also* Moors murders
"Death at One's Elbow" 48
"Death of a Disco Dancer" 48
deCordova, Richard 96, 107
Deevoy, Adrien 62, 116–117
Depardieu, Gérard 104–105
"Dial-a-Cliché" 52
"Disappointed" 55
"Do Your Best and Don't Worry" 64
Downey, Lesley Ann *see* Moors murders
Doyle, Tom 183
"Driving Your Girlfriend Home" 56
Du Noyer, Paul 41–42
Dublin 135, 138
Dwyer, Elizabeth 17, 23, 166
Dyer, Richard 8, 95–97, 98, 99–100, 107, 119
Dylan, Bob 11, 45

Eliot, T.S. 190
Ellis, John 95, 127–128
enigma 1, 2, 4, 5, 6, 7, 9, 11, 13, 16, 18, 22–24, 56, 88, 94–95, 107, 108, 159, 160, 162–165, 173, 179, 180–182
Erlewine, Stephen Thomas 73
eroticism 20–21, 90, 94, 108
Evans, Edward *see* Moors murders
Evans, Paul 62
Everett-Green, Robert 141
"Everyday Is Like Sunday" 50–51, 167, 169

Fadele, Dele 25
Farber, Jim 47, 49, 53
"The Father Who Must Be Killed" 71
Feist, Leslie 187–189
Felder, Rachel 57
Finsbury Park 24
"First of the Gang to Die" 32, 69, 134, 170
Foucault, Michel 105–106
fourth gender 20, 109, 112–113, 143–144; *see also* Hubbs, Nadine
"Frankly, Mr. Shankly" 42, 89
Frith, Simon 26, 78–79, 80, 81, 92, 106, 144

Gable, Clark 168
Gallagher, Noel 23
"Girl Afraid" 38
Girlfriend in a Coma (novel) 48; *see also* Coupland, Douglas
"Girlfriend in a Coma" 48, 145, 184
"Glamorous Glue" 31–32, 57–58; *see also* "The National Front Disco"
God 54–55, 66, 71, 72; *see also* Catholicism; Christianity; God; Jesus
Godard, Jean-Luc 186
Goddard, Simon 33
"Golden Lights" 47
the grain of the voice 9, 13, 89–92, 107, 122, 190–191; *see also* Barthes, Roland
Greatest Hits (Morrissey album) 73
Gross, Joe 75

Haas, George 159
"Hairdresser on Fire" 52
"Half a Person" 46
Hall, Stuart 82
"Hand in Glove" 22, 34, 35
"Handsome Devil" 38
Haraway, Donna 111–112
Hatful of Hollow 37–39
Hawkins, Stan 7, 15, 142–143, 146–150, 155–156, 158, 191
"He Cried" 66
"He Knows I'd Love To See Him" 54, 72
"The Headmaster Ritual" 39, 41
Heath, Stephen 90
"Heaven Knows I'm Miserable Now" 38, 114
Hendrickson, Matt 67
Henke, James 19, 21, 112–113, 143
hermeneutic code 12, 95, 107, 161, 182; *see also* Barthes, Roland; *S/Z*
Hill, Harry *see Stars in Their Eyes*
Hindley, Myra *see* Moors murders
Holby City 176
"Hold On to Your Friends" 34, 60
Holmes, Tim 41
Hopps, Gavin 190
"How Can Anybody Possibly Know How I Feel?" 69, 70
"How Soon Is Now?" 37–38

Hsu, Melinda 109, 138
Hubbs, Nadine 6, 8, 14, 30, 108, 109, 112, 114–115, 142–146, 147, 158
Hulmerist 53
Hunter, James 70

"I Am Hated for Loving" 61
"I Am Two People" 10
"I Don't Mind If You Forget Me" 52
"I Don't Owe You Anything" 35
"I Have Forgiven Jesus" 17, 68, 116; *see also* Jesus
"I Just Want to See the Boy Happy" 54, 72
"I Knew I Was Next" 76
"I Know It's Gonna Happen Someday" 59
"I Know It's Over" 42, 44
"I Like You" 70
"I Want the One I Can't Have" 40
"I Will See You in Far Off Places" 71
"I Won't Share You" 49; *see also* crooning
Idov, Michael 70–71
"I'll Never Be Anybody's Hero Now" 72
illness 35, 72, 73, 76; *see also* lack
I'm a Celebrity 176
"I'm Not Sorry" 68–69
"I'm OK By Myself" 75
"(I'm) the End of the Family Line" 56; *see also* celibacy; loneliness
"I'm Throwing My Arms around Paris" 74
The Importance of Being Morrissey 22, 23, 26
"In the Future When All's Well" 71
inactivity 6, 8, 15, 108, 119 128, 143, 144, 146, 147, 156–158, 159
injury 14, 109–110, 113, 115–116, 117, 121–123, 128–129, 132
"Interlude" 60, 62, 132
Introducing Morrissey 60, 62, 116, 132, 154, 156, 158, 159
Ireland 4, 17, 18, 31–32; *see also* nationalism
"Irish Blood, English Heart" 4, 32, 68
"It's Not Your Birthday Anymore" 16, 187–190

"Jack the Ripper" 138–139
Jackson, Michael 30
Jensen, David 37; *see also Hatful of Hollow*
Jesus 54, 55, 68, 69, 118, 138–139; *see also* Catholicism; Christianity; God
jhai 188
Joan of Arc 43, 49
"Johnny Get Angry" 84
Jones, Tom 140
jouissance 91
Joyce, Mike 34, 39, 61, 66, 67

Kaige, Chen 104
Keats (John) 42
Kelly, Danny 36
Kelly, Nick 135
Kilborn, Craig 4, 8, 15, 160, 165–170, 172, 177–178
Kilbride, John *see* Moors murders
Kill Uncle 55–57, 60, 115, 118
Kimono My House 17
King, Barry 96, 107
King, Scott Benjamin 101–102
"King Leer" 56
King of the Children see Kaige, Chen
Koestenbaum, Wayne 9, 93–94, 107, 187, 189
Kristeva, Julia 116

Lacan, Jacques 89
lack 13, 56, 108, 109, 113, 116–117, 127, 128, 148, 181, 185
lang, k.d. 84
Larken, Philip 30, 190
Las Vegas 140
The Last Laugh 103
"Last Night I Dreamt That Somebody Loved Me" 48
"The Last of the Famous International Playboys" 54
"Late Night, Maudlin Street" 51, 60, 65
Latino 4, 17, 18, 32, 69
"The Lazy Sunbathers" 62
Let It Die 188
"Let Me Kiss You" 69
Levarie, Siegmund 156–157; *see also* inactivity
Levy, Earnst 156–157; *see also* inactivity
"Life Is a Pigsty" 71–72, 73
"Lifeguard Sleeping, Girl Drowning" 61–62
"Little Man, What Now?" 50
Live at Earls Court 70–71, 134
Liverpool 79–80, 106–107
Loder, Kurt 36
London 24, 30, 31–32, 57, 118, 182
"London" (song) 45
loneliness 39, 40, 41, 42, 44, 46, 56, 64, 68, 76; *see also* "What Difference Does It Make?"
Long, Janice 3, 8, 16, 32, 161, 174, 175–177, 178, 182
Los Angeles 4, 11, 18, 31, 57, 69, 165, 168, 182
Louder Than Bombs 44–47, 50
Lowe, Zane 32
"Lucky Lisp" 55; *see also* Christianity; Jesus

Maconie, Stuart 55
Madness 25
Madonna 30
Magnani, Anna 7, 183; *see also* "You Have Killed Me"
Maladjusted (album) 57, 64–67, 73
"Maladjusted" 64–65

"Mama Lay Softly on the Riverbed" 73
Mamma Roma 183; *see also* Pasolini, Pier Paolo
Manchester 17, 30, 35–36, 39, 41, 75, 182
Manchester United football club 66
"Margaret on the Guillotine" 52–53; *see also* Thatcher, Margaret
Marr, Johnny 34, 35, 39, 40, 50, 61, 67
Marshall, P. David 8, 97–98, 107
McBay, Nadine 75–76
McClary, Susan 6, 82–84, 107, 115, 142
McCracken, Allison 79, 81
McCullough, Dave 20
McRobbie, Angela 78–79, 80, 81, 92, 106, 144
Meat Is Murder (album) 39–42, 44
"Meat Is Murder" 41, 42
metrosexual 124–125, 140, 175
Metz, Christian 7, 126–128
"Mexico" 32
Miami Vice 7, 101–102
Middleton, Richard 9, 29–30, 92, 93, 132–133, 157
Monro, Matt 148
Moors murders 35–36
Mordue, Mark 136
"The More You Ignore Me, the Closer I Get" 61, 115; *see also* Joyce, Mike
Morgan, Robert 28–29
Morley, Paul 182–183
Morricone, Ennio 16
Morrissey-Solo (website) 112, 137
Mulvey, Laura 6, 8, 13, 77, 94 99–100, 105, 106, 107, 126
Murnau, F.W. 100, 103
"Mute Witness" 56; *see also* lack

Nagy, Evie 75
"The National Front Disco" 24–26, 57–58, 153; *see also* racism
nationalism 11–12, 18, 25–26, 27–32, 58, 59; *see also* racism
Needham, Alex 72–73
Negus, Keith 29–30
Nelson, Jim 32
"Never Had No One Ever" 42, 44; *see also* crooning
new lad 124–125; *see also* new man
new man 105–106, 117, 123–124; *see also* new lad
New Musical Express 3, 12, 17, 18, 24–26, 34, 36, 42, 50, 72–73; *see also* racism
Newley, Anthony 64
Nixon, Sean 105–106, 123
nostalgia 31, 65, 71, 141
"November Spawned a Monster" 54, 60, 114–115
"Now My Heart Is Full" 60
"Nowhere Fast" 40

Oasis 23
O'Brien, James 119, 132
O'Hagan, Sean 123, 136
"On the Streets I Ran" 72
"One Day Goodbye Will Be Farewell" 57, 74
"The Operation" 63
"The Ordinary Boys" 52
organicism 28
"Oscillate Wildly"
"Ouija Board, Ouija Board" 54
"Our Frank" 55, 115

"Paint a Vulgar Picture" 46, 49
"Panic" 45
"Papa Jack" 65
Papamarko, Sofi 140
Pareles, Jon 147–148
Pasilas, Loretta 163–164
Pasolini, Pier Paolo 7, 183; *see also* "You Have Killed Me"
Pavone, Rita 7, 185; *see also* "You Have Killed Me"
Peel, John 37; *see also Hatful of Hollow*
"Piccadilly Palare" 53, 145
Potter, John 9, 92–93
Presley, Elvis 20, 140
Press, Joy 116–117; *see also* lack
"Pretty Girls Make Graves" 34, 36, 61; *see also* "Hold On to Your Friends"
"The Public Image" 4

Quantick, David 64
the Queen 40, 42
The Queen Is Dead (album) 42–44
"The Queen Is Dead" 42, 49

racism 18, 24–27, 32, 51, 59
Raging Bull 7, 102
Raihala, Ross 73
Railton, Diane 81–82, 107
Rank 49–50, 53, 134
Ratliff, Ben 75, 88
"Reader Meet Author" 63
"Redondo Beach" 175
"Reel Around the Fountain" 34, 36
Reid, Pat 108, 109, 112
Reimer, David 111; *see also* asexuality
religion 49, 68, 76, 157; *see also* Catholicism; Christianity; God; Jesus
Renan, Ernest 28
Reynolds, Simon 116–117; *see also* lack
Riley, Julia 108, 131, 136–138, 141
Ringleader of the Tormentors 7, 16, 45, 54, 71–73, 182–186
Robertson, John 22
Rocco e i suoi fratelli 183; *see also* "You Have Killed Me"
Rogan, Johnny 24, 25, 37, 50

Rogers, Jude 67
Rolling Stone 12, 19, 21, 23, 34, 49, 53, 59, 67, 70, 112–113, 143
Rome 4, 12, 16, 182–183
Ross, Jonathan 8, 16, 160, 171–175, 177–178
Rough Trade 37
Rourke, Andy 39
"Roy's Keen" 66
"A Rush and a Push and the Land Is Ours" 47–48, 49
"Rusholme Ruffians" 40

Saddleworth Moor *see* Moors murders
San Diego 118
Santoro, Gianni 182, 184
Sarrasine (novella) 160, 161–165, 178
Sarrasine 163–164
"Satan Rejected My Soul" 56–57, 66–67, 71, 74; *see also* God; religion
Schindler, Stephan 100–101
Schoenberg, Arnold 83
Scott, Bruce 139–140
Seal Hunt, Canadian 16, 186–187; *see also* animals, ethical treatment of
Sean-nós 134–135
"Seasick, Yet Still Docked" 58–59
"Shakespeare's Sister" 45, 46
"Sheila Take a Bow" 47
Shepherd, John 85–86, 107, 144
"Shoplifters of the World Unite" 45
Shostakovich (Dmitri) 63
Simpson, Mark 14, 20–22, 24, 59, 109, 118, 121, 124–125, 139, 140, 164–165, 169–170, 174–175; *see also* metrosexual
"Sing Your Life" 55–56
Sioux, Siouxsie 132
skinhead (subculture) 26, 31
Skryabin (Alexander) 29
Smith, Patti 175
Smith, Stevie 190
The Smiths (album) 34–36, 37, 38, 39
Snow, Mat 132
Snowsell, Colin 19–20
"Some Girls Are Bigger Than Others" 44
"Something Is Squeezing My Skull" 73
Sommer, Joanie 84
"Sorrow Will Come in the End" 66
"Sorry Doesn't Help" 74–75
"Southpaw" 64–71
Southpaw Grammar 63–64, 67, 115, 121
Sparks 17
"Speedway" 62
"Spring-Heeled Jim" 121
Stallone, Sylvester 103; *see also Copland*
Stars in Their Eyes 173–174
Sterling, Linder 118
"Still Ill" 35, 69, 70, 134–135
"Stop Me If You Think You've Heard This One Before" 48, 49, 114

Strangeways, Here We Come 46, 47–49
"Stretch Out and Wait" 46
Stringer, Julian 5, 148
suedehead (subculture) 25, 26; *see also* skinhead (subculture)
"Suedehead" 51–52, 170
"Suffer Little Children" 35–36
Swords 75–76
S/Z 5, 16, 160, 161–165; *see also* Barthes, Roland; *Sarrasine* (novella)

Talking Heads 50
Taruskin, Richard 28
"The Teachers Are Afraid of the Pupils" 63, 71
teenybop 78–79, 81
"That Joke Isn't Funny Anymore" 40, 44
Thatcher, Margaret 26, 53, 68
"There Is a Light That Never Goes Out" 43
"There's a Place in Hell for Me and My Friends" 56–57, 74
"These Things Take Time" 37
"This Charming Man" 113–114, 173
"This Night Has Opened My Eyes" 38
Thornton, Anthony 75
"Tomorrow" 59
Toronto 130, 139
"Trouble Loves Me" 65
True to You (website) 131, 137, 186; *see also* Riley, Julia

Uhelszki, Jaan
"Unhappy Birthday" 48
Union Jack 4, 25, 31
"Unloveable" 46
"Used to Be a Sweet Boy" 189

Vallee, Rudy 79
Vauxhall and I 34, 60–62, 115, 149, 189
vegetarianism 3, 20, 41, 44, 173; *see also* "Meat Is Murder"
Venkateswaran, Mona 130
Vernallis, Carol 13, 121–123
"Vicar in a Tutu" 43, 44, 49
Viitamäki, Taina 109, 112
Vincendeau, Ginette 104–105
violence 5, 16, 35, 36, 38, 39, 40, 41, 43, 58, 61, 63, 65, 76, 115, 165, 187–190
Visconti, Luchino 183; *see also* "You Have Killed Me"
Visconti, Tony 16
Viva Hate 50–53, 55, 60
Volk, Steven 62

Wagner, Richard 84
Walser, Robert 8, 135–136, 187
Watson, Don 36
"We Hate It When Our Friends Become Successful" 58

Weisel, Al 64
"Well I Wonder" 41
"We'll Let You Know" 8, 15, 26, 57–58, 121, 142, 150–156, 157, 181
West Ham United (football club) 30, 118
"What Difference Does It Make?" 35, 114
"What She Said" 41
"When Last I Spoke To Carol" 74
White, Armond 26
White, Michael 70, 76
Who Put the "M" in Manchester? 140
"Why Don't You Find Out for Yourself" 61
Whyte, Alain 34, 59, 61, 185–186
"Wide to Receive" 65–66
Wilde, Oscar 24, 31, 42, 137, 172, 175
"Will Never Marry" 56
"William, It Was Really Nothing" 37
Williams, Sean 135
Wood, Elizabeth 86–87, 107, 187, 189
"The World Is Full of Crashing Bores" 68
World of Morrissey 62
The World Won't Listen 44–46

Years of Refusal 16, 47, 57, 73–75, 137, 187
Yeats (William) 42
"Yes, I Am Blind" 54–55; *see also* Catholicism; Christianity; God
You Are the Quarry 14, 67–70, 76, 116, 131, 136, 139, 174, 175
"You Have Killed Me" 16, 183
"You Just Haven't Earned It Yet, Baby" 46
"You Know I Couldn't Last" 70
"You Were Good in Your Time" 47, 74
Young, Neil 75
"The Youngest Was the Most Loved" 71
Your Arsenal 18, 24, 27, 30, 57–60, 63, 117–118, 132, 153
"You're Gonna Need Someone on Your Side" 57
"You're the One for Me, Fatty" 30, 58

La Zambinella 163–165; *see also Sarrasine* (novella); *S/Z*
Zuberi, Nabeel 31

www.ingramcontent.com/pod-product-compliance
Ingram Content Group UK Ltd.
Pitfield, Milton Keynes, MK11 3LW, UK
UKHW041952140426
5217IPUK00015B/765